WORKPLACE ACCOMMODATIONS

for Disability and Religion

2nd Edition

Burton J. Fishman, Esq.
Barbara S.Magill, Esq.

D1708777

Thompson Publishing Group, Inc.
805 15th St. NW, Ste. 300
Washington, DC 20005
202-872-4000 (Editorial Offices)
800-677-3789 (Customer Service)
www.thompson.com

THOMPSON

Insight you trust.

⋔ THOMPSON

Thompson Publishing Group, Inc.

Thompson Publishing Group is a trusted name in authoritative analysis of laws, regulations and business practices that helps corporate, government and other professionals develop regulatory compliance strategies. Since 1972, thousands of professionals in business, government, law and academia have relied on Thompson Publishing Group for the most authoritative, timely and practical guidance available.

Thompson offers looseleaf services, books, specialty newsletters, audio conferences and online products in a number of subject and regulatory compliance areas. These Thompson products provide insightful analysis, practical guidance and real-world solutions to the challenges facing human resources professionals today and beyond. More information about Thompson's product offerings is available at http://www.thompson.com.

To order any Thompson products or additional copies of this book, please contact us:

Call: 800-677-3789
Online: www.thompson.com
Fax: 800-999-5661
Email: service@thompson.com
Mail: Thompson Publishing Group
Subscription Service Center
PO Box 26185, Tampa, FL 33623-6185

❦❦❦❦❦❦❦❦❦❦❦❦❦

Authors: Burton J. Fishman, Esq., and Barbara S. Magill, Esq.
Desktop Publisher: Laurie S. Clark
Cover design: Ellen Hamilton

Workplace Accommodations for Disability and Religion, 2nd Edition is published by Thompson Publishing Group, Inc., 805 15th St. N.W., Ste. 300, Washington, DC 20005.

ISBN-13: 978-1-933807-23-2

Printed in the United States

About This Book

Employers are prohibited by federal law from discriminating in the workplace on a number of bases, including race, gender, national origin, age, pregnancy, religion and disability. However, there are only two – religion and disability – that require employers to go beyond merely treating members of the protected class equally with everyone else. For religious beliefs and people with disabilities, employers are required to provide reasonable accommodations so the employees can do their jobs without violating the tenets of their faith (in the case of religion) or can overcome their physical limitations (in the case of disability).

Workplace Accommodations for Disability and Religion explains what employers are required to do when an employee requests an accommodation. Just as important, it explains what employers are *not* required to do.

Accommodations for people with disabilities have been part of the workplace since the enactment of the Americans With Disabilities Act in 1992. Indeed, reasonable accommodation is really the heart of the Americans With Disabilities Act. Providing a real equal opportunity means making facilities accessible so mobility-impaired workers can get to their offices or workstations. It means providing aids such as amplified telephones and larger computer screens so people with hearing and vision impairments can do the essential functions of their jobs.

It never was enough under the ADA just to permit those with disabilities to apply for jobs; the law requires employers to make changes in policies, procedures and physical spaces so individuals with disabilities were given a realistic opportunity to work.

Religious accommodation is guaranteed by Title VII of the 1964 Civil Rights Act. Prior to Sept. 11, 2001, there was not really a lot employers were required to do, beyond avoiding outright discrimination. If it was not too difficult and did not cause too much trouble, an employee who could not work on a certain day due to religious beliefs had to be permitted to swap days off with a willing co-worker or modify a work schedule or, most likely, lose a day's pay or vacation, but that was about it. An accommodation that created an "undue hardship" for the employer was not required, and it was not difficult to cross the undue hardship threshold.

After Sept. 11, 2001, however, there was renewed vigor in the subject of religious accommodation. The Equal Employment Opportunity Commission (EEOC) issued new guidances on religious discrimination in the workplace in which it pointed out that leave for religious observances, breaks during the workday to pray, and permission to wear some religious garb were all reasonable accommodations that could be required under most circumstances.

Now the courts are taking a harder look at what constitutes an undue hardship and requiring employers to make a real effort at accommodation.

There are more than 40 years of court decisions and federal agency guidance on religious accommodation, but there has been a change in the last few years. There are only about 15 years of court decisions since the ADA became law and reasonable accommodation under that act is still evolving. *Workplace Accommodations for Disability and Religion* is designed to help employers sort through the changing rulings and directives to determine what is required of them under various circumstances so they can avoid litigation and effectively manage their workforces.

What's Inside

Workplace Accommodations is divided into two sections: religious accommodation and disability accommodation.

The section on disability accommodation explains what a disability is under the ADA, what kinds of reasonable accommodations might be required and what constitutes an undue hardship.

The section on religious accommodation explains what a religion is under Title VII, what reasonable accommodations are and what an undue hardship is. It also addresses harassment.

Sample policies are included and the text of some of the EEOC's regulations and guidances are in the appendix. We think you will find this the easiest to understand and most complete book on workplace accommodation available.

Our Guarantee

Please take a minute to review *Workplace Accommodations for Disability and Religion*. You have our 30-day risk-free guarantee. We are confident that the book will become a trusted resource for your HR program. If you don't agree, just return the book to us with the enclosed invoice.

If we can be of any assistance, please do not hesitate to contact our customer service department at 1-800-677-3789.

About the Authors

Burton J. Fishman, Esq., is an attorney with Fortney & Scott, LLC in Washington, D.C., and is recognized as one of the nation's leading authorities on workplace law. He has devoted his practice to developing the "law of the workplace," an interdisciplinary approach that offers employers counsel and representation on a broad range of matters growing out of government regulation of business. A former deputy solicitor of the U.S. Department of Labor, his experience extends to the full spectrum of employment and labor matters. A well-known speaker and writer, Fishman has written over 100 books and articles in the employment field, including *The ADA: Ten Years After, HR Guide to Employee Management* and *The HR Question and Answer Book,* and edited *Workplace Privacy: Real Answers and Practical Solutions,* the latter three published by Thompson Publishing Group. He is a Fellow of the College of Labor and Employment Lawyers and has been named "Super Lawyer" in the field and labor and employment law.

Barbara S. Magill, Esq., is a senior managing editor at Thompson Publishing Group. She is a recognized authority on the Americans With Disabilities Act, having written the first authoritative report on the employment portion of the law and its EEOC regulations. She has written and edited numerous books and articles on employment law, including *Sex Discrimination Handbook, HR Series: Fair Employment Practices, Workplace Accommodations Under the ADA, HR Question and Answer Book* and *Workplace Privacy: Real Answers and Practical Solutions 2nd Edition,* the latter three published by Thompson Publishing Group. She served as an HR generalist prior to joining Thompson with responsibilities for benefits, equal employment opportunity and the company's affirmative action plan. Before beginning a career in publishing, she was in private law practice in Illinois.

Table of Contents

Section I: Accommodations for Disabilities

Accommodating qualified employees with disabilities is at the center of the employment provisions of the Americans With Disabilities Act (ADA) because many individuals with disabilities cannot do things in the same way as their able-bodied counterparts. Provided with accommodations that enable them to get into buildings, maneuver within workspaces, answer telephones and use computers to perform essential job functions, individuals with disabilities have a real opportunity to compete on an equal basis with other employees. Without such accommodations, these potential workers are shut out of the workforce.

Reasonable accommodation is not specifically defined in the ADA. The Equal Employment Opportunity Commission (EEOC), the agency that enforces the law's employment provisions, gave numerous examples of reasonable accommodations in its implementing regulations, Technical Assistance Manual on Title I and its various guidances, especially the 1999 "Reasonable Accommodation and Undue Hardship Under the Americans With Disabilities Act" (amended in 2002). The courts have provided others.

No matter how many examples there are, however, they can never cover every situation and claims of failure by employers to provide reasonable accommodations is one of the most litigated issues under the ADA. Moreover, there is no agreement among the courts about what accommodations are required, even when the situations are virtually the same. To make matters worse, the courts do not always agree with the EEOC.

For example, in its original guidance on the issue, the EEOC said "reasonable" meant "effective" and cost had no relevance. The U.S. Supreme Court ruled that "reasonable" does *not* mean "effective"; it "is the word 'accommodation,' that conveys the need for effectiveness" (*U.S. Airways, Inc. v. Barnett*, 535 U.S. 391 (2002)). A number of courts have ruled that reasonable means costs do not greatly exceed the benefits.

Reasonable accommodation applies to all employees of covered employers, including those who are part-time or probationary, according to the EEOC. Reasonable accommodation can apply to the job application process, the manner or circumstances in which a job is performed, and access to the benefits and privileges of employment. Types of accommodations include making facilities accessible, restructuring jobs, changing work schedules, providing new or adaptive equipment, changing application processes and modifying company policies.

Employees may request accommodations at any time and do not have to use specific words to do so, the EEOC says, and employers must respond to requests for accommodation within a "reasonable amount of time," with "reasonable" depending on the availability of suitable accommodation alternatives. To the extent that it relates to the request for accommodation, an employer may request medical documentation of the disability.

The ultimate choice of an accommodation is the employer's to make, but the EEOC stresses the need for an interactive process in which the employee and employer work together to arrive at an accommodation that will enable the employee to perform the essential functions of the job without causing the employer an undue hardship in its business. Courts usually will rule against the party, whether employer or employee, that causes a breakdown in the interactive process.

Although most federal courts that have decided the issue have found that regular attendance is an essential function of most jobs, the EEOC is not a strong supporter of that position. Attendance policies are not sacred, according to the EEOC, which stresses that reasonable accommodation may include granting additional leave time beyond that of a company policy or even of the Family and Medical Leave Act.

Moreover, according to the commission, an employer may have to grant a leave request even if the employee cannot provide a fixed day of return. Most courts agree that leave may be a required reasonable accommodation, as long as the leave leads to "regular, reliable, predictable attendance." The EEOC's guidance includes no such caveat.

Reassignment is listed in the law as a form of reasonable accommodation. The EEOC insists that an employee with a disability who can no longer perform the essential functions of the current job and who is qualified for a vacant job should get the position without having to compete for it, even if that employee is not the best qualified applicant. On the other hand, many courts have held that employees who cannot perform the essential functions of their current jobs are not "qualified individuals" under the ADA and, therefore, are not eligible for reassignment.

The EEOC guidance addresses job restructuring and modified work schedules; telecommuting; access to communications, benefits and privileges of employment; and accommodations for job applicants. In its guidance, it discusses the concept of undue hardship, which is a defense in the law to reasonable accommodation, pointing out that cost is not always enough to amount to an undue hardship. The commission also insisted that conflict with a collective bargaining agreement was not always enough to amount to an undue hardship, but the U.S. Supreme Court made it clear that a bona fide seniority policy, even one that is not part of a union contract, trumps a reasonable accommodation that conflicts.

This section of *Workplace Accommodations for Disability and Religion* examines accommodations for employees with disabilities by beginning as an employer must, with determining whether an individual who requests a reasonable accommodation has a disability as defined by the ADA. In June 1999 the U.S. Supreme Court ruled in a series of cases that individuals whose conditions are mitigated by modified behaviors, medications or corrective devices or equipment may not have ADA-covered disabilities. This was in direct conflict with the EEOC's position that disabilities should be examined in their unmitigated state to determine if they affected a major life activity and thus were covered by the ADA.

The previous year the Supreme Court seemed to expand the meaning of disability when it ruled that an individual with asymptomatic HIV was limited in the major life activity of reproduction and, therefore, had an ADA-covered disability. That decision upheld EEOC pronouncements. In addition to the Supreme Court, federal courts of appeals have issued decisions on various aspects of disability and ADA coverage. Pertinent decisions and opinions by experts about what those rulings mean are discussed in **Chapter 1**.

Defining reasonable accommodation by drawing from the language of the statute, the EEOC's regulations, the Technical Assistance Manual on Title I and the commission's guidances and then determining what, if any, accommodation is needed, are the next steps in the process of providing an individual with a disability an equal job opportunity. These are discussed in **Chapters 2** and **3**.

Job applicants as well as employees must be provided with reasonable accommodations that do not impose an undue hardship on the employer's business. There are rules about what information can be obtained from job applicants concerning their disabilities both before and after a job offer has been made. The rules and accommodation requirements are explained in **Chapter 4**.

The types of employment-related activities and benefits that must be accommodated are discussed in **Chapter 5** and the specific types of accommodations that may be required are analyzed in **Chapter 6**. Retaliation and other issues concerning accommodation, such as an employee's refusal to take prescribed medication, are discussed in **Chapter 7**.

Chapter 8 examines the issues concerning the undue hardship defense to making reasonable accommodations. The cost/benefit analysis favored by some courts and rejected by the EEOC and the impact of collective bargaining agreements and seniority policies are discussed.

In the **Appendix** are lists of low-cost accommodations that employers have found effective for workers with various types of disabilities and resources for more information about accommodations. Court case and topic indexes provide quick references.

What Disabilities Require Reasonable Accommodation?

1

Reasonable accommodations are required only for those employees and job applicants who have ADA-covered disabilities and only if the employer knows about the disability, either because it is obvious or because the employee reveals it.

The statute defines "disability" as:

- a physical or mental impairment that substantially limits one or more of an individual's major life activities;

- a record of such an impairment; or

- being regarded as having such an impairment (42 U.S.C. §12102(2)).

This vague definition has been the subject of interpretation by the courts since the law was passed. The Equal Employment Opportunity Commission attempted to explain what Congress meant in its regulations, Technical Assistance Manual on Title I and its various guidances. The real problem is that whether a specific individual has a disability has to be determined on a case-by-case basis, which means no general definition has general application, a condition that can seriously impact the major life activities of one individual may be no more than an inconvenience to another, depending both on the person and the job. There is no list of disabilities employers can consult.

When most people think of disabilities, what immediately comes to mind are individuals with obvious mobility, visual and hearing impairments. Of course individuals who are in wheelchairs or are blind or deaf are not the ones employers have difficulty identifying as in need of accommodations. As a matter of fact, many of these "obviously disabled" individuals may not even need an accommodation to do a particular job. It is those people with back or other soft-tissue injuries, those with intellectual and mental impairments, and those with illnesses that vary in impact who are not only more difficult to classify as in need of accommodation, but also more difficult to accommodate.

The only way to begin to understand what a disability is under the ADA is to examine the law's definition part by part. The fact that the Supreme Court has returned to this subject on a number of occasions should make it clear that the task is not an easy one.

Meaning of 'Qualified'

The statute does not make our task any easier. The law provides:

> A qualified individual with a disability is one with an ADA-covered disability who can perform the essential functions of the job that the individual holds or desires (42 U.S.C. §12111(8)).

Because the parts of this definition are interconnected, the analysis can begin anywhere: Are the job functions really "essential"? Is the impairment truly a "disability"? We will begin with What is "qualified"?

"Qualified" means that the individual has the experience and requisite training, certifications and licenses, if any are required, to be considered for the job. A bus driver who cannot meet U.S. Department of Transportation requirements for a commercial driver's license is not qualified and neither is an applicant for a teaching job who does not have a state teaching certificate.

Being *un*qualified can involve a less clearly identifiable deficit than not having the required license. A data entry employee, even one with a disability, must meet the company standard for entering words per minute. A stock loader must be able to carry the required load. A receptionist must be able to show up on time, despite his obsessive compulsive disorder, complete assignments, get along with colleagues and supervisors, and work under the stress of the job.

Being qualified also means an ability to perform the essential functions of a job, with or without accommodation. The courts have made this very clear.

Example: An employee who suffered a severe head injury when he fell from a fence was *not qualified* to perform any of the jobs at the manufacturing plant where he had worked prior to his injury, because he had lost his sense of balance, could not work under time pressure, had lost his fine manual dexterity and had cognitive and memory losses. The employee was not qualified to perform any of the jobs at the plant, even with the accommodation of a job coach, an appeals court ruled (*Kleiber v. Honda of America*, 485 F.3d 862 (6th Cir. 2007)).

Example: An employee at a cheese factory with a vision impairment who failed to perform many of the essential tasks of his job, worked too slowly to keep up with the speed of the production line, had "a poor attitude and performed many of his tasks carelessly and without regard for his safety or that of his co-workers" and could not show any accommodation that would have enabled him to do his job was *unqualified*, an appeals court ruled (*Hammel v. Eau Galle Cheese Factory*, 407 F.3d 852 (7th Cir. 2005)).

Example: A police officer with multiple sclerosis who could no longer run, arrest or restrain individuals was *not qualified* because he could not perform the essential functions of his job. There was no accommodation that would enable him to do so, the 10th U.S. Circuit Court of Appeals held (*Frazier v. Simmons*, 254 F.3d 1247 (10th Cir. 2001)).

Examples: Also *unqualified* was an employee in a manufacturing plant who could not meet more than 30 percent of his hourly production quota (*Denczak v. Ford Motor Co.*, 215 Fed. Appx. 442 (6th Cir. 2007) (unpublished)) and one who admitted there was no accommodation that would enable him to perform the essential functions of his cable splicing job (*Miller v. Ameritech Corp.*, 214 Fed. Appx. 605 (7th Cir. 2007) (unpublished)).

Physical and Mental Impairments

Reasonable accommodations are required for the known physical or mental impairments of an otherwise qualified job applicant or employee with a disability, unless those accommodations would impose an undue hardship on the employer's business (42 U.S.C. §12112(5)(A)). A *physical impairment* is a "physiological disorder or condition, cosmetic disfigurement, or anatomical loss that affects one or more of the following body systems:

* neurological;

* musculoskeletal;

* special sense organs;

* respiratory (including speech organs);

* cardiovascular;

* reproductive;

* digestive;

* genito-urinary;

* hemic and lymphatic;

* skin; and

* endocrine" (29 C.F.R. §1630.2(h)).

A *mental impairment* is a "mental or psychological disorder such as mental retardation, organic brain syndrome, emotional or mental illness and specific learning disabilities" (29 C.F.R. §1630.2(h); EEOC's Technical Assistance Manual on Title I §2.2(a)(i)).

Neither the law nor enforcement regulations list all of the diseases or conditions that could be physical or mental impairments. On the other hand, they do state what are not impairments. The ADA does not cover homosexuality, bisexualism, transvestitism, transsexualism, compulsive gambling, kleptomania, pyromania, pedophilia, exhibitionism, voyeurism, those with gender identity disorders not resulting from physical impairments or other sexual behavior disorders. In addition, because the use of illegal drugs and current addiction to illegal drugs are not considered disabilities, neither are psychoactive substance use disorders resulting from the current illegal use of drugs (42 U.S.C. §12211).

The law also does not cover individuals who are currently engaging in the illegal use of drugs (42 U.S.C. §12210). However, it does cover rehabilitated drug users who are no longer using, and it covers alcoholics, even those who continue to drink. But employers can enforce policies prohibiting alcohol on the premises and can discipline, including fire, employees who show up at work after they have been drinking.

The ADA does not cover physical characteristics, such as eye or hair color or left handedness. Nor does it cover physiological conditions such as pregnancy (although complications that cause a disability may be covered) or predispositions to diseases that would not be impairments. Personality traits, such as poor judgment, quick temper or irresponsible behavior; or environmental, cultural or economic disadvantages such as lack of education or a prison record also are not within the ADA's protective scope (EEOC's Technical Assistance Manual on Title I §2.2).

These distinctions are often more complicated than they appear. The EEOC gave the examples of two people with the same difficulty: an inability to read. However, one individual has dyslexia and one is illiterate due to lack of education. The first person has a disability that requires an attempt at accommodation. The second has no disability.

Whether the individual could have prevented the condition that results in a disability is not relevant. For example, the EEOC and some courts hold that morbid obesity is a disability, even though the individual might be able to lose weight. The same is true of cardiovascular disease that may be caused or worsened by smoking or an unhealthy diet. (See, for example, *Cook v. Rhode Island Dept. of Mental Health, Retardation & Hospitals*, 10 F.3d 17 (1st Cir. 1993).)

Direct Threat to Self or Others

The ADA does not require an employer to hire or retain an employee who poses a direct threat to the health or safety of him- or herself or others. The statute states that "direct threat" means "a significant risk to the health or safety of others that cannot be eliminated by reasonable accommodation." The EEOC added "substantial harm to the health or safety *of the individual* or others" in its regulations (29 C.F.R. §1630.2(r)).

In a unanimous decision, the U.S. Supreme Court held that the ADA's direct threat provision applied to an employee's own health in light of the Occupational Safety and Health Act (*Chevron v. Echazabal*, 536 U.S. 73 (2002)). The case involved a worker with hepatitis C. The employer was concerned that substances in its workplace would endanger the worker's health. If employers could not keep workers with disabilities who pose a direct threat to their own health from the workforce, the companies' duty to comply with the ADA would be "at loggerheads with the competing policy of OSHA to ensure the safety of each and every worker," the Court said.

The statute also states that individuals with infectious or communicable diseases that can be transmitted to others through the handling of food do not have to be hired or retained if there is no reasonable accommodation that can eliminate the threat (42 U.S.C. §12113(d)(2)). Individuals with contagious diseases such as AIDS may have a covered disability, but an employer does not have to hire them if they would pose a direct threat to the health or safety of themselves or others in the workplace and no reasonable accommodation can reduce or eliminate the threat.

The regulations explain that determining whether an individual poses a "direct threat" must "be based on an individualized assessment of the person's present ability to safely perform the essential functions of the job." An assessment is to be "based on reasonable medical judgment that relies on the most current medical knowledge and/or the best available objective evidence" (29 C.F.R. §1630.2(r)).

To establish that a direct threat exists, the employer must show the following:

- "a significant risk of substantial harm;

- the specific risk must be identified;

- it must be a current risk, not one that is speculative or remote;

- the assessment of risk must be based on objective medical or other factual evidence regarding a particular individual; and

- even if a genuine significant risk of substantial harm exists, the employer must consider whether the risk can be eliminated or reduced below the level of a direct threat by reasonable accommodation" (EEOC's Technical Assistance on Title I §4.5).

Specific factors to consider in determining whether an individual poses a direct threat, the Supreme Court has said, include (1) the duration of the risk; (2) the nature and severity of the potential harm; (3) the likelihood that the potential harm will occur; and (4) the imminence of the potential harm (see *School Bd. of Nassau County v. Arline*, 480 U.S. 273 (1987)).

Employers cannot assume an individual with a disability will have an increased risk of injury and a potential for higher workers' compensation or insurance costs is not a defense to discrimination under the ADA. The employer must conduct a fact-based, individualized assessment that takes into account the person's specific circumstances, including:

- whether the prior injury was related to the individual's disability;

- the circumstances surrounding the prior injury;

- whether the injury involved hazards not associated with the current job;

- the individual's current physical condition;

- the number and frequency of prior injuries;

- how long the individual has been injury free; and

- whether the threat can be lowered or eliminated with reasonable accommodations (EEOC Enforcement Guidance on Workers' Compensation and the ADA, 9/3/96).

Especially with respect to individuals who are already employees when a threat to health or safety arises, the EEOC maintains that employer are required to provide a reasonable accommodation if doing so would eliminate the threat. For example, an applicant for a kitchen job in a restaurant who has an infectious disease that can be transmitted through the food supply can be rejected. If current kitchen employee develops such an illness, the employer would be obligated to attempt to find a reasonable accommodation to eliminate the risk, such as reassignment to another job in the restaurant.

However, the courts are divided on whether reassignment is a reasonable accommodation, especially in light of the rights and expectations of other workers seeking new positions.

Physical illness is not the only type of threat covered by these provisions. Employers can fire employees for unacceptable behavior or misconduct, especially when a threat of some kind is involved. The fact that the behavior or conduct was precipitated by a disabling condition is not an issue under the ADA. The law does not require employers to retain potentially violent employees (see *Palmer v. Circuit Court of Cook County, Ill.*, 117 F.3d 351 (7th Cir. 1997)).

Example: The firing of a teacher who told nine students she was going to "kill" them did not violate the ADA, a federal district court ruled. The fact that the teacher had a psychological disability as the result of a severe head injury did not protect her from discipline that would be imposed on any other teacher (*Macy v. Hopkins County Bd. of Ed.*, 429 F. Supp. 2d 888 (W.D. Ky. 2006)).

Example: Making a threat is not the same as posing a threat. When an employee threatens someone in the workplace, there is no need to make an individualized assessment of the danger. Making a threat is "a legitimate, non-discriminatory reason for termination" (*Sista v. CDC IXIS North America, Inc.*, 445 F.3d 161 (2d Cir. 2006)).

Example: The termination of an employee who threatened violence during an exchange with his supervisor did not violate the ADA because this conduct rendered the employee unqualified for his job. An employee whose unacceptable behavior threatens the safety of others need not be retained even if the behavior stems from a mental disability, the 1st U.S. Circuit Court of Appeals ruled in *Rose v. Laskey* (110 Fed. Appx. 136 (1st Cir. 2004) unpublished) quoting the 5th Circuit (*Hamilton v. Southwestern Bell Tel. Co.*, 136 F.3d 1047 (5th Cir. 1998)).

Because the direct threat exception is an affirmative defense, the employer generally bears the burden of proving that the threat actually exists (see *EEOC v. Wal-Mart Stores, Inc.*, 477 F.3d 561 (8th Cir. 2007)). In that case, the employer failed to show that a mobility-impaired applicant for the job of store greeter or cashier posed a direct threat to the health or safety of others.

Temporary and Intermittent Conditions

Temporary non-chronic conditions, such as broken ankles, that do not last for long and have little or no lasting impact usually are not impairments covered by the ADA. They can become impairments, however, due to complications. The important question is whether the impairment substantially limits one or more major life activity. The answer is found by examining the extent, duration and impact of the impairment.

The EEOC and a number of courts agree that if the impairment lasts several months, it is not short term. (See, for example, *Aldrich v. Boeing Co.*, 146 F.3d 1265 (10th Cir. 1998), in which the duration of the employee's condition was indefinite; *Katz v. City Metal Co.*, 87 F.3d 26 (1st Cir. 1996), in which a condition that was expected to last at least several months could be a disability.)

On the other hand, some courts have held that an impairment must be permanent to be covered by the ADA. (See, for example, *Pangalos v. Prudential Ins. Co. of America*, 118 F.3d 1577 (3d Cir. 1997), in which the court said to be a disability a condition must be permanent or at least of indefinite duration.)

An intermittent impairment may be a disability under the ADA. As one federal appeals court explained, often "the disabling aspect of a disability is, precisely, an intermittent manifestation of the disability, rather than the underlying impairment."

The employee in the case was paralyzed from the waist down as the result of a spinal cord tumor. Her paralysis made her prone to develop pressure ulcers. Treatment of those ulcers required her to stay home, sometimes for several weeks. The employer argued that there was no duty to accommodate her ulcers because they did not fit the statutory definition of a disability. Intermittent, episodic impairments were not disabilities, the employer claimed.

On the contrary, the court ruled, an intermittent impairment that is a characteristic manifestation of an admitted disability is a part of the underlying disability and, thus, must be reasonably accommodated. For example, the AIDS virus progressively destroys the infected person's immune system, resulting in a series of opportunistic diseases that often prevent the employee from working. If they are not part of the disability, the court said, then people with AIDS do not have a disability, "which seems to us a very odd interpretation of the law and one expressly rejected in the regulations."

The court found that the employee's pressure ulcers were part of her disability and the employer had a duty to reasonably accommodate them (*Vande Zande v. State of Wisconsin Dept. of Admin.*, 44 F.3d 538 (7th Cir. 1995)).

Limitations Caused by Disability

The *Vande Zande* case leads to the question of whether employers are required to accommodate only the disability and the substantial limitations it causes, or also the limitations that result from having the disability. The EEOC took the broad approach, stating in a friend of the court brief that accommodations are for any known physical or mental limitations flowing from the disability even if the substantially limited major life activity is not related to the accommodation (*Felix v. New York City Transit Authority*, 324 F.3d 102 (2d Cir. 2003) brief filed 12/14/01).

Some courts have held that there must be a causal connection between the major life activity that is substantially limited by the disability and the accommodation. If a mobility restriction affects only an employee's ability to reproduce, a reasonable accommodation must relate to reproduction (*Nuzum v. Ozark Automotive Distributors, Inc.*, 432 F.3d 839 (8th Cir. 2005)). Because the ADA requires employers to reasonably accommodate limitations to major life activities, not disabilities, another court decided, accommodations need not be provided if they are not related to a limitation (*Wood v. Crown Redi-Mix, Inc.*, 339 F.3d 682 (8th Cir. 2003)).

Courts seem to agree that the accommodation must be needed because of limitations flowing from a disability. Thus, an employer was not required to change its workplace policy that employees requesting light-duty assignments had to submit documentation. Failing to submit documentation had nothing to do with the disability of an employee who wanted a vacant light-duty position as an accommodation (*Peebles v. Potter*, 354 F.3d 761 (8th Cir. 2004)).

Major Life Activities

An ADA-covered disability is a physical or mental impairment that substantially limits one or more major life activities (42 U.S.C. §12101(2)). Major life activities are things an average person can perform with little or no difficulty. There is some controversy over what are major life activities and the EEOC has added to the list it gave in its original regulations. The commission gives the following examples:

- walking;

- seeing;

- speaking;

- hearing;

- breathing;

- learning;

- performing manual tasks;

- caring for oneself; and

- working.

The agency says other examples include sitting, standing, lifting and reaching (29 C.F.R. Part 1630 App. §1630.2(i)). Also included in major life activities are thinking, concentrating, interacting with others and sleeping (EEOC Enforcement Guidance on the ADA and Psychiatric Disabilities (3/25/97)). In a friend of the court brief, the commission stated that the ability to control bodily functions, such as one's bowels, is a major life activity.

Some courts have disagreed with some of the elements on the EEOC's list. One appeals court found, for example, that while sleeping was a major life activity, concentrating was merely a component of other life activities such as working, learning or speaking (*Pack v.*

Kmart Corp., 166 F.3d 1300 (10th Cir. 1999)). Another court declared that interacting with others is not a major life activity. While it is a skill to be prized, the court declared, it is not the same as breathing or walking (*Soileau v. Guilford of Maine*, 105 F.3d 12 (1st Cir. 1997)).

Numerous cases have dealt with activities that are not on the EEOC's list. Courts have held that throwing, squatting, running, eating, reading and traveling freely are major life activities. An activity does not have to have a public, economic or daily dimension to be a major life activity, the U.S. Supreme Court said in a case in which it held that reproduction is a major life activity and suggested that sex itself also might be one (*Bragdon v. Abbott*, 524 U.S. 624 (1998)).

On the other hand, courts have held that driving, shopping, skiing, golfing, painting, shoveling snow and climbing are not major life activities. Indeed, one court held that awareness is not a major life activity and that, therefore, an individual with epilepsy whose seizures caused temporary loss of awareness did not have a disability (*Deas v. River West*, 152 F.3d 471 (5th Cir. 1998)).

Sometimes a plaintiff's case concentrates so hard on showing that the employee could do the job, the need to present evidence that he or she has a disability that substantially impacts a major life activity is overlooked. An intellectually disabled applicant for a job at Wal-Mart lost his case because by arguing how well he could do the job, his attorney forgot to emphasize that his client had difficulty with the major life activities of thinking and communicating. The court ruled in an unpublished decision that the plaintiff was not disabled under the law (*Littleton v. Wal-Mart Stores Inc.*, No. 05-12770 (11th Cir. 2007) unpublished).

Reproduction as Major Life Activity

One of the body systems listed in the EEOC's regulations as being affected by a physical impairment is the reproductive system. The commission is silent, however, in its regulations and Technical Assistance Manual on Title I of the ADA about whether infertility, or a communicable disease that makes it wise not to engage in unprotected sexual activity, is a disability that affects a major life activity.

Some courts have ruled that having and caring for children is not a major life activity. For example, an employee sued under the ADA, claiming her employer's health plan violated the law because it excluded coverage for infertility. "To treat reproduction and caring for others as major life activities under the ADA would be inconsistent with the illustrative list of activities in the regulations and a considerable stretch of federal law," the federal appeals court said (*Krauel v. Iowa Methodist Medical Ctr.*, 95 F.3d 674 (8th Cir. 1996)).

Although the commission has taken no official position on infertility as a disability, one of its field offices issued a determination letter on April 27, 1999, stating that an employer-sponsored insurance plan's denial of coverage for an employee's infertility treatment may be a violation of the ADA.

The employee was diagnosed with a hormonal imbalance and her doctor prescribed oral medication. The employee became pregnant, but later miscarried. Subsequent diagnostic and genetic tests were performed to determine the cause of the miscarriage. The woman also underwent surgery to prevent infection and potential bleeding.

The employer-sponsored insurance plan allegedly denied coverage for all related medical treatment except the oral medication. The determination letter said that the employee was protected by the ADA because she suffered from a pregnancy-related medical impairment

The U.S. Supreme Court ruled that reproduction is a major life activity, but not whether infertility is a disability under the ADA. The case involved a dental patient with asymptomatic HIV. She sued the dentist who refused to do the routine filling of a cavity in his office. Due to fear of contracting the disease, the dentist insisted that the patient be treated in a hospital, where she would have been charged hospital fees as well as the usual dental fee. The dentist insisted that the woman was not protected by the ADA because she was not substantially limited in a major life activity.

Because of the danger of passing HIV to a partner and an unborn child, the patient insisted her disease, even though it had no symptoms, substantially limited her ability to reproduce. Reproduction cannot be regarded as any less important than working and learning, the Supreme Court said, noting that the sexual dynamics surrounding reproduction are central to the life process itself. The Court ruled that reproduction is a major life activity and that HIV substantially limited that activity, making asymptomatic infection with the virus a disability under the ADA (*Bragdon v. Abbott*, 524 U.S. 624 (1998)).

There is reason to believe that *Bragdon* is a product of the "AIDS hysteria" of the last century, and, therefore, not a compelling precedent. Lower courts have found ways to distinguish it and avoid dealing with the notion of an asymptomatic disability.

Substantially Limited

To be covered by the law, an individual has to prove that he or she has a recognized impairment, identify one or more appropriate major life activities and show that the impairment "substantially limits" one or more of those activities (see *Holt v. Grand Lake Mental Health Center, Inc.*, 443 F.3d 762 (10th Cir. 2006)).

"Substantially limits" means the individual is unable to perform or is significantly limited in the ability to perform an activity compared to an average person in the general population. A substantial impairment is one "that prevents or severely restricts" a person "from doing activities that are of central importance to most people's daily lives" and that is "permanent or long term," the Supreme Court explained (*Toyota Motor Manufacturing v. Williams*, 534 U.S. 184 (2002)).

There are three factors to consider in determining whether an individual's impairment substantially limits a major life activity:

- its nature and severity;

- how long it will last or is expected to last; and

- its permanent or long-term impact or expected impact (EEOC's Technical Assistance on Title I §2.2(a)).

It is not the name of the condition or impairment, but the effect that condition or impairment has on the life of the individual that determines whether the person is protected by the ADA, the EEOC explained. While some impairments by their nature are substantially limiting, such as blindness, deafness or AIDS, other impairments may be disabling for some individuals and not others.

Example: The example the commission gives in its Technical Assistance Manual is cerebral palsy. Cerebral palsy can be a debilitating condition for some people, interfering with speech, the ability to walk and perform manual tasks. Individuals with mild conditions may have only a slight speech impairment and no other significant impairments of major life activities. The latter would not have a disability under the ADA.

Example: A mobile phone company employee had multiple sclerosis. Although she was impaired – she tired easily and had to rest often – she could not show that the impairment substantially limited any of her major life activities. Her medical records showed that many of her symptoms were addressed with medication. The appeals court ruled that she was not substantially limited, and, therefore, was not a person with a disability as defined by the ADA (*Berry v. T-Mobile USA, Inc.*, 2007 WL 1830755 (10th Cir. 2007)).

Example: An employee with acute stress disorder and generalized anxiety alleged that she was substantially limited in her ability to think and work. She was able to complete work assignments at home with no problem, and requested full-time telecommuting as an accommodation. The fact that she could work at home indicated "she was not significantly impaired from thinking," the appeals court found. That fact also showed that she was not substantially limited in her ability to work. Because she was not substantially limited in a major life activity, she did not have an ADA-covered disability (*Ashton v. American Telephone and Telegraph Co.*, 2007 WL 595251 (3d Cir. 2007)).

Individuals may have two or more impairments, neither of which by itself substantially limits a major life activity but together, do. That individual has a disability, the EEOC's Technical Assistance Manual on Title I of the ADA states, giving the example of an employee who has mild arthritis and osteoporosis, which together significantly restrict the worker's ability to lift and perform manual tasks.

Determining whether an individual is substantially limited is always based on the effect of the impairment on that individual's life activities, the commission explained. One individual with a back injury may have constant pain that interferes with walking, sitting, standing and other mobility-related activities, while another may have good pain control and be able to pursue an active lifestyle. Only the individual whose impairment substantially limits everyday activities has an ADA-covered disability.

Courts generally find that an impairment that affects but does not substantially interfere with a major life activity is not a disability. Pain in walking, depression that causes some anxiety, some difficulty in sleeping, inability to sit or stand for very long or to walk or run briskly or for extended distances are not substantially limiting impairments. Neither is below average physical ability in such activities as lifting, pulling or pushing.

Often, courts look at what an individual *can* do when determining whether he or she has a substantial impairment. An individual with asthma who can play football, run, sing and water ski was found not to be substantially impaired in breathing. An individual with a knee injury who could still walk, do yard work, engage in recreational activities and drive was not substantially limited in a major life activity. Each case must be examined on an individual basis.

Substantially Limited in Working

There is an issue about whether "working" can even be considered a major life activity. The Supreme Court has questioned it, without specifically deciding, saying the justices were "hesitant to decide that working could be a major life activity" (*Toyota Motor Manufacturing v. Williams*, 534 U.S. 184 (2002)) and that "there may be some conceptual difficulty in defining 'working' as a major life activity" (*Sutton v. United Air Lines*, 527 U.S. 492 (1999)).

In any event, even the EEOC pointed out in its Technical Assistance Manual on Title I that whether an individual is substantially limited in the major life activity of working need not be determined if there is a substantial limitation to another major life activity. For example, an individual who is blind, deaf or confined to a wheelchair has a disability under the ADA because of a substantial limitation to the major life activity of seeing, hearing or walking. There is no need to consider whether the individual is also substantially limited in working.

Some employers have objected to the EEOC's position, arguing that if an impairment does not interfere with an individual's ability to work, it is irrelevant in the workplace. Most courts have not agreed, finding that if there is any substantial impairment of a major life activity, the individual has an ADA-covered disability. Working is just one of the possible major life activities that may be substantially limited, one court said (*Davidson v. Midelfort Clinic*, 133 F.3d 499 (7th Cir. 1998)).

"Proving that an employee is disabled in the major life activity of working takes the plaintiff to the farthest reaches of the ADA," according to the 6th U.S. Circuit Court of Appeals (*Ross v. Campbell Soup Co.*, 237 F.3d 701 (6th Cir. 2001)). An employee is substantially limited in the major life activity of working only when an impairment significantly restricts the employee's ability to perform either a *class of jobs* or a *broad range of jobs* in various classes when compared to the average person with comparable training, skills and abilities. An employee is not substantially limited in working if he or she is unable to perform only a single job (29 C.F.R. §1630.2(j)).

An individual who cannot qualify as a commercial airline pilot because of a minor vision impairment, but who can fly in other capacities is not substantially limited in working, the EEOC said in its Technical Assistance Manual. A pitcher who can no longer pitch, or a quarterback who can no longer throw would not be substantially limited in working, presuming it is only those specialized jobs they can no longer perform.

Example: A welder whose arm injury prevented her from lifting heavy objects and doing repetitive rotational movements, but not the normal activities of daily living, was not substantially limited in her ability to perform a large class of jobs. Consequently, her discharge for being unable to climb a ladder, which was a requirement of her job, was not a violation of the ADA (*Dutcher v. Ingalls Shipbuilding*, 53 F.3d 723 (5th Cir. 1995)).

Example: Similarly, a car paint inspector with carpal tunnel who could not perform the task of wiping down freshly painted cars because of the repetitive motions required was not substantially limited, the U.S. Supreme Court ruled, because responsibilities unique to a job "are not necessarily important parts of most peoples' lives." The woman could brush her teeth, wash her face, bathe, tend her flower garden, fix breakfast, do laundry and pick up around the house, the Court found, and even though she stopped or reduced the amount of time she spent doing some common activities, the change was not enough to show a substantial limitation (*Toyota Motor Manufacturing v. Williams*, 534 U.S. 184 (2002)).

An individual need not be totally unable to work to be considered substantially limited in working. In its regulations, the EEOC says the following factors may be considered when determining if an individual is substantially limited in the major life activity of working:

- The geographical area to which the individual has reasonable access.

- The *class of jobs* from which the individual has been disqualified due to an impairment. That is, the number and types of jobs in the geographical area that use similar training, knowledge, skills or abilities.

- The *range of jobs* from which the individual has been disqualified because of an impairment. That is, the number and types of other jobs within the geographical area that do not require similar training, knowledge, skills or abilities from which the individual is also disqualified due to the impairment (29 C.F.R. §1630.2(j)).

For example, an individual is significantly restricted in a *class of jobs* if a back injury prevents him or her from doing heavy labor. An individual is considered significantly limited in the ability to perform a *broad range of jobs* if he or she has an allergy to a substance found in most office buildings in the area and the allergy causes extreme difficulty in breathing.

The final decision can come down to numbers. A former courier who had a 30-pound lifting restriction due to a back injury and could no longer do his job or even 57 percent of the job titles in the geographical area for which he would have qualified absent the injury, was not substantially limited in his ability to work because he was able to perform his daily activities and qualified for over 1,400 job titles and over 130,000 actual jobs in the geographic region (*Taylor v. Federal Express Corp.*, 429 F.3d 461 (4th Cir. 2005) *cert. denied*, No. 05-1023, 5/22/06).

It must be remembered that the regulation requires that an individual be restricted in the ability to perform *either* a class of jobs *or* a broad range of jobs (29 C.F.R. §1630.2(j)(3)(i)). If an employee is significantly restricted in the ability to perform most of the jobs in his or her geographical area that require training, knowledge, skills and abilities similar to the job from which he or she has been disqualified, that individual is substantially limited in the major life activity of working, according to the 3rd U.S. Circuit Court of Appeals, regardless of whether there is a broad range of jobs the individual could perform (*Williams v. Philadelphia Housing Authority Police Dept.*, 380 F.3d 751 (3d Cir. 2004)).

An employer can *regard* an employee as substantially limited in working, according to the 6th U.S. Circuit Court of Appeals. A hospital administrator was perceived to be an alcoholic by his boss, and therefore unable to perform the essential functions of his job. The court found that the administrator's employer perceived him to be unable to perform a broad class of jobs – essentially all of those requiring senior management skills – and violated the ADA by firing him while he was undergoing rehabilitation (*Moorer v. Baptist Memorial Health Care System*, 398 F.3d 469 (6th Cir. 2005)).

The U.S. Supreme Court has questioned whether working is a major life activity at all. It noted that "there may be some conceptual difficulty in defining 'major life activity' to include work" (*Sutton v. United Air Lines*, 527 U.S. 492 (1999)), but the Court did not rule specifically on the issue. In any event, employees who claim the major life activity in which they are substantially impaired is working generally find it difficult to prove their cases. Courts look not just at what jobs the employees cannot do, but what jobs they can do.

The *Toyota* case has made it clear that even if working were a major life activity, not being able to do one's job as a result of physical or intellectual impairments does *not* implicate the ADA. One's limitations must reach beyond the workplace and affect the common daily activities of one's life.

Mitigating Measures

The ADA itself does not discuss mitigating measures, such as medication or assistive devices, and their effect on whether an individual is substantially limited in a major life activity. In its Technical Assistance Manual on Title I, the EEOC insisted that an individual's impairment must be determined without regard to medication or assistive devices. A person with epilepsy whose medication controls seizures or someone who walks with an artificial leg has an impairment, even if the medicine or prosthesis reduces the impact of that impairment, the commission said.

Most federal appeals courts that ruled on the issue agreed with the EEOC's position that disabilities should be determined without reference to mitigating measures. (See, e.g., *Baert v. Euclid Beverage*, 149 F.3d 626 (7th Cir. 1998); *Matczak v. Frankford Candy & Chocolate Co.*, 136 F.3d 933 (3d Cir. 1997); *Arnold v. United Parcel Service*, 136 F.3d 854 (1st Cir. 1998).) However, the U.S. Supreme Court did not see it that way in three decisions handed down in June 1999. Employers and courts now have to determine whether individuals still have impairments that substantially limit major life activities if they use medication, assistive devices or other aids.

The disability cases the Supreme Court chose to rule on involved myopia corrected with eyeglasses, high blood pressure somewhat controlled with medication and monocular vision for which the individual involved had learned to compensate. Two of the cases also involved safety rules issued by federal agencies.

Sutton v. United Air Lines

Twin sisters Karen Sutton and Kimberly Hinton, both of whom had myopia of 20/200 in one eye and 20/400 in the other, correctable to 20/20 vision with glasses or contact lenses, sued United Air Lines after they were rejected for positions as commercial airline pilots, claiming that United discriminated against them on the basis of their disability in violation of the ADA.

United, which requires its pilots to have uncorrected vision of 20/100 or better, argued that the sisters did not meet its minimum standards and that they were not disabled because when corrected, their vision was identical to individuals who had no impairment. The Supreme Court held that because the women were not substantially limited in a major life activity when they wore glasses or contact lenses, they were not disabled under the ADA (*Sutton v. United Air Lines*, 527 U.S. 492 (1999)).

Stating that the EEOC had not been delegated the authority to interpret the term "disability," the Supreme Court noted that the commission's guidance called for determining whether an individual had a substantially limiting impairment without regard to mitigating measures and concluded that this was an impermissible interpretation of the law.

"Looking at the act as a whole, it is apparent that if a person is taking measures to correct for, or mitigate, a physical or mental impairment, the effects of those measures – both positive and negative – must be taken into account when judging whether that person is 'substantially limited' in a major life activity and thus 'disabled' under the act," the Court said.

A disability exists only when an impairment actually limits a major life activity, the Court explained, not when it might, could or would be limiting if mitigating measures were not taken. A "person whose physical or mental impairment is corrected by mitigating measures still has an impairment, but if the impairment is corrected it does not 'substantially limit' a major life activity."

Moreover, the Court said, the EEOC's approach runs directly counter to the individualized inquiry mandated by the ADA. Under this view, "courts would almost certainly find all diabetics to be disabled," even those whose condition does not impair daily activities. In addition, the commission's approach could "lead to the anomalous result that in determining whether an individual is disabled, courts and employers could not consider any negative side effects suffered by an individual resulting from the use of mitigating measures, even when those side effects are very severe," the Court pointed out.

Finally, the Court looked to the law's preamble to support its position that medication or other measures should be taken into account in determining whether an individual has an ADA-covered disability. The preamble stated that "some 43,000,000 Americans have one or more physical or mental disabilities." The number of people with vision impairments alone is 100 million, the Court said, insisting that had Congress intended to include all persons with corrected physical limitations among those covered by the law, it would have cited a much higher number of disabled persons in its findings.

"The use or nonuse" of corrective devices "does not determine whether an individual is disabled," the Court said. "[T]hat determination depends on whether the limitations an individual with an impairment actually faces are in fact substantially limiting." While the law does not define substantially limits, "'substantially' suggests 'considerable' or 'specified to a large degree,'" the Court explained.

Murphy v. United Parcel Service

Vaughn Murphy was diagnosed with high blood pressure as a child. With medication his pressure still was higher than normal, but he was not significantly restricted in his activities and could function normally. He was hired by United Parcel Service as a mechanic, a position that required him to have a commercial motor vehicle license. To be licensed, Murphy had to meet federal Department of Transportation requirements, including health standards for blood pressure.

Even though his medicated blood pressure exceeded DOT regulations, Murphy was erroneously certified to drive a commercial vehicle. A month after he was hired, a UPS medical supervisor discovered the error and Murphy was fired.

Murphy sued, claiming discrimination on the basis of his disability in violation of Title I of the ADA. UPS insisted it did not terminate Murphy because of an unsubstantiated fear that he would suffer a heart attack or stroke, but because his blood pressure exceeded the DOT's requirements. Murphy was not disabled because in his medicated state, he functioned normally, the Supreme Court decided. Moreover, UPS did not regard him as disabled, only uncertifiable under DOT regulations, the Court held (*Murphy v. United Parcel Service*, 527 U.S. 516 (1999)).

Citing its decision in *Sutton*, the Court ruled that whether an individual is disabled should be determined with reference to the mitigating measures the individual uses. As for being regarded as substantially limited in the major life activity of working, the Court said, at most Murphy showed that he was regarded as unable to perform only a particular job. That "is insufficient, as a matter of law, to prove that [he] is regarded as substantially limited" in working, the Court decided.

Albertsons v. Kirkingburg

Hallie Kirkingburg was erroneously certified as meeting DOT vision standards of at least 20/40 in each eye. In fact, Kirkingburg's left eye was only 20/200 and was not correctable. Two years later his vision was correctly assessed and he was told he would have to get a waiver of DOT standards under a program begun that year.

The employer fired him for not meeting DOT's vision standard and refused to rehire him even after he received the waiver. Kirkingburg sued under the ADA, claiming discrimination on the basis of his disability. The Supreme Court held that although he saw differently than others, Kirkingburg did not have an impairment that substantially limited a major life activity because he compensated by adjusting his behavior (*Albertsons v. Kirkingburg*, 527 U.S. 555 (1999)).

The ADA requires individuals claiming its protection to prove they have a disability that causes a substantial restriction on a major life activity. The appeals court found that there was a significant difference between the manner in which Kirkingburg saw and that in which most people see, the Supreme Court noted. "By transforming 'significant restriction' into 'difference,' the [appeals] court undercut the fundamental statutory requirement that only impairments that substantially limit the ability to perform a major life activity constitute disabilities."

Moreover, the appeals court seemed to suggest that it need not take into account an individual's ability to compensate for an impairment, even though it acknowledged that Kirkingburg's brain had subconsciously done just that. "[M]itigating measures must be taken into account in judging whether an individual possesses a disability," the Court ruled.

And finally, "the appeals court did not pay much heed to the statutory obligation to determine a disability's existence on a case-by-case basis." Some impairments invariably cause a substantial limitation on a major life activity, the Supreme Court acknowledged, but monocularity is not one of them, because it encompasses a group of individuals whose conditions vary in numerous ways, including the degree of visual acuity in the weaker eye, the extent of compensating adjustments, and the ultimate scope of the restrictions on visual abilities.

The Court went on to say that the employer's job qualification was not of its own devising, but was the standard of the federal Motor Carrier Safety Regulations. An employer that requires as a job qualification that an employee meet an otherwise applicable federal safety regulation does not have to justify enforcing the regulation solely because its standard may be waived experimentally in an individual case, the Court held.

EEOC's Revised Guidance

A month after the Supreme Court's *Sutton*, *Murphy* and *Albertsons* decisions, the EEOC issued instructions to its field offices, noting that "consistent with the Court's approach" in *Bragdon v. Abbott* (524 U.S. 624 (1998)) the agency would continue to give broad interpretation to the terms "impairment," "major life activity," and "substantial limitation." The agency also reminded its field staff that the list of major life activities in its regulations and enforcement guidelines "is not exhaustive."

Regarding the Court's 1999 trilogy of cases, the commission stated the following:

- any determination of whether a person has a disability must be made on a case-by-case basis;

- a disability determination must be based on an individual's actual condition at the time of the alleged discrimination – speculation regarding whether the person would have been substantially limited if he or she used a mitigating measure is irrelevant; and

- even with the use of mitigating measures, or perhaps because of the use of those measures, a person may be substantially limited in a major life activity.

The Court held that determining whether an individual has a disability under the ADA includes an analysis of whether the person has a record of or is regarded as having a disability, the EEOC's instructions stated. (See Chapter 2 for discussion of "record of" and "regarded as.") Employers should not misinterpret the Supreme Court's rulings as meaning certain conditions are automatically excluded from the ADA's coverage, the commission added.

For example, someone with Parkinson's disease may take medication, but still suffer from severe trembling. An individual who has a hearing aid may be able to hear low and high pitches, but not actual words. A person with monocular vision may make behavioral modifications that address that person's problems with distance vision, but not close-range vision, the EEOC explained.

Field investigators were advised to consider whether the mitigating measure or compensating behavior fully or only partially controlled the symptoms or limitations of the impairment. In making an individualized determination of whether someone using mitigating measures or compensating behavior had a disability, investigators were advised to consider several questions, including the following:

- Does the mitigating measure control the symptoms or limitation all or only some of the time?

- Do any limitations remain despite a compensating behavior?

- Does the mitigating measure become less effective under certain conditions, such as adverse weather?

There is not much new to be gleaned from the Court's decisions about the major life activity of working, the instructions asserted. Individuals who could not work as global pilots were not substantially limited in the major life activity of working because global piloting is not a broad range of jobs, but rather one job. Likewise, an individual who could not work as a mechanic required to drive commercial vehicles was not substantially limited in working, because those types of mechanics do not constitute a broad range of jobs, the EEOC said.

Mitigating measures themselves might cause substantial limitations of major life activities, the commission noted. Major life activities such as thinking, standing, lifting, walking, eating, caring for oneself, sleeping, performing manual tasks, reproduction and working might be substantially limited by certain medications, the instructions explained.

For example, an individual who treats a psychiatric illness or epilepsy with medication might be substantially limited in thinking or concentrating because the medication makes the person groggy, disoriented or slow. Someone with diabetes might be substantially limited in eating because they must adhere to extensive dietary restrictions. Individualized analysis of the effect of medications on different people was imperative, the agency said.

Meaning for Employers

Employers need only provide reasonable accommodations for ADA-covered disabilities, but it is difficult to predict what conditions will be considered disabilities by the EEOC and the courts. The safest course is for employers to respond to requests for accommodations by initiating an interactive process (see chapter 4) with the employee to determine what kind of difficulties the worker is having in performing the job's essential functions and what reasonable accommodations might alleviate the problems.

If the accommodations can be provided without much difficulty or expense, the employer should provide them. If the requested accommodations would disrupt the workplace, be difficult or expensive to provide, the employer might explore whether the employee making the request has an impairment that substantially limits a major life activity and/or whether providing the accommodation would impose an undue hardship on the employer's business.

Congressional Reaction

In the wake of a number of Supreme Court decisions, legislation has been introduced in both houses of Congress to "restore" the ADA. The proposals simplify and broaden the meaning of "disability" and largely erase the Supreme Court's mitigating measures rulings. If these proposals become law, the ADA will be very different from what it is now.

What 'Reasonable Accommodation' Means

2

Congress did not define the term "reasonable accommodation" other than by giving examples of the modifications or aids that might be provided to qualified individuals with disabilities to enable them to perform the essential functions of a job. There are no quantitative, financial or other limitations on the term to guide employers on the extent of their obligations, other than to say that an accommodation that would cause an "undue hardship" on the employer's business is "not reasonable."

Reasonable accommodations can include "making existing facilities used by employees readily accessible to and usable by individuals with disabilities; and job restructuring, part-time or modified work schedules, reassignment to a vacant position, acquisition or modification of equipment or devices, appropriate adjustment or modifications of examinations, training materials or policies, the provision of qualified readers or interpreters, and other similar accommodations," according to the statute (42 U.S.C. §12111(9)).

The EEOC interpreted the requirement to mean that reasonable accommodation included "modifications or adjustments":

- to a job application process;

- to the work environment or the manner or circumstances under which the position is customarily performed; or

- that enable the employee with a disability to enjoy benefits and privileges of employment equal to those of similarly situated employees without disabilities (29 C.F.R. §1630.2(o)).

The interpretive guidance appended to the EEOC's regulations explained that reasonable accommodation could include permitting the use of accrued paid leave or providing additional unpaid leave for necessary treatment, making employer-provided transportation accessible or providing reserved parking spaces. Providing personal assistants or travel attendants on business trips could also be a reasonable accommodation, as could making facilities such as break rooms, lunchrooms, training rooms and restrooms accessible (29 C.F.R. Part 1630 App. §1630.2(o)).

Again, these are just examples, not a real definition. The EEOC attempted to provide a definition in its Technical Assistance Manual on Title I of the ADA. Reasonable accommodation "is any change in the work environment or in the way things are usually done that results in equal employment opportunity for an individual with a disability."

Reasonable accommodations remove workplace barriers for individuals with disabilities, which is the goal of the ADA – to "assure equality of opportunity" to the estimated 43 million Americans who have one or more physical or mental disabilities (42 U.S.C. §12101(a)(8)). But what the term "reasonable" means has created a great deal of controversy.

'Effective' as 'Reasonable'

The EEOC said a reasonable accommodation is one that is "effective." It must enable the employee to perform the essential functions of the job and to have an equal opportunity to enjoy the benefits and privileges of employment. For job applicants, a reasonable accommodation must enable them to have an equal opportunity to participate in the application process and to be considered for employment on an equal basis.

The U.S. Supreme Court said a reasonable accommodation is one that "seems reasonable on its face" (*U.S. Airways, Inc. v. Barnett*, 535 U.S. 391 (2002)). The Court referred to the practical approach adopted by the 1st U.S. Circuit Court of Appeals in *Reed v. Lepage Bakeries, Inc.* (244 F.3d 254 (2001)). A reasonable accommodation must consider "the difficulty or expense imposed on the one doing the accommodating" the *Reed* court stated. It must, at least on its face, be feasible for the employer under the circumstances. The difficulty of providing an accommodation "will often be relevant both to the reasonableness of the accommodation and to whether it imposes an undue hardship," the 1st Circuit said.

Most federal appeals courts have adopted a form of "cost/benefit analysis" (discussed in detail in Chapter 8) to determine whether an accommodation is reasonable, but the Supreme Court neither approved nor rejected that approach. The EEOC, however, soundly rejected it, stating cost/benefit analysis "has no foundation in the statute, regulations, or legislative history of the ADA" in its updated Enforcement Guidance on Reasonable Accommodation and Undue Hardship released in October 2002.

The Supreme Court did reject the position taken by the EEOC that "reasonable" has no independent definition, simply meaning "effective" (29 C.F.R. §1620.9 App.; EEOC's Enforcement Guidance on Reasonable Accommodation and Undue Hardship, 3/1/99). In its 2002 update of the guidance, the EEOC modified its position slightly by stating that an accommodation must be both "reasonable" and "effective," which is no definition at all.

Clearly, an accommodation that does not accomplish the purpose of enabling an employee to do the essential functions of his or her job is not "reasonable" (see *EEOC v. Sears*, 417 F.3d 789 (7th Cir. 2005)). Perhaps as clearly, there is an understood if not clearly articulated limit to what an employer must do to meet a disabled employee's requests. Despite the EEOC's expansive interpretation, courts will require that there be a relationship between the cost of the accommo-

> ### EXAMPLES OF EFFECTIVE ACCOMMODATIONS
>
> A stool for a cashier who becomes easily fatigued can be an effective accommodation if it provides the employee with an equal opportunity to perform as well as any other cashier. Conducting an employment interview in an accessible room is effective if it permits applicants with disabilities an equal opportunity to participate in the process. These are examples of reasonable accommodations that meet the ADA's requirements because they provide equality of opportunity, courts have found.

dations and the value added to the company (*Vande Zande v. State of Wisconsin Dept. of Admin.*, 44 F.3d 538 (7th Cir. 1995)).

Associated With, Record of and Regarded as Disabled

The law prohibits discrimination against individuals who have a relationship or association with a person who has a disability (42 U.S.C. §12112(b)(4)). The association can be through family, business, social or other relationships. The idea behind the provision was to prevent employers from refusing to hire individuals who had family members with disabilities to keep their health insurance costs from rising.

It also was meant to keep fears and prejudices about some illnesses from impacting hiring decisions. As the U.S. Supreme Court said, "society's accumulated myths and fears about disability and diseases are as handicapping as are the physical limitations that flow from actual impairments" (*School Board of Nassau County v. Arline*, 480 U.S. 273 (1987)).

There is nothing in the ADA that requires reasonable accommodations for an employee who associates with an individual who has a disability (see *Den Hartog v. Wasatch Academy*, 129 F.3d 1076 (10th Cir. 1997); and *Larimer v. IBM Corp.*, 370 F.3d 898 (7th Cir. 2004)).

Few courts have addressed the issue of association. Those that have, have determined that employers may not harass employees because of their association with someone with a disability, or because of a perception that an employee would have to miss work or could not undertake some project because of the association (see *Overley v. Covenant Transportation, Inc.*, No. 05-5280 (6th Cir. 2006) unpublished; and EEOC's Enforcement Guidance on Unlawful Disparate Treatment of Workers With Caregiving Responsibilities, 5/23/07).

None has found that accommodation is necessary because of the disability of another person as opposed to the employee's own disability.

Accommodations for 'Record of' Disability

The ADA also prohibits discrimination against individuals who have "a record of" or are "regarded as" having a disability (42 U.S.C. §12102(2)(B) and (C)). The EEOC explained that having a record of an impairment means having a history of or being misclassified as having a mental or physical impairment that substantially limits one or more major life activities (29 C.F.R. §1630.2(k)).

In friend of the court briefs, the EEOC has taken the position that reasonable accommodations are required in "record of" disability cases. It apparently is a fine line between having a *record of* a disability and *currently having* that disability. Reasonable accommodations might be required for an individual with a record of a disability even though he or she cannot currently prove the presence of an impairment that substantially limits a major life activity (*Davidson v. Midelfort Clinic, Ltd.*, 133 F.3d 499 (7th Cir. 1998)).

The 7th Circuit said in the *Davidson* case that reasonable accommodations were appropriate for ongoing or recurrent limitations. It is not clear why "ongoing" or "recurrent" limitations would not qualify as regular disabilities, rather than just a record of a disability. Indeed, some courts have not distinguished between actual disabilities and record of or even regarded as having disabilities. The real question is whether an accommodation would enable the employee to perform the essential functions of the job at hand (see *Amadio v. Ford Motor Co.*, 238 F.3d 919 (7th Cir. 2001)).

Accommodation for 'Regarded as' Disabled

Being regarded as having a disability, according to the EEOC, means:

1. having a physical or mental impairment that does not rise to the level of a covered disability because it does not substantially limit a major life activity, but the employer acts as if it does;

2. having an condition that is limiting only because of the attitudes of others; or

3. having no impairment but being treated as if there is one that substantially limits a major life activity (see 29 C.F.R. §1630.2(l)).

In these cases, courts focus on the employer's perception, not an actual disability. That is why supervisors are advised not to ask about the health condition of an employee who requests an accommodation. If something goes wrong with the accommodation process, the employee has less chance of making a "regarded as" claim if the employer did not know about the worker's medical condition.

The EEOC considers the employer's knowledge of an employee's medical condition to be a critical piece of the "regarded as" issue. The less an employer, through its supervisors and managers, knows about its employees' health, the better.

Whether an accommodation is required in a "regarded as" case is unsettled. Certainly *providing* an accommodation does not, by itself, impute knowledge to an employer or show that it regarded the employee as having a disability. A statement by the 7th Circuit is illustrative: "decent managers try to help employees cope with declining health without knowing or caring whether they fit the definition in some federal statute" (*Cigan v. Chippewa Falls School District*, 388 F.3d 331 (7th Cir. 2004)). However, just as Title VII of the 1964 Civil Rights Act does not create a code of civil conduct in the workplace, the ADA does not require that managers be "decent."

Another court said providing minor accommodations was a sensible way to avoid litigation, liability and confrontation (*Colwell v. Suffolk County Police Dept.*, 158 F.3d 635 (2d Cir. 1998)). Helping an individual to perform better without delving into why the person needs help does not prove that an employer regarded the worker as disabled.

Similarly, providing information on or referring a worker to an employee assistance program, with nothing more, does not show the employer regarded the employee as having a disability. Even sending an employee for a medical exam, by itself, generally is not sufficient to show the employer regarded the worker as disabled.

With "regarded as" cases, the courts seem to want the supposed impairment to be one that, if it existed, would qualify as a disability under the ADA (see *Sutton v. Lader*, 185 F.3d 1203 (11th Cir. 1999)). Courts generally find that the employer must have considered the condition it thought the employee had to be substantially limiting and long term.

At least two federal appeals courts have said that employees who are regarded as disabled by their employers are entitled to reasonable accommodations that would enable them to perform the essential functions of their jobs, even if their conditions would not rise to the level of an actual disability under the ADA. This raises an internal conflict. Those who seek relief under the "regarded as" prong of the ADA insist that they are *falsely* regarded as disabled and are being prevented from doing a job they can do. For this class of employee, it is hard to imagine what accommodation could be provided or sought.

Example: An employee who worked as a product transporter suffered from vertigo. Her job required her to move products from one end of the line to another in and out of freezers, stack pallets and work around moving equipment. She handled these essential functions without difficulty. Then a new supervisor required her to work on a conveyer belt and she suffered an attack of vertigo. After receiving a note from her doctor stating that she should not work on the conveyer belt, the company fired her, claiming she posed a safety hazard. The employee sued.

Because her vertigo prevented her from holding only a narrow category of jobs and did not substantially impair her ability to work or perform other major life activities, the court found that the employee was not disabled. Her employer treated her as if she were, however, and so regarded her as disabled.

The ADA provides "no basis for differentiating among the three types of disabilities [actual, regarded as and association with those who are disabled] in determining which are entitled to a reasonable accommodation and which are not," the appeals court said (*D'Angelo v. ConAgra Foods, Inc.*, 422 F.3d 1220 (11th Cir. 2005)).

The 3d Circuit also required accommodations for a worker who was regarded as disabled (see *Williams v. Philadelphia Housing Authority Police Dept.*, 380 F.3d 751 (3d Cir. 2004)). The 1st Circuit indirectly agreed in a decision in which it assumed that the ADA requires accommodations for "regarded as" employees, but it did not expressly so hold (*Katz v. City Metal Co.*, 87 F.3d 26 (1st Cir. 1996)).

The 5th, 6th, 8th and 9th Circuits ruled the other way (*Newberry v. East Texas State Univ.*, 161 F.3d 276 (5th Cir. 1998); *Workman v. Frito-Lay, Inc.*, 165 F.3d 460 (6th Cir. 1999);

Weber v. Strippit, Inc., 186 F.3d 907 (8th Cir. 1999); *Kaplan v. City of North Las Vegas*, 323 F.3d 1226 (9th Cir. 2003)).

These courts reasoned that requiring accommodations for workers who are regarded as disabled would "create a disparity in treatment among impaired but non-disabled employees, denying most the right to reasonable accommodations but granting to others, because of their employers' misperceptions, a right to reasonable accommodation no more limited than that afforded actually disabled employees" (*Weber v. Strippit, Inc.*, 186 F.3d 907 (8th Cir. 1999)).

Meaning for Employers

What should an employer take from this? If an employee asks for a reasonable accommodation to enable him or her to do the essential tasks of the job and that assistance would not be an undue hardship on the employer's business, should the employer find a way to provide it?

Perhaps, but bear in mind that this is a broad, one-way street. Offers of accommodation to those who are not disabled under the law must be given without regard to any other classification, to avoid being accused of other forms of discrimination. Some employers believe that the safest way is the way proscribed by the law, which means going through the process of determining first if the individual is qualified to perform the job's essential functions and if so, then determining whether he or she has an ADA-covered disability.

In general, if it is determined that an accommodation would be appropriate, the quick fix – if available – is usually the best, even if the adjustment is not actually required by the ADA. Assuming the employee has been performing competently, when he or she asks for some sort of accommodation due to a health condition, the normal response is "How can I help you? What do you need?" There is no requirement to determine whether the employee has a disability as defined by the law, even though doing so may be a good idea.

Regardless, whatever assistance is given should be documented. If it works, the problem was easily solved to everyone's satisfaction. The "Seven Steps to a Smooth Accommodation Process" on the next page shows the accommodation process.

If, on the other hand, the requested accommodation is too difficult or would be too disrupting to provide, the employer should document that as well. Something else might work, and the logical thing to do is to pursue with the employee an alternative.

Often it is not the competent employee, but rather the problem one who asks for help to do the job. The employer needs to look at the situation objectively and use the same strategy for all employees. Is the requested accommodation simple and easy to provide and would it make a difference? If so, the safest course is probably to provide it. The employee's performance should have been and continue to be documented. Employees with disabilities can be held to the same production and behavior standards as any other worker, even though accommodations may be needed.

SEVEN STEPS TO A SMOOTH ACCOMMODATION PROCESS

If a formal interactive accommodation process becomes necessary, following the steps below can make it easier.

The employee asks for a reasonable accommodation.

The employer examines the employee's job for its purpose and essential functions.

The employer and employee confer to identify any physical and mental abilities and limitations as they relate to the essential job functions.

The employer determines if the employee has an ADA-covered disability, and whether the individual is qualified with or without a reasonable accommodation.

With medical and other evidence, the employer determines whether the employee poses a direct harm threat to him/herself or others. The employer determines whether a reasonable accommodation can remove the threat.

The employer and employee identify possible accommodations. The employer consults with other experts on making accommodations.

The employer considers the employee's preferred accommodation, cost, feasibility and other factors such as whether a particular accommodation would impose an undue business hardship.

If one is available, the employer selects a reasonable accommodation.

Essential Functions Need Not Be Eliminated

When designing an accommodation, employers never have to eliminate essential functions of the job at issue, or lower production standards, either qualitative or quantitative, as long as those standards are uniformly applied to all similarly situated employees. Accommodations are provided to help the employee *perform* the essential functions.

In its regulations, the EEOC defines "essential functions" as "the fundamental job duties of the employment position" (29 C.F.R. §1630.2(n)). Functions may be essential, the commission said, because:

- they are the reason the position exists;

- there is a limited number of employees who can perform the functions; and/or

- the functions are highly specialized and the person in the position was hired for his or her expertise or ability to perform the particular function.

For a proofreading job, the ability to proofread is an essential function. It is the reason the job exists. If an employee can no longer wipe down the car, he or she cannot be the final inspector on an auto manufacturing plant's assembly line.

The employer's judgment will usually suffice, within reason, for determining what job functions are essential. Written job description can provide evidence of essential functions, but those functions also can be determined by the amount of time spent performing them, the consequences of not performing them, the terms of a collective bargaining agreement, the work experience of incumbents in the job and/or the experience of incumbents in similar jobs (see 29 C.F.R. §1630.2(n)(3)).

There is, of course, nothing to prevent an employer from eliminating an essential function or lowering production standards if it wishes, either as an accommodation or because it deems a change is needed.

Job duties that are not critical to the performance of the job at hand may not be used as criteria to determine whether the individual is qualified. The fact that a predecessor in an administrative assistant's job occasionally drove a company car to perform errands did not make that an essential function of a job that was secretarial in nature. Under the ADA, a job applicant who did not have a driver's license due to a disability could not be rejected for the administrative assistant's job on that basis.

WRITING JOB DESCRIPTIONS

The utility of a job description depends on the nature of the job. The more mechanical a job is, the easier it is to write a description. Not all experts are in favor of job descriptions. A big concern is that jobs can change over time and if the descriptions are not reviewed and updated regularly, they can be worthless.

Job descriptions can be of any length and specificity. The company's needs dictate the amount of detail. For those employers that have or want to have job descriptions, the following is an outline of the most comprehensive job description that can be adapted.

- **Basic facts** – The job's title, geographic location, place in the organization chart and reporting structure, salary range, special benefits, work hours and overtime requirements and prerequisites.

- **Purpose** – The main purpose of the position and how it contributes to the company's business.

- **Responsibilities** – The things the company expects the holder of this position to achieve. This should focus on the outcomes or ultimate results, rather than the way in which they are accomplished.

- **Duties or tasks** – How the job holder accomplishes the functions listed above.

Determining Essential Job Functions

The essential functions of a job are those that are fundamental, not marginal "other duties as assigned." For example, in a secretarial position, using a computer and answering the telephone may be essential functions, while running errands are marginal duties.

When identifying essential job functions, employers need to focus on the task itself, not how it is done. While the ability to use a computer may be an essential function for the job of secretary, it is not essential that information be entered manually or read visually. An computer that has been made accessible might be a reasonable accommodation for an individual with a vision impairment that would enable him or her to perform the essential function of word processing.

In addition to specific skills, education and certifications that may be required to perform a job's essential functions, the ability to get along with co-workers and supervisors and to be at work on a regular and predictable basis usually will be required (see, for example, *Grenier v. Cyanamid Plastics*, 70 F.3d 667 (1st Cir. 1995)). These factors must be examined on an individual basis for each job, however.

While they are not required, well drafted job descriptions prepared prior to the application process can provide sound evidence of essential job functions. Job descriptions should be logical with major tasks listed first, followed by less important or less frequently performed ones. Tasks should be specifically quantified when possible. For example, rather than listing "heavy lifting required," the job description should state that "packages weighing up to 50 pounds must be lifted." Care must be taken to list specific tasks, not how those tasks are to be performed.

Software programs are available to help employers write good job descriptions and a number of materials are available in print. There also are consultants who will develop job descriptions for a fee.

Examples of Essential Functions

Court cases provide some examples of what were and were not considered essential functions in various workplaces. Attendance and punctuality are two of the more common job requirements employers have insisted are essential functions.

Attendance has been identified as an essential function by most of the courts that have ruled on the issue. The 7th Circuit has held that the "Inability to work for a multi-month period removes a person from the class protected by the ADA" (*Byrne v. Avon Products, Inc.*, 328 F.3d 379 (7th Cir. 2003)). "The rather common-sense idea is that if one is not able to be at work, one cannot be a qualified individual," the court said (*Waggoner v. Olin Corp.*, 169 F.3d 481 (7th Cir. 1999)).

The list of occupations in the 7th Circuit requiring attendance as an essential function "has grown to include, in addition to clerical worker, the positions of teacher, account representative, production employee and plan equipment repairman, (citations deleted)" the court noted (*Amadio v. Ford Motor Co.*, 238 F.3d 919 (7th Cir. 2001)).

The 4th Circuit reached the same conclusion more than a decade ago by finding that an employee who could not meet her job's attendance requirements was not otherwise qualified under the ADA (*Tyndall v. National Educational Ctrs.*, 31 F.3d 209 (4th Cir. 1994)).

Punctuality has been ruled an essential job function in some circumstances. However, when an employee's tardiness was due to his mobility impairment and the employer's failure to provide any accommodation, such as a van-accessible parking space, the 11th Circuit found that whether punctuality was an essential function was a question of fact, and the district court erred by granting summary judgment to the employer (*Holly v. Clairson Industries*, 2007 WL 2050769 (11th Cir. 2007)).

Ability to evacuate a chemical plant in case of emergency was found not to be an essential function by the 5th Circuit. While agreeing that safety measures are extremely important in such workplaces, an employer must make an "individualized assessment of the individual's present ability to safely perform the essential function of the job," the court said, quoting *Chevron v. Echazabal* (536 U.S. 73 (2002)), and held that the jury's decision that the employee could evacuate even though it would take her longer would not be disturbed (*EEOC v. DuPont*, 480 F.3d 724 (5th Cir. 2007)).

Limitations on Reasonable Accommodations

Personal use items needed both on and off the job do not have to be provided by employers, the EEOC said in its guidance on accommodation. Prosthetic limbs, wheelchairs, eyeglasses and hearing aids are not reasonable accommodations for that reason. Items that might otherwise be considered personal may be reasonable accommodations "if they are specifically designed or required to meet job-related rather than personal needs," the guidance stated.

Personal use amenities such as refrigerators are not required unless also provided to nondisabled employees in the regular course of employment. Similarly, only accommodations related to the individual's disability are covered by the ADA, not accommodations requested for some other reason. The EEOC gave as an example in its Technical Assistance Manual a request for a transfer because a blind employee wanted to work in a warm climate, not because the transfer would enable the employee to better perform the essential functions of the job.

Collective bargaining agreements and bona fide seniority agreements limit employers' obligations to provide reasonable accommodations (see Chapter 8 for further discussion of union and seniority agreements).

The definition of reasonable accommodation given in the statute does not include any quantitative, financial or other limitations on the extent of an employer's obligation to make changes to a job or work environment. The only limitation provided is that an accommodation is not reasonable if it causes an "undue hardship" on the employer's business (see chapter 8 for a discussion of undue hardship).

Each employee with a disability must be considered on a case-by-case basis and accommodations must be tailored to meet the employee's specific needs. While the accommodation does not have to be the one the employee prefers, it does have to meet the employee's needs so that he or she can perform the job's essential functions.

Contingent Workers

The EEOC stated in its Enforcement Guidance on the Application of the ADA to Contingent Workers Placed by Temporary Agencies and Other Staffing Firms, released in 2000, that the ADA's reasonable accommodation provisions apply to contingent workers. Both the staffing firm and the client need to comply, absent undue hardship, and if they have notice of the need for accommodation. The responsibilities of each party for accommodations may be set out in their contracts.

Small Employers

Employers with 15 employees have the same responsibilities for reasonable accommodation as those with 1,050 or more. The only difference is that a small employer will find some accommodations to be an undue hardship because of its lack of resources.

For example, a small employer might have difficulty reassigning job duties to other workers because each employee is critical to the operation of a small business. Larger employers have more flexibility is assigning duties. The EEOC's guidance, Small Employers and Reasonable Accommodation, issued in 1999, sheds no further light on the issue.

Social Security Disability Claimants

A claim of total disability and inability to work on a Social Security Disability Insurance application form does not necessarily defeat a claim for reasonable accommodation under the ADA. In spite of "the appearance of conflict that arises from the language of the two statutes, the two claims do not inherently conflict to the point where courts should apply a special negative presumption," the U.S. Supreme Court explained. "That is because there are too many situations in which an SSDI claim and an ADA claim can comfortably exist side by side." (*Cleveland v. Policy Management Systems Corp.*, 526 U.S. 795 (1999)).

The Court went on to say that the ADA allows reasonable accommodation of a person's disability, while the Social Security Administration does not when determining SSDI eligibility. The U.S. Court of Appeals for the 7th Circuit noted that, "Sufficient divergence exists between the definitions of 'disability' under the ADA and SSDI that, in some circumstances, an individual can claim truthfully both that she is unable 'to engage in any substantial gainful activity' under the SSDI, but is also a 'qualified individual with a disability' under the ADA" (*Feldman v. American Memorial Life Insurance Co.*, 196 F.3d 783 (7th Cir. 1999)).

An ADA claimant cannot just ignore the apparent contradiction that he or she cannot work for SSDI purposes, but can under the ADA. There must be sufficient evidence that the individual could perform the essential functions of the job with or without reasonable accommodations.

In a case in which an employee with severe epilepsy received SSDI benefits after being fired and also filed an ADA lawsuit against his former employer, the 7th Circuit found that his SSDI application precluded the ADA claim because the claimant merely argued that he was "mistaken" on his SSDI application. "Contradictions are unacceptable," the appeals court held. An individual who applies for disability benefits "must live with the factual representations made to obtain them, and if these show inability to do the job then an ADA claim may be rejected without further inquiry" (*Johnson v. Exxon Mobil Corp.*, 426 F.3d 887 (7th Cir. 2005) quoting *Opsteen v. Keller*, 408 F.3d 390 (7th Cir. 2005)).

How To Know When, and What, Accommodation Is Needed

3

Employers are required to make reasonable accommodations to the *known* physical or mental limitations of an otherwise qualified individual with a disability who is an applicant or employee. Employers may not deny employment "if such denial is based on the need … to make reasonable accommodation to the physical or mental impairments of the employee or applicant" (42 U.S.C. §12112(b)(5)).

But how is an employer supposed to know when an accommodation is needed? To violate the ADA provision, an employer must know that the employee or job applicant has a physical or mental limitation that requires accommodation. Questions about disabilities, however, are generally prohibited.

Some limitations are obvious, of course, but many disabilities are hidden and even when they are obvious, an employer may not know that an accommodation is required. The burden is on the applicant or employee to make it known that accommodation is needed. After that is done, the process of determining an appropriate accommodation can begin.

This chapter examines how and what notice is appropriate and then discusses how an employer should go about finding and providing an effective accommodation.

Accommodation Must Be Requested

Employers are forbidden from asking job applicants whether they have a disability or about the nature or severity of disabilities, although they may ask about the ability to perform job-related functions (49 U.S.C. §12112(d)). On the other hand, employers are not required to accommodate disabilities of which they are unaware. If an employee with a known disability is having difficulty performing a job, the EEOC explains, an employer may ask whether an accommodation would help (29 C.F.R. Part 1630 App. §1630.9), but there really is no obligation on the employer's part.

Unless the disability is obvious, the employee usually must inform the employer that an accommodation is needed. In general, "it is the responsibility of the individual with a disability to inform the employer that an accommodation is needed," the EEOC noted (29 C.F.R. §1630.9 App.; EEOC's Enforcement Guidance on Reasonable Accommodation and Undue Hardship, 10/17/02).

Courts have agreed that the employee must make the initial request (see *Brown v. Lucky Stores*, 246 F.3d 1182 (9th Cir. 2001)). Only after an employee requests an accommodation and the employer fails to provide it, can a discrimination claim be made (see *Gaston v. Bellingrath Gardens & Home, Inc.*, 167 F.3d 1361 (11th Cir. 1999)).

On the other hand, if an employer knows about a disability and the need for an accommodation, it probably would be obligated to provide one, even though no express request was made. Such was the case when an employee, after being promoted, requested that some duties be assigned to another worker. The employer was aware of the supervisor's disability and that she needed to avoid working overtime so as not to exacerbate her medical condition. Moreover, the employer, the U.S. Postal Service, was large enough to provide the accommodation without any undue burden and had accommodated the worker prior to her promotion (*Smith v. Henderson*, 376 F.3d 529 (6th Cir. 2004)).

In addition, the EEOC said that even though an employee generally must ask for an accommodation, if, because of the disability, the employee is unable to request the accommodation, the employer might still be held liable for providing one. The example the agency gave is an employer that knows about a disability and recognizes that the employee is having difficulty doing his or her job, and knows that the disability prevents the employee from asking for an accommodation.

Form of Request

When asking for an accommodation, the employee does not have to use any specific words. It is enough to let the employer know that a disability exists and that an accommodation is required because of it (*EEOC v. Sears*, 417 F.3d 789 (7th Cir. 2005)). There is no "magic language" that is required, not even the words "reasonable accommodation."

In the case of employees who are rendered disabled by on-the-job injuries, courts have suggested that it is sufficient for the employee to say "I want to keep working for you; do you have any suggestions?" A statement such as that triggers the employer's duty to find out if there is some job the employee can fill (*Robinson v. Excel Corp.*, 154 F.3d 685 (7th Cir. 1998)).

There is nothing in the law that requires an individual to use specific terms or to anticipate information an employer may need to provide a reasonable accommodation, although some courts have ruled that the individual must say enough so that the employer is aware of its duty to investigate whether reasonable accommodations may be required. Telling a supervisor that the employee's wheelchair will not fit under an office desk, requesting time off for a medical procedure or requesting a change of schedule for medical treatments all constitute requests for accommodation, the EEOC points out in its guidance.

There does have to be enough information to put an employer on notice that a disability is involved and that an accommodation is needed, though (see *Conneen v. MBNA America*

Bank, 334 F.3d 318 (3d Cir. 2003)). Requesting leave or some other adjustment for "a medical condition" is not enough (EEOC Enforcement Guidance on Reasonable Accommodation and Undue Hardship Under the ADA, 10/17/02).

Thus, an employee who told his supervisor he was "ill" did not make "a request for leave as an accommodation for his diabetes" because the statement would not apprise the employer that the absence was related to a disability (*Brenneman v. MedCentral Health System*, 366 F.3d 412 (6th Cir. 2004)). The request must be sufficiently direct and specific and must in some way explain how the accommodation asked for is linked to a disability (see *Reed v. Lepage Bakeries, Inc.*, 244 F.3d 254 (1st Cir. 2001)).

Requests for accommodation do not need to be in writing. Employers may require their employees to fill out forms, but they cannot ignore oral requests for accommodation (EEOC's Enforcement Guidance on Reasonable Accommodation and Undue Hardship Under the ADA, 10/17/02).

FAILURE TO GIVE ENOUGH INFORMATION

A county government required its job applicants to take a written test. The vocational rehabilitation counselor for a job applicant with a developmental disorder asked the county to permit the counselor to read the test to the applicant because she was illiterate. Neither the counselor nor the applicant told the county that the applicant had a developmental disorder.

The county refused the request that the test be read to the applicant, believing the ability to read was an essential requirement of the job at issue. The applicant sued, claiming the failure to accommodate violated the ADA. The case was dismissed because the court found the applicant had not provided enough information to notify the county she had a disability (*Morisky v. Broward County*, 80 F.3d 445 (11th Cir. 1996)).

Requests do not have to come from the individual with a disability. A family member, friend, health professional or other representative may request accommodation on behalf of the job applicant or employee, according to the EEOC's guidance.

A spouse may call to notify the employer that the employee had a medical emergency due to a covered disability and that would be enough to alert the employer that a reasonable accommodation (leave) has been requested, the commission explained. An employee's doctor may release an injured employee to return to work with some restrictions and a letter listing those restrictions would be a request for reasonable accommodation.

A request for an accommodation can be made at any time during the application process or during employment. Obviously it is in the employee's best interest to request an accommodation before performance suffers, but sometimes it takes time for an employee to realize that a disability is interfering with performing essential job functions. Then too, a disability may not occur until after an employee has been in the job for some time and subsequently develops a disease or is injured.

Even if the disability existed prior to hiring, the law does not preclude an employee from requesting an accommodation at any time, regardless of whether one was asked for during the hiring process.

Employer's Right to Information

If the employer needs more information, it can ask for it. While questions about disabilities generally may not be asked of job applicants, if an applicant or employee requests an accommodation, the employer may ask for information. Specifically, the employer is entitled to documentation about the disability and any functional limitations it causes.

The employer may ask for documentation describing the impairment; the nature, severity and duration of the impairment; the activity or activities that the impairment limits; and the extent to which the impairment limits the employee's ability to perform the activity or activities.

In other words, if an employee with a disability that is not obvious requests an accommodation, the employer does not have to take the employee's word for it (see *EEOC v. Prevo's Family Market, Inc.*, 135 F.3d 1089 (6th Cir. 1998)). If the employee provides insufficient information, the employer may require that he or she go to a health professional of the employer's choice. However, the employer must explain why the documentation is insufficient, permit the individual to provide the missing information and pay all costs associated with an examination by the chosen health professional. Any medical examination conducted at the request of the employer must be job related and consistent with business necessity.

The employer may ask for written documentation from any relevant professional who has knowledge of the employee's condition. The type of professional will depend on the disability and the functional limitation it imposes. If both the disability and need for reasonable accommodation are obvious, or the individual has provided the employer with sufficient information to substantiate the existence of an ADA-covered disability and need for reasonable accommodation, the employer may not ask for further documentation.

The EEOC's guidance limits the documentation to what is reasonable and what is needed to establish that the employee has an ADA disability that requires reasonable accommodation. An employer cannot request complete medical records, for example, that are likely to contain information unrelated to the specific disability at issue. If more than one disability exists, only information about the one at issue may be requested.

To protect doctors and other health care professionals from violating patient confidentiality, the guidance warns employers that they must obtain a release from the employee permitting the health care worker to answer relevant questions. The employer should be clear about what type of information is needed and the release should correspond to that. Confidentiality by the employer must be maintained concerning any medical information received during the documentation process.

Of course an employer may choose to discuss the disability and functional limitations with the employee rather than requiring formal documentation. In any event, if the disability and need for accommodation are not obvious and the employee or job applicant refuses to provide requested documentation, the employer is not required to provide reasonable accommodation, according to the EEOC's guidance (see *Beck v. University of Wisconsin Bd. of Regents*, 75 F.3d 1130 (7th Cir. 1996)).

If the accommodation sought is a leave covered by the Family and Medical Leave Act (FMLA), different rules apply. The FMLA permits covered employees of covered employers (those with 50 or more employees) to take up to 12 weeks of unpaid leave in any 12-month period for, among other things, an employee's serious health condition, and the employer must comply with the requirements of that law when requesting documentation. The FMLA permits employers to request medical certification of an employee's serious health condition from the employee's health care provider after the employee has requested FMLA leave.

Only information on the U.S. Department of Labor's Certification Statement (Form WH-380) may be requested. The form includes the following information:

- the name and type of practice of the health care provider;

- a statement regarding the type of serious health condition and medical facts supporting the certification;

- the approximate date the health condition began and its probable duration, including the probable duration of the employee's present incapacity;

- whether the employee needs to take leave intermittently or work on a reduced schedule;

- if the condition is pregnancy or a chronic condition, whether the employee is presently incapacitated and the likely duration and frequency of episodes of incapacity;

- if additional treatments will be required for the condition, an estimate of the probable number of treatments;

- if the employee's incapacity will be intermittent or require a reduced schedule, an estimate of the probable number of and interval between the treatments, actual or estimated dates of treatments, if known, and any required recovery period; and

- whether the employee is unable to perform work of any kind, is unable to perform any one or more of the essential functions of the job or must be absent from work for treatment.

The employer may only request certification of the condition for which the employee requested FMLA leave. Unlike under the ADA, the employer may not have any direct contact with the employee's health care provider and if the certification form is complete, may not request additional information from the health care provider unless the employee is receiving workers' compensation and state law permits such contact. However, the employer may have its doctor contact the employee's health care provider, with the employee's permission, to clarify and verify the medical certification.

Notice of Employee Rights

Employers must let job applicants and employees know that they may be entitled to reasonable accommodations for covered disabilities. Notices of the ADA's provisions are required to be posted in conspicuous places, such as employment offices where applicants and employees can readily see them (49 U.S.C. §12115).

The EEOC provides posters for this purpose. Information about an employer's obligation to provide reasonable accommodations also can be included in job application forms, job advertisements and personnel manuals, or communicated orally.

Determining What Is Needed

A request by an employee or job applicant for an accommodation does not necessarily mean the employer is required to provide one. The request is merely the first step. Before addressing the merits of the request, the employer needs to determine whether the individual has a disability as that term is defined by the law. (See Chapter 1 for a discussion of what is a disability.)

A request for a new office chair because the old one is uncomfortable does not constitute a request for an accommodation, because there is nothing to indicate the request is due to a disability. While the employer might want to keep the employee happy by providing a new chair, no ADA requirement is implicated. Only those individuals with ADA-covered disabilities are entitled to reasonable accommodations.

If a request for a reasonable accommodation is from a qualified individual with an ADA-covered disability, the employer is required to make a reasonable effort to determine if an appropriate accommodation is available. The EEOC explains in the appendix to its regulations that this is best done through a flexible, *interactive process* involving both the employer and employee or job applicant (29 C.F.R. Part 1630 App. §1630.9).

The commission advises employers to:

1. analyze the job involved and determine its purpose and essential functions;

2. consult with the employee to be accommodated to find out the precise job-related limitations imposed by the individual's disability and how those limitations could be overcome with a reasonable accommodation;

3. in consultation with the employee, identify potential accommodations and assess the effectiveness each would have in enabling the employee to perform the job's essential functions; and

4. consider the employee's preference and select and implement the accommodation that is most appropriate for both the employer and employee or job applicant.

Often the appropriate accommodation will be so obvious that a step-by-step process is not necessary. For example, if a request for leave for medical treatment is granted, the accommodation has been requested, identified and provided with no real interactive accommodation process being evident.

If the accommodation is not evident, however, a problem solving process may be required. A new hire may not know enough about the company or the job to be able to suggest anything specific. The employer may not know enough about the limitations the disability imposes or assistive equipment available to identify an accommodation. That is when a process to assess the requirements of the job and the individual's physical or mental limitations may be necessary.

Interactive Process

The ADA favors an informal, interactive discussion between the employer and the individual who needs accommodation after a request has been made. During this process, the employer and employee identify the limitations imposed by the disability and available accommodations that would overcome those limitations to enable the employee to perform the essential functions of the job.

Some courts have said the burden of identifying an accommodation that would enable the employee with a disability to perform a job's essential functions rests with the individual, as does the burden of showing that an accommodation is reasonable (*Willis v. Conopco*, 108 F.3d 282 (11th Cir. 1997); *Stewart v. Happy Herman's Cheshire Bridge*, 117 F.3d 1278 (7th Cir. 1997)).

Other courts have stated that the interactive process requires the employer to take some initiative (*Taylor v. Phoenixville School Dist.*, 184 F.3d 296 (3d Cir. 1999)). "[T]he interactive process would have little meaning if it was interpreted to allow employers, in the face of a request for accommodation, simply to sit back passively, offer nothing, and then, in post-termination litigation, try to knock down every specific accommodation as too burdensome. That's not the proactive process intended," the *Taylor* court stated. "The obligation to participate in the process falls on both parties," the 5th Circuit ruled (*Cutreau v. Board of Supervisors of Louisiana State Univ.*, 429 F.3d 108 (5th Cir. 2005)).

Most courts have recognized that the interactive process is an important part of the reasonable accommodation process under the ADA and some appeals courts have stated or at least suggested that it may be a requirement. There "is a mandatory obligation to engage in an informal interactive process," the 9th Circuit said (*Vinson v. Thomas*, 288 F.3d 1145 (9th Cir. 2002)). The interactive process means "a great deal of communication between the employee and employer" and the "employer's refusal to participate in the process may itself constitute evidence of a violation of the statute," the 1st Circuit said (*Calero-Cerezo v. U.S. Department of Justice*, 355 F.3d 6 (1st Cir. 2004)).

Moreover, there is some chance an employer may not avoid liability merely by acceding to an employee's requested accommodation without more. The employer has some responsibility for identifying an accommodation that is appropriate. The "determination of a reasonable accommodation is a cooperative process in which both the employer and the employee must make reasonable efforts and exercise good faith," one appeals court said, noting that reasonableness depends on "a good-faith effort to assess the employee's needs and respond to them," (*Feliberty v. Kemper Corp.*, 98 F.3d 274 (7th Cir. 1996)).

There must be an individual assessment of the job, which involves analyzing all of the functions performed and determining the job's true purpose, so that the essential functions can be identified. It is only the essential functions that the employee can be required to perform; if the disability prevents performance of marginal ones, those functions should be reallocated or eliminated.

After determining what the job's essential functions are, the employer should discuss with the employee the specific limitations his or her disability imposes on the performance of those functions. This will expose any barriers and enable the employer and employee to determine the accommodations that will overcome those barriers (see *Barnett v. U.S. Air, Inc.*, 228 F.3d 1105 (9th Cir. 2000) and *Williams v. Philadelphia Housing Authority Police Dept.*, 380 F.3d 751 (3d Cir. 2004)).

Often the employee will be able to suggest what is needed or between them the employer and employee will arrive at a solution. If that does not happen, there are extensive public and private resources to help employers identify accommodations. (See the resource list at the end of this book.)

There is no independent legal violation of the ADA for failing to engage in the interactive process, but not doing so may result in no appropriate solution, which in turn can lead to a claim of failure to accommodate (see *Mengine v. Runyon*, 114 F.3d 415 (3d Cir. 1997).) On the other hand, engaging in good faith in the interactive process of assessing the job, the employee's limitations in performing the job's essential functions, and identifying potential accommodations, can provide a defense to the employer if the employee later sues.

An employer can show good faith in the interactive process by taking the following steps:

* meeting with the employee who requested an accommodation;

* requesting information about the condition and what limitations the employees has;

* asking the employee what he or she specifically wants;

* showing some sign of having considered the employee's request; and

* offering and discussing available alternatives when the request is too burdensome (*Taylor v. Phoenixville School Dist.*, 184 F.3d 296 (3d Cir. 1999)).

The effort the employer gives in the attempt to find an accommodation bears a direct relationship to potential damages in a suit for failure to accommodate. When an employer can show a good faith effort in consultation with the employee who needed accommodation "to identify and make a reasonable accommodation that would provide such individual with an equally effective opportunity," by law, punitive and certain compensatory damages may not be awarded (42 U.S.C. §1981A). Some courts have found the employer is not liable for discrimination at all when it makes a good faith effort to accommodate, although others merely limit damages.

SILENT EMPLOYEE LOSES ACCOMMODATION RIGHT

An employee who maintained a "stony silence" during continuing talks with her employer about possible work accommodations for her bad back lost her protection under the ADA. "The process broke down because she stayed silent," the U.S. Court of Appeals for the 5th Circuit said, adding that not holding her responsible for participation in a process that was designed for her own benefit would reward her withdrawal.

The employee was a laboratory technician who injured her back while moving a container at work. She returned to work with a 35 pound lifting restriction, which ultimately was reduced to 10 pounds following back surgery. Initially, the restriction was not a problem because contract workers provided help when she needed heavy containers moved, which all lab technicians were required to do on a rotating basis. Then a new policy, requiring technicians to move containers themselves, was put in place.

The employer held a meeting to discuss the use of equipment that would accommodate the employee's disability. She said nothing at the meeting and failed to raise the issue of accommodation with anyone. A week before the next rotation that would have required her to move heavy containers, the employee quit her job and sued, claiming the employer refused to reasonably accommodate her.

Because she failed to take part in the interactive process and quit before the adequacy of the employer's proposed accommodation could be tested, the employer was not liable under the ADA, the appeals court held, finding that it was the employee who was responsible for the breakdown in the interactive process (*Loulseged v. Akzo Nobel*, 178 F.3d 731 (5th Cir. 1999)).

If the employee has caused a breakdown in the process through no fault of the employer, courts usually will find the employer has no liability (see, e.g., *Beck v. University of Wisconsin Bd. of Regents*, 75 F.3d 1130 (7th Cir. 1996)).

 "Liability simply cannot arise under the ADA when an employer does not obstruct an informal interactive process; makes reasonable efforts to communicate with the employee and provide accommodation based on the information it possesses; and the employee's actions cause a breakdown in the interactive process," the U.S. Court of Appeals for the 7th Circuit said in *Stewart v. Happy Herman's Cheshire Bridge* (117 F.3d 1278 (1997)).

In the Stewart case, the court found that the employee failed to engage in the interactive process after the employer offered her several potential accommodations. "[S]he did not provide Happy Herman's with any substantive reasons as to why all five of the proffered accommodations were unreasonable given her medical needs," the court said.

Both parties are responsible for helping to find a reasonable accommodation and neither should be able to cause a breakdown in the process "for the purpose of either avoiding or inflicting liability." Courts "should attempt to isolate the cause of the breakdown and then assign responsibility," (EEOC v. Sears, 417 F.3d 789 (7th Cir. 2005)).

These cases turn heavily on their facts and a determination of the reasonableness of both parties' behavior. Open communication on the part of both the employer and employee is critical to the process envisioned under the ADA.

HOW NOT TO CONDUCT INTERACTIVE PROCESS

An employer put workers who were injured on the job in temporary light-duty positions while they were recovering. Once they reached maximum recovery, if they were unable to return to their original jobs, a company nurse evaluated each employee's abilities to see if there was any job the employee could perform with or without accommodation. The nurse compared the employee's restrictions to job descriptions for available positions, consulted with the employee and others about what the jobs required and observed the jobs being performed. If no job was available, the employee could examine the company's job postings.

An ergonomics monitor compared the employee's restrictions with job descriptions to confirm whether the employee could perform a job with accommodation. The employee was given a complete tour of the plant to view other production jobs and could inquire about non-production jobs. The employee also could suggest accommodations that might enable him or her to perform an available job. If no job was available, the employee was put on medical layoff status and the company automatically bid the worker on vacant production jobs. Employees were told to call once a week while on medical layoff to inquire about jobs. When they did, they were always told no jobs existed.

This seemingly thorough medical policy nevertheless violated the ADA's interactive process requirement. First, the employees were not automatically bid on non-production desk jobs, which they were more likely able to do. Second, the automatic bid procedure precluded any chance for job accommodation. Third, the company nurse unilaterally determined whether an employee was capable of performing the job in question.

"There was no discussion of accommodation because there was no mention that a potential job existed," the court pointed out. Essentially, the accommodation dialogue was terminated by the employer before it began. The company's methodology was directive, not interactive, the court said. What the ADA requires is a flexible, interactive process in which both the employer and the employee investigate cooperatively whether it is possible to accommodate the employee's disability, the court explained (*Robinson v. Excel Corp.*, 154 F.3d 685 (7th Cir. 1998)).

Similarly, telling an employee who could no longer perform the essential functions of his job due to his disability to look online for jobs for which he might be qualified did not meet the requirements of the interactive process (*Liner v. Hospital Service Dist. No. 1 of Jefferson Parish*, 2007 WL 1111565 (5th Cir. 2007)).

Response to Accommodation Request

An employer should respond promptly to a request for a reasonable accommodation, and if an interactive process needs to take place, it should begin as soon as possible. The employer should then provide the accommodation promptly. "Unnecessary delays can result in a violation of the ADA," the EEOC's guidance warns.

Relevant factors in determining if a delay has occurred include:

1.   the reason for the delay;

2.   the length of the delay;

3.   how much the employee and employer each contributed to the delay;

4.   what the employer was doing during the delay; and

5.   whether the required accommodation was simple or complex to provide.

REASONABLE ACCOMMODATION PROCESS

This chart outlines the steps in the reasonable accommodation process, which, according to the EEOC, includes: determining a job's essential functions; consulting with the employee with a disability to determine his or her abilities and needs; identifying potential accommodations in consultation with the employee; and selecting the best accommodation.

An employee requests a reasonable accommodation.

The employer examines the employee's job and determines its essential functions.

The employer consults with the employee to find out his or her physical or mental abilities and limitations as they relate to performing the job's essential functions.

The employer determines if the individual has a disability covered by the ADA.

The employer makes an individualized determination, based on objective medical or other evidence, of whether a person with a disability poses a direct threat of harm to himself or herself or others and if so, whether the threat can be removed by reasonable accommodations.

The employer and employee identify potential accommodations. The employer may consult with other experts on accommodating individuals with disabilities.

If more than one accommodation would be effective, the individual's preference is considered but the employer makes the final choice and may choose an accommodation that is less expensive or easier to provide.

The employer must consider, on a case-by-case basis, whether a reasonable accommodation would impose an undue hardship on the business. If a particular accommodation would impose an undue hardship, it does not have to be provided, but the employer must consider whether an alternative accommodation is available that would not impose a hardship.

If a reasonable accommodation that would not cause an undue hardship is available, the employer provides it in a timely manner.

Sometimes it takes time to obtain needed equipment. An employer will not be penalized for acting promptly on an individual's request but not being able to provide the accommodation for several months because the equipment cannot be obtained any sooner. On the other hand, sitting on a request without taking any action can amount to a denial of a reasonable accommodation and leave the employer vulnerable to liability in an ADA lawsuit.

After potential accommodations have been identified, the employer should assess the effectiveness of each in helping the employee overcome the barriers to performing the essential functions of the job. If more than one accommodation would work or the individual prefers to provide his or her own, the individual's preference should be given consideration, according to the EEOC's guidance. It is ultimately the employer's decision, however.

The least expensive or easiest way to provide accommodation may be chosen as long as it is effective in enabling the employee to perform the essential functions of the job. The employer does not have to provide the specific accommodation requested by the employee and does not have to show that providing an accommodation other than the one chosen would impose an undue hardship (29 C.F.R. Part 1630 App. §1630.9). If more than one accommodation will enable the individual to perform the essential functions of the position, the employer can choose whichever it wishes to provide (*Kiel v. Select Artificials, Inc.*, 169 F.3d 1131 (8th Cir. 1999); see also *Rehling v. City of Chicago*, 207 F.3d 1009 (7th Cir. 2000)).

Indeed, some courts have said the word "reasonable" would be superfluous if employers were required to provide employees the maximum accommodation in every case (see *Stewart v. Happy Herman's Cheshire Bridge*, 117 F.3d 1278 (7th Cir. 1997)).

Accommodations Issues for Hiring, Testing and Medical Exams

4

Whether and when to ask job applicants and employees questions about their health or to require physical examinations can be a quagmire for employers. Basically, the ADA addressed three stages of the employment relationship: pre-job-offer, post-job-offer and during actual employment. The limits on disability-related inquiries and the ability to require medical examinations are different at each stage and apply to all employees of a covered employer, regardless of whether any of them has a disability.

During the application stage prior to making a job offer, an employer generally may not ask any disability-related questions or require any medical examinations, including tests that may reveal mental disabilities, even if those questions or exams are related to the job.

After an applicant is offered a job but before he or she starts work, an employer may ask disability-related questions and conduct medical examinations regardless of whether they are job related, as long all entering employees in the same job category are required to take the same tests and answer the same questions. In the event questioning or an exam reveals a condition that might interfere with the potential employee's ability to perform the job's essential functions, the employer is obligated to determine whether a reasonable accommodation would enable the person to do the job.

During employment, employers may make only those disability-related inquiries and require only those medical examinations that are job related and consistent with business necessity. That means that based on objective evidence, the employer reasonably believes the employee will be unable to perform the job's essential functions because of a medical condition, or the employee will pose a direct threat to the health or safety of him- or herself or others. (For more on "direct threat," see Chapter 1.)

Employers also may seek medical information about an employee when:

- a reasonable accommodation has been requested and the disability is not obvious;

- a federal law or regulation requires it;

- voluntary health programs are offered; or

- affirmative action is required by law or undertaken voluntarily to benefit individuals with disabilities.

In its Enforcement Guidance on Disability-Related Inquiries and Medical Examinations of Employees Under the ADA, the EEOC explained that disability-related inquiries are questions such as whether the individual has a disability, the types of prescription drugs he or she is taking and the results of genetic tests. Questions about medications that could result in a direct threat to the safety of others, such as those taken by airline pilots that could affect their ability to fly or by construction workers or users of heavy machinery, may be permissible.

This chapter discusses the types of accommodations that may be required for job applicants throughout the hiring process and then explains the rules that apply to various types of tests, including medical exams.

Accommodations for Job Applicants

Individuals with disabilities cannot have equal employment opportunities if they cannot apply for available jobs. Consequently, such things as barriers that prevent potential employees from entering buildings or taking required employment tests are prohibited by the ADA. The law also prohibits discrimination in regard to advertising, recruiting and hiring for jobs.

The EEOC suggested that job notices include a statement that the employer does not discriminate on the basis of race, religion, color, sex, age, national origin or disability. It also suggested that information about job openings should be accessible to all individuals and that while there is no obligation to provide written job advertisements in various formats, the information should be made available in an accessible format on request.

The ADA's nondiscrimination requirements for job applicants apply to all selection standards and procedures, including:

- education and work experience;

- physical and mental requirements;

- safety requirements;

- paper and pencil tests;

- physical or psychological tests;

- interview questions; and

- rating systems.

The ADA restricts the type of information an employer can solicit before a job offer has been made. Prior to making a conditional offer of employment, an employer may not ask any health-related or disability-related questions, unless the disability is obvious or the applicant has mentioned it, in which case some limited questions about accommodations may be asked. Job-related medical examinations and health inquiries required for insurance purposes may be requested only after a conditional job offer has been made.

In its Enforcement Guidance on Disability-Related Inquiries and Medical Examinations of Employees Under the ADA, the EEOC explained that while disability-related inquiries about job applicants – which can include questions to co-workers, family members and doctors, not just the individual – are prohibited, questions about general well-being, such as "how are you today," the ability to perform job functions and about current illegal use of drugs are always permitted.

Before Job Offer Is Made

Employers must provide reasonable accommodations to qualified applicants with disabilities to enable them to participate in the application process and be considered for a job on an equal basis, unless doing so would impose an undue hardship on the employer's business, the EEOC said in its guidance on reasonable accommodations. Essentially, job applicants have the same rights to reasonable accommodation as existing employees do, although obviously employers do not have to provide some types of accommodations, such as reassignment, to applicants that may be available to employees.

Employers should let applicants know what will be required during the application process and offer to make reasonable accommodations, but may not ask if the applicant has a disability or if an accommodation will be necessary, unless the disability is apparent. In fact, before a job offer has been made, employers may not ask job applicants about the existence, nature or severity of a disability, only about their ability to perform specific job functions.

An individual should not be excluded from the application process even if the employer believes, based on a request for an accommodation, that the individual cannot be sufficiently accommodated to perform the job's essential functions. An assessment about job accommodations should be made separately from those for the application process, the EEOC advised.

The ADA prohibits employers from entering into contracts that violate the law, including contracts with employment agencies. In its Technical Assistance Manual on Title I of the ADA, the EEOC advised employers to inform employment agencies with which they work about the ADA's requirements concerning qualification standards, pre-employment inquiries and reasonable accommodation.

Under the ADA, employers may set their own job qualification standards, including the following:

- education;

- skills;

- work experience;

- licenses or certifications;

- physical and mental abilities;

- health and safety standards; and

- other job-related requirements, such as judgment or interpersonal skills.

The law does not interfere with an employer's right to establish job qualification standards or to hire the best qualified individual who can perform the job effectively and safely. Nor do employers have to lower qualification standards as a reasonable accommodation if those standards are uniformly applied to all applicants.

However, all qualification standards must be job related and necessary for the operation of the employer's business to withstand a protest by an individual with a disability. In addition, if a standard screens out or tends to screen out an individual with disabilities, the employer must show that there is no reasonable accommodation that would enable that individual to perform the job's essential functions.

Even though general job requirements can be established and employers do not have to consider reasonable accommodations when they set qualification standards, each job applicant must be considered on an individual basis to determine whether a reasonable accommodation exists for that person. Standards that tend to screen out entire classes of individuals, such as those with back injuries, should be examined carefully. Blanket exclusions often will not meet the ADA's requirements.

Example: An employer required all of its truck drivers to pass the Department of Transportation's hearing test for those who drove trucks of 10,001 pounds or more, even though none of its trucks were that size. The test disqualified hearing-impaired driver applicants. The 9th Circuit said the company's blanket test was discriminatory because there was no evidence that all deaf truck drivers posed a significant risk (*Bates v. United Parcel Service,* 465 F.3d 1069 (9th Cir. 2006)).

Example: In a case in which an employer refused to hire someone because of his "uncontrolled" diabetes, the 5th Circuit stated that such a policy "embraces what the ADA detests: 'reliance on stereotypes and generalizations' about an illness when making employment decisions" (*Rodriguez v. ConAgra Grocery Prods. Co.,* 436 F.3d 468 (5th Cir. 2006)).

Some basic qualifications, such as licenses and certifications that are job related and a business necessity, will determine whether the applicant is qualified. Reasonable accommodations have to be made only for qualified individuals with disabilities. For example, if an applicant for an attorney's position is not a member of the state bar, that individual is not qualified and no accommodation need be made for a disability, because state licensing is required for the practice of law.

On the other hand, while a job requirement that the individual be able to lift a minimum of 50 pounds might be an essential function, it is not such a basic qualification that no accommodation can be considered. Aids in lifting or the availability of other employees might be reasonable accommodations, depending on the circumstances.

Employers may set physical or mental qualifications when necessary to perform specific jobs, such as those in the transportation or construction industry, or police, firefighter or other jobs involving protection of public health and safety, according to the EEOC's Technical Assistance Manual on Title I. The standard must be job related and consistent with business necessity, however. "Job related" means the standard is a legitimate measure or qualification for the specific job it is being used for, according to the EEOC, while "business necessity" means it is related to the essential functions of the job under consideration.

Job Application Forms

While job application forms may reflect a job's qualification standards by asking questions related to education, certifications and licenses, and experience, questions not related to the specific job should be avoided. Questions that would result in information about disabilities nearly always violate the ADA.

Application forms should not include questions about the applicant's health, medical treatment, prior drug use, workers' compensation claims or the number of sick days used in previous jobs.

Employers may ask about an applicant's current drinking habits, but may not ask questions that reveal an applicant's current or former alcoholism. For example, asking whether an applicant drinks alcohol is permitted, but asking how much the applicant drinks or whether he or she has participated in a behavior modification program to curb alcohol consumption is not.

Individuals with disabilities may need reasonable accommodations for filling out the application form. A blind individual may need to have the questions read and the answers written by someone else, or an individual with a mobility impairment may need an accessible location for filling out the form.

Employers that have federal affirmative action reporting requirements are advised to request relevant information about whether the job applicant considers him- or herself to have a disability on a separate form that is not given to persons who will be making hiring decisions. Job applicants should be informed that the requested information is strictly voluntary and will have no bearing on hiring.

The EEOC addressed the issue of affirmative action with regard to Internet job applications that bar job-seekers from proceeding with an online application until they complete a voluntary EEOC questionnaire that includes asking for health information. In a 2005 advisory letter, the commission said those questionnaires are lawful if they are truly voluntary. The information should not be available to hiring officials, should be kept confidential and should be collected solely to comply with recordkeeping requirements of the nondiscrimination laws and rules, 29 C.F.R. Part 1607 and 41 C.F.R. Part 60-1, the EEOC said.

FORBIDDEN PRE-EMPLOYMENT INQUIRIES

Questions employers should eliminate from application forms and interviews include the following:

✔ Have you ever had or been treated for any of the following conditions or diseases (followed by a list)?

✔ Have you ever been hospitalized?

✔ Have you ever been treated for a mental disorder?

✔ How many days were you absent from work last year due to illness?

✔ Do you have any known physical disabilities?

✔ Are you taking any prescription medicines?

✔ Have you ever been treated for alcoholism or drug addiction?

✔ Do you have any physical or mental impairments that would affect your job performance?

✔ Have you ever filed a workers' compensation claim?

These questions and variations of them are prohibited by the ADA.

Personal Interviews

Reasonable accommodations must be provided to enable job applicants to have an equal opportunity during personal interviews. Accommodations may include:

• an accessible location;

• an interpreter for an individual with a hearing impairment; or

• a reader for an individual with a vision impairment.

Employers cannot ask during personal interviews (or in background or reference checks) any questions that are not permitted on job application forms. Anything about the existence of, nature or severity of a disability is prohibited. If an applicant has a disability that is obvious or that is disclosed by the individual to the employer, the interviewer may ask the applicant to describe or demonstrate how an essential job function would be performed with or without a reasonable accommodation.

Before a job offer is made, employers generally may not ask whether a reasonable accommodation will be needed, the EEOC noted in its guidance. The only exception is for a known disability. If the applicant answers that no accommodation is necessary, the inquiry must stop there. If, however, the applicant replies that an accommodation will be needed, the interviewer may ask what type. (42 U.S.C. §12112(d) and 29 C.F.R. §1630.13(a)) Interviewers should be wary about asking follow-up questions related to the disability rather than reasonable accommodations. Questions should be phrased in terms of how the applicant would perform specific essential job tasks.

Anyone who will be conducting job interviews should be trained in what questions may and may not be asked. Interviewers should be familiar with the specific job so they are better able to determine whether an applicant is qualified to perform the job's essential functions regardless of whether the applicant has a disability. Scripts are a good idea to ensure that all applicants are asked the same questions and that prohibited questions are not included.

In addition, it is helpful if interviewers are trained in communicating with individuals with disabilities and have some general knowledge about the more common types of disabilities. In its Technical Assistance Manual on Title I, the EEOC gives as an example individuals with cerebral palsy. Certain characteristics of this condition, such as indistinct speech and involuntary movements, may give an uninformed interviewer the impression that the individual has limited intelligence when, in fact, cerebral palsy does not affect intelligence at all.

Background and Reference Checks

Employers may not request any information from a previous employer, family member, reference or other source that cannot be asked of the job applicant before a conditional job offer has been made. Just as with employment agencies, if the employer uses an outside firm to perform background checks, it has an obligation to make sure that firm knows and complies with the ADA's requirements concerning pre-employment inquiries, and can be held liable for any violations.

Before a conditional job offer is made, employers may not ask references or other sources about the applicant's disabilities, illnesses or workers' compensation history. Questions concerning functions, tasks and duties performed in a previous job, the quality and quantity of work, how job functions were performed, attendance record (overall, not sick days) and other job-related issues that have nothing to do with disability may be asked, the EEOC explained in its Technical Assistance Manual on Title I of the ADA.

If an applicant has a known disability and indicates a reasonable accommodation would be necessary, the EEOC stated that a previous employer may be asked about accommodations it made.

Accommodations for Testing

Reasonable accommodations may be required during the application process for testing procedures. Test sites must be accessible and tests must measure the ability to perform essential job functions and be the same for all applicants for the same job. Formats should not require the use of an impaired skill unless that is the job-related skill the test is designed to measure.

For example, a reader, large print, Braille or an oral test may be required for applicants with vision impairments. Accommodations are not required if the individual being tested does not request them, but employers have a responsibility to let applicants know in advance that the test will be given.

The EEOC gives the following examples of alternative test formats and accommodations that may be required, depending on the situation:

- substituting a written test for an oral one or vice versa;

- administering a test in large print, Braille, orally or on a computer;

- permitting test answers to be recorded or dictated;

- allowing extra time to complete the test;

- simplifying test language;

- scheduling rest breaks;

- providing an accessible test site;

- providing a quiet setting for test taking; and

- evaluating the skill or ability being tested through some means other than a formal test.

Medical Exams and Other Types of Tests

Prior to Employment Offer

Prior to an offer of employment, an employer may not require any medical examinations, even if they are related to the job. A "medical examination" is a procedure or test, usually given by a health care professional or in a medical setting, that seeks information about an individual's physical or mental impairments or health. Medical examinations include vision tests; blood, urine and breath analysis; blood pressure screening and cholesterol testing; and diagnostic procedures, such as X-rays, CAT scans and MRIs.

The rules about testing under the ADA seem clear. Absolutely no testing that is likely to elicit medical information is permitted before a clear offer of employment is made. The rule is aimed at preventing discrimination against job applicants with disabilities. If an employer does not know about a disability, it cannot discriminate on the basis of one.

Pre-offer tests designed to evaluate skills necessary for the particular job are permitted. For example, physical agility tests for firefighters or typing tests for secretaries are not considered medical examinations. Demonstrations of an applicant's ability to perform job tasks are not considered medical examinations. They are skills tests, and may be given to job applicants. Honesty tests, polygraphs and tests designed to elicit information about an individual's tastes and habits generally are not considered medical examinations either, according to the EEOC in its Technical Assistance Manual on Title I.

Tests for illegal drugs are not considered medical examinations and current illegal drug users are not protected by the ADA. Tests to determine alcohol use are medical examinations if they require blood, urine, breath samples or the like and may not be administered at the pre-offer stage, the EEOC warned.

Employers that require a medical release to assure that applicants will not be harmed by physical agility tests may request the applicant's physician to respond to an inquiry that describes the test and asks if the applicant can safely perform it, the EEOC explained. The applicant can be asked to sign a waiver, or the test can be given after a conditional job offer is made, when relevant medical information can be gathered. The same tests and medical releases or information must be required of all similarly situated job applicants.

Whether a paper and pencil psychological or personality test is considered a medical examination depends on the purpose for which it is given. Tests designed to measure honesty, tastes, habits and other personality traits were okayed by the EEOC in its guidance. Tests meant to discern whether an applicant has a mental disorder were prohibited as medical examinations. Questions about the use of mental health services, drugs or alcohol were prohibited even if the rest of the paper and pencil test was not.

There is no universal agreement on which personality tests are meant to illicit more than just likes and dislikes.

Example: An employer gave its employees who sought promotions to managerial positions a battery of tests, including the Minnesota Multiphasic Personality Inventory (MMPI), in an effort to determine if the candidates were suited by personality to manage others. The employer used a vocational scoring protocol, not a clinical one, to assess the MMPI results and the test was administered by HR staff. Nevertheless, the court held that the test was a prohibited medical exam. Some questions were "designed, at least in part, to reveal mental illness" and hurt the promotion prospects of those with mental disabilities, the court decided (*Karraker v. Rent-a-Center*, 411 F.3d 831 (7th Cir. 2005)).

Example: The use of the same MMPI test was approved by another appeals court as job related and consistent with business necessity when it was used to screen police officers at the post-job-offer stage. "We easily conclude that appropriate psychological screening is job related and consistent with business necessity where the selection of individuals to train for the position of police officer is concerned," the court said (*Miller v. City of Springfield*, 146 F.3d 612 (8th Cir. 1998)).

Personality tests must be chosen with care. The company that publishes the MMPI recommended use of its test in employment only in the identification of suitable candidates for high-risk public safety positions and only after a conditional job offer has been made.

Promotions for which employees must compete generally are viewed the same as an initial job for ADA purposes, according to the EEOC and some courts, so the same medical examination prohibitions apply. The employee is more like an applicant than an existing employee, according to the commission and those courts that agree with this position. They hold that the prohibition against medical examinations and questions applies for promotions, regardless of the fact that such information more than likely is already available in the employee's files. On the other hand, there is no reason non-disability questions and skills tests cannot be required for promotions the same as for first-time job applicants.

After Conditional Job Offer

While the ADA prohibits medical examinations or even medical questions before an offer of employment has been made, after an employee has been offered a job but before he or she begins work, even medical examinations are permitted for insurance and other purposes, as long as everyone in the same job category is treated the same.

"Post-offer" stage means after all conditions for an offer have been met under the employer's usual policy and practices. If a background check generally must be completed before a real job offer can be made, for example, medical information cannot be collected until after the background check is done (see *Leonel v. American Airlines, Inc.*, 400 F.3d 702 ((9th Cir. 2005)).

At the post-offer stage, employers may obtain any information they believe might be relevant to the employee's ability to perform the job or important for the employer to know. Physicals can be required and the initial offer can be conditioned on the results (29 C.F.R. §1630.14 (b)).

These examinations do not have to be limited to the individual's ability to perform job functions, be job related or consistent with business necessity, but all entering employees in the same job category must be subject to the same examinations. Not all employees, only all of those in the same job category, must be subject to the same medical examination (29 C.F.R. §1630.14(b)(3)). If a physical reveals a medical problem, the employee may be required to take additional tests or asked to provide additional information that is not requested of other employees.

Employees may be asked to take voluntary medical examinations after a job offer has been made as part of an employee wellness program or for insurance purposes. All medical information, whether obtained from a required or voluntary examination, must be kept strictly confidential.

Employers may not discriminate on the basis of the results of a post-offer medical examination. If an applicant is rejected for employment on the basis of a physical, the employer must be able to show that the rejection is job related and a business necessity and that there is no reasonable accommodation that would enable the individual to perform the job's essential functions, the EEOC warned in its regulations (29 C.F.R. §1630.14(b)(3)).

If the rejection is on the basis that the individual poses a threat to the safety of him- or herself or others, the employer must be able to show that there is a direct threat based on objective evidence and that the individual poses a significant risk of substantial harm. (For more information about the direct threat exception, see Chapter 1.) Moreover, the employer must be able to show that there is no reasonable accommodation that would reduce the risk to an acceptable level. Employers may not make class-wide exclusions based on fears about future medical, insurance or workers' compensation costs.

After making a job offer, employers may ask job applicants about workplace injuries and workers' compensation claims, as long as all employees entering the same job category are asked the same questions. However, the EEOC warned employers that they may not obtain specific information about workplace injuries or workers' compensation claims from third parties, including former employers or state workers' compensation employees.

After Employment Begins

An employer may make disability-related inquiries and require medical examinations of current employees only if they are job related and consistent with business necessity. Job related and consistent with business necessity means that the employer has a reasonable belief based on objective evidence that the employee will be unable to perform the essential functions of his or her job because of a medical condition, or the employee will pose a direct threat because of a medical condition.

Employers may ask employees about their health when sick leave is involved, the EEOC said in its Enforcement Guidance on Disability-Related Inquiries and Medical Examinations of Employees Under the Americans With Disabilities Act. An employer is entitled to know in general terms why the employee is taking sick leave and may request a doctor's note or other explanation. The requirements must apply to all employees.

Employers also may ask questions or require a medical exam when an employee wants to return to work from sick leave if there is any doubt about the employee's ability to perform essential job functions or whether the employee will pose a direct threat. Inquiries or exams must be limited to what is needed to determine whether the employee is able to work.

Employers may require employees who are injured while on the job to undergo a medical examination either at the time of the injury or when the employee asks to return to work. Unlike medical examinations required of all employees in a job category after a conditional offer of employment is made, examinations of employees due to workplace injuries must be job related and a business necessity as, for example, when the employer is trying to ascertain the extent of its workers' compensation liability, reasonably believes that the injury will impair the employee's ability to perform essential job functions, or believes that because of the injury the employee will pose a direct threat to the health and safety of him- or herself or others.

The examination must be limited to the scope of the specific workplace injury; the employer may not request far-ranging disability-related information or require medical examinations unrelated to the injury.

Employers also may obtain medical information about an employee when he or she has requested an reasonable accommodation and the disability or need for accommodation is not obvious.

Public safety personnel may be required to take periodic fitness-for-duty medical exams, so long as they are strictly job related. A police department could not test officers to determine whether they are HIV-positive, the EEOC noted, because such a diagnosis by itself would not result in a direct threat.

Drug and Alcohol Tests

Drug tests are not considered medical examinations. Alcohol tests, on the other hand, are, and the EEOC said employers generally may not subject employees to periodic alcohol testing. However, rules prohibiting employees from being under the influence of alcohol in the workplace may be enforced and alcohol testing is permitted when there is a reasonable belief that an employee has been drinking on the job.

Employers may hold employees with alcohol and other drug use problems to the same standards as all other employees and may enforce federal, state and local alcohol- and drug-free workplace laws and company policies. The ADA specifically provides that employers may discharge or deny employment to current illegal drug users on the basis of that use without being liable for discrimination, because current illegal drug users are not individuals with disabilities protected by the law (42 U.S.C. §12210). No reasonable accommodation for those individuals is required.

Illegal drugs as defined in the EEOC's Technical Assistance Manual on Title I include the illegal use of prescription drugs that are controlled substances. They do not include drugs taken under the supervision of a licensed health care professional.

The law provides limited protection for recovering drug addicts and alcoholics. Alcoholics are individuals with disabilities, but employers may discipline or discharge any employee whose drinking impairs job performance or causes misconduct in the workplace and employers may prohibit the use of alcohol on company property. Alcoholics may be held to the same standards of performance as all other employees but may not be disciplined more harshly than other employees for the same performance or conduct (EEOC's Technical Assistance on Title I §8.4).

SUCCESSFUL ACCOMMODATIONS FOR ALCOHOLISM

There are numerous accommodations that might benefit employees with alcoholism, but based on calls to the Job Accommodation Network, the most frequently requested accommodations are flexible scheduling, stress reduction, leave and avoiding work-related events where alcohol is served.

Examples of successful accommodations include the following:

- An office manager was allowed leave time for in-patient treatment for alcoholism. After returning to work, his employer provided him with a flexible schedule that allowed him to do his job but also attend AA meetings.

- A lawyer with alcoholism and stress from family problems had difficulty attending social events with clients where alcohol was served. Her employer excused her from attending the events until she was able to deal with her family problems.

For more information about accommodating alcoholism in the workplace, see http://www.jan.wvu.edu.

Individuals who have successfully completed supervised drug rehabilitation programs and are no longer using illegal drugs, or who have otherwise been successfully rehabilitated and are not using illegal drugs, are participating in a rehabilitation program and not using illegal drugs, or who are erroneously regarded as engaging in illegal drug use, are protected from discrimination by the ADA.

These employees may even be entitled to reasonable accommodations such as modified work schedules to permit attendance at ongoing rehabilitation meetings (EEOC's Technical Assistance on Title I §8.7). Employers may adopt policies, including drug testing, to ensure that rehabilitated employees are no longer engaging in the use of illegal drugs (42 U.S.C. §12114(b)).

Interestingly, casual past illegal drug users who did not become addicted are not protected by the ADA. The reasoning is that casual users were not substantially limited in a major life activity because of their drug use and therefore were not disabled by it.

"Current" drug use is not specifically defined. The EEOC said it must be determined on a case-by-case basis, but the use of drugs does not have to be on the day discipline is imposed or the day a drug test is administered. The use, as shown by a valid drug test, must only have occurred recently enough to justify the employer's reasonable belief that it is an ongoing problem, the commission said.

REASONABLE ACCOMMODATIONS FOR DRUG TESTING

A power company required one of its employees, a former drug user, to submit to monthly random drug testing. Employees who were not former drug users were randomly tested once every five years.

The employee had a neurogenic bladder that made it difficult for him to urinate on command. When he could not provide a urine sample in the allotted time during one test, he was fired, in spite of his providing a blood sample. The employee claimed the employer's refusal to reasonably accommodate his neurogenic bladder condition amounted to discrimination on the basis of his former drug use.

The federal appeals court agreed, finding that under the employer's drug policy, former drug users with neurogenic bladders would be fired after one month, presuming they could not supply a urine sample, while other employees with the same condition would be fired only after an average of five years. The differential treatment discriminated on the basis of the ADA-covered disability of former drug use, the court held.

While the employer did not have to change its drug testing policy, it did have to provide reasonable accommodations, such as allowing more time or substituting blood samples, for former drug users who could not easily provide urine samples (*Buckley v. Consolidated Edison Co.*, 127 F.3d 270 (2d Cir. 1997)).

Employers may fire or refuse to hire individuals with a past history of illegal drug use in occupations such as law enforcement or health care, if it can be shown that the policy is job related and consistent with business necessity. Employment also can be denied when it can be shown that the individual poses a direct threat to health or safety because of the likelihood the person would return to drug use.

The showing of significant risk of substantial harm must be based on an assessment of the individual involved, not solely on statistics, the EEOC warned.

Drug Testing Policies

While the ADA neither encourages nor authorizes drug testing by employers, it does state that drug testing is not considered a medical examination, which means testing can be required prior to making a conditional job offer. In addition, the law does not restrict employers' rights to test employees for illegal drug use or to fire employees who test positive (42 U.S.C. §12114(d)).

Drug testing does not have to be job related or a business necessity. On the other hand, invasive alcohol tests are medical examinations, according to the EEOC, and may be required only in conformance with ADA requirements for such exams, which means, for one thing, only after a conditional offer of employment has been made.

If drug tests reveal the use of lawful prescription drugs or the presence of a disability, the information must be kept confidential just as any other medical record must be.

Catch-22 – There is a Catch-22 to employer drug testing. Tests may reveal drugs that are being taken legally. If the employee or applicant is denied a job or fired because he or she was erroneously believed to be an illegal drug user, the employer would be liable for discrimination under the ADA. To avoid this liability, the employer could ask the individual about prescription drugs, but this is not permitted before a conditional job offer has been made.

The EEOC suggests in its Technical Assistance Manual on Title I that employers make conditional job offers prior to requiring drug tests. Applicants who test positive for illegal drug use are not protected by the ADA, so the employer can withdraw the job offer on that basis but still be able to determine whether the test results were due to authorized prescription drugs. Questions should be limited to medications that could have caused the positive drug test.

However, questions about prescription drugs should be asked only *after* a positive test result. While drug testing does not have to be job related or consistent with a business necessity, requiring employees to answer questions about prescription drugs does. An employer that asked employees to disclose all prescription drugs they took prior to drug testing violated the ADA, according to a federal appeals court that found there was no business necessity for asking the question (*Roe v. Cheyenne Mountain Conference Resort*, 124 F.3d 1221 (10th Cir. 1997)).

Moreover, an employee does not have to be a qualified individual with a disability to be protected from medical questions, because the ADA's prohibition on disability-related inquiries that are not job related and a business necessity applies to all employees (*Roe v. Cheyenne Mountain Conference Resort*, 124 F.3d 1221 (10th Cir. 1997); see also *Griffin v. Steeltek*, 160 F.3d 591 (10th Cir. 1998), *cert. denied*, 119 S. Ct. 1455 (1999)). Needless to say, employers should tread carefully when doing drug testing, especially if testing is not required in the employer's industry by a federal law.

Accommodations for Benefits and Privileges of Employment 5

The ADA requires employers to provide reasonable accommodations that will enable individuals with disabilities to have an equal opportunity in every aspect of employment, unless doing so would impose an undue hardship on the employer's business. Employers may not limit, segregate or classify individuals with disabilities in any way that negatively affects them in terms of job opportunity and advancement. All employment decisions are to be based on objective, factual evidence about each individual, not on assumptions or stereotypes about the individual's abilities.

Under these basic premises, employers may not discriminate against qualified employees with disabilities in any of the following areas:

- promotions;

- awarding tenure;

- evaluations, discipline or firing;

- transfers;

- compensation;

- assignments;

- classification;

- fringe benefits;

- training;

- social and recreational programs; or

- any other term, condition or privilege of employment.

Not discriminating means providing reasonable accommodations as needed, unless doing so would result in an undue hardship.

This chapter discusses reasonable accommodations that may be required for individuals with disabilities to fully participate in the benefits and privileges of employment, including job conditions, training, services, fringe benefits, and social and recreational activities. Without access to facilities, there can be no participation, so the chapter begins with a discussion of the ADA's requirements concerning access to buildings.

Access to Facilities

Reasonable accommodation in employment may include "making existing facilities used by employees readily accessible to and usable by individuals with disabilities" (42 U.S.C. §12111(9)(A)). In the appendix to its regulations, the EEOC explained that this applies to both areas that must be used by the employee to perform essential job functions and non-work areas used by employees for other purposes such as break rooms, lunchrooms, training rooms and restrooms (29 C.F.R. Part 1630 App. §1630.2(o)).

The commission explained in its Technical Assistance Manual on Title I that the ADA establishes different requirements for making facilities accessible under different sections of the law. A private employer's obligation to make its workplace accessible to job applicants and employees under Title I differs from that of a place of public accommodation to provide access in existing facilities for its customers and clients, and from the obligation of public accommodations and commercial facilities to provide accessibility in renovated or newly constructed buildings under Title III of the law.

General Requirements Under Title I

Unless it would cause an undue hardship, employers are required to provide access to their facilities so that a job applicant with a disability can participate in the job application process and an employee with a disability can perform the essential functions of his or her job, including having access to the workstation, equipment and all other facilities, such as lunchrooms, that are used by employees.

Employers are not required to make facilities accessible until a job applicant or an employee needs the accommodation, and then, assuming there is no undue hardship in doing so, the structural modifications should meet the work needs of the individual, the EEOC said. The employer does not have to provide access to places or facilities that will not be used by the individual (EEOC's Technical Assistance on Title I §3.9).

On the other hand, Title III requires places of public accommodation to make their goods and services accessible in general to all individuals with disabilities. Architectural barriers and communication barriers that are architectural in nature and an integral part of the physical structure, such as signs and alarm systems, must be removed if doing so is readily achievable. If removal is not readily achievable, services must be provided in some alternative manner that makes them accessible, if that is readily achievable (EEOC's Technical Assistance on Title I §3.9).

"Readily achievable" means easily accomplished and able to be carried out without much difficulty or expense. There is no numerical formula or cost threshold provided by the law or regulations for what is readily achievable, so determinations must be based on all the circumstances and done on a case-by-case basis. The requirement is designed to be flexible, with the size and nature of the business serving as key components in a final decision.

Of course employers' businesses often will also be places of public accommodation and the EEOC suggested that when making changes to facilities under Title I, employers consult applicable Department of Justice accessibility guidelines. (Justice enforces Title III.)

It is wise, the EEOC pointed out, to make structural changes that conform to the Title III guidelines if they meet the employee's needs and do not impose an undue hardship on the employer's business, but the commission warned that even though modifications meet the standards established under Title III, a different or further modification might be required to meet the needs of a particular employee. For example, a restroom that is modified to meet general accessibility standards may need a lower grab bar installed for a very short employee in a wheelchair.

Even though the requirements for accessibility to a workplace are triggered by the needs of a specific individual, the EEOC said employers should consider initiating changes that provide general accessibility so that job applicants will be accommodated in advance. Accommodation can be as simple as relocating employment offices and interview facilities to an accessible ground floor area. Job information can be made accessible in an alternative format for visually impaired individuals.

Other accommodations that may be needed to make workplace facilities accessible include:

- installing ramps at building entrances;

- removing raised thresholds;

- providing reserved parking spaces that are wheelchair accessible close to an accessible entrance to the building;

- making restrooms accessible;

- rearranging office furniture and equipment;

- providing accessible paths of travel to equipment and employee facilities;

- removing potential hazards from the paths of employees with visual impairments; and

- providing flashing lights that accompany alarm bells warning of fire and other emergencies.

IRRITANT FREE ENVIRONMENTS

Employees with multiple-chemical sensitivities present a unique problem for employers. At least one appeals court ruled that employers are not required to make the workplace free of perfumes, scents and other irritants. An employer is not required to create a wholly isolated work space that is free from numerous possible irritants, the court decided (*Buckles v. First Data Resources, Inc.*, 176 F.3d 1098 (8th Cir. 1999)).

In a formal agency decision (*Roberts v. Slater* (2000)) the EEOC ruled that an entirely fragrant free environment is not a reasonable request for accommodation. It would be impractical and cause an undue hardship on the employer.

Renovation and New Construction

Employers' accessibility requirements to existing structures under Title I have to do with making reasonable accommodations for specific employees and job applicants. As with any accommodation, if making structural modifications imposes an undue hardship on the employer's business, doing so is not reasonable and not required. If an employer decides, for whatever reason, to make renovations or to undertake new construction, accessibility requirements are much more extensive.

In discussing alterations and new construction, Title III of the ADA refers to not just places of public accommodation, but to "commercial facilities." These are defined as any nonresidential facility whose operations affect commerce and include office buildings, factories and warehouses. In other words, most workplaces must conform to the rules incorporated in Title III if they undergo major construction work. Those rules are the ADA Accessibility Guidelines (ADAAG) from the Justice Department's regulations.

Only alterations that affect the usability of a facility are covered by the ADAAG. Routine maintenance is not included. Relocating a doorway would be a covered alteration, for example, but putting a new roof on an existing structure would not, according to the EEOC in its Technical Assistance Manual on Title I. Included under covered alterations are remodeling (more extensive than projects such as painting and wallpapering), renovation, rehabilitation, reconstruction, historic restoration (unless doing so would threaten or destroy historic features), changes or rearrangement in structural parts or elements, and changes or rearrangement in the plan configuration of walls and full-height partitions (28 C.F.R. §36.402(b)).

Each area that is altered must comply with the ADAAG. A relocated doorway must be wheelchair accessible, for example, and if a bathroom is renovated at the same time, it, too, must be made accessible.

The theory behind covering all commercial facilities that are renovated or newly constructed is that making buildings accessible when they are built or remodeled will not add much cost to the project and eventually there will be little need for individualized reasonable accommodations.

Newly constructed buildings and those that undergo major renovations must be made readily accessible to and usable by individuals with disabilities. Employees must be able to approach, enter and use the building easily and conveniently. While not every part of every area of a facility has to be accessible, there must be a high degree of accessibility, including to a primary entrance, parking areas, paths of travel into and from the building, restrooms and water fountains, and work areas.

Not every individual workstation needs to be accessible – modifications may be required as reasonable accommodations to suit the needs of a specific worker with a disability – but paths of travel and facilities such as lunchrooms used by all employees must be built so they are accessible. Moreover, employee work areas must be constructed so that workers with disabilities can approach, enter and exit.

Elevators do not have to be installed in buildings that have fewer than three stories or those that have less than 3,000 square feet per story. Shopping centers, shopping malls and the professional offices of health care providers are not covered by this elevator exemption.

Access to Privileges, Responsibilities

The ADA prohibits employers from limiting, segregating or classifying employees with disabilities in a way that adversely affects their employment opportunities or status (29 C.F.R. §1630.5). Job opportunities may not be restricted on the basis of stereotypes or myths about an individual's abilities. Capabilities must be determined on an individualized, case-by-case basis, the EEOC noted.

Employers may not segregate employees with disabilities into separate work areas, break rooms, lunchrooms or lounges. It also is discriminatory to provide separate lines of advancement. Limiting an employee's duties or assignments because the employer makes a presumption about what is "best" violates the law, the EEOC explained. Employees with disabilities must be given the same assignments as all other employees in the same job category, regardless of whether a reasonable accommodation is needed to enable them to perform essential job functions.

Similarly, it is illegal discrimination to adopt a separate job track for promotions or progression based on an assumption that an employee with a disability is uninterested in or incapable of performing certain jobs.

Compensation and Advancement

Employees with disabilities must be given compensation that is equal to all similarly situated employees without disabilities. An employer may not deduct the cost of an accommodation from the employee's pay and may not pay employees with disabilities any less than other employees in the same job category. Employers also may not reduce the pay of an employee with a disability because marginal job functions were eliminated as a reasonable accommodation, although the employer may give the employee other job functions to make up for the ones that were eliminated (EEOC's Technical Assistance on Title I §7.8).

If an employee is assigned to a lower-level job or provided with a part-time job as a reasonable accommodation, the employer may pay the worker the lower compensation applicable to such positions, as long as doing so is consistent with overall compensation practices, the EEOC said in its Technical Assistance Manual.

Promotions and advancement for employees with disabilities should be determined on the same basis as for all other employees. Employers may not deny promotions or advancement on the basis of the employee's disability or because the employee may require a reasonable accommodation to perform the essential functions of a higher-level job.

Evaluations and Discipline

Employees with disabilities need not be given special treatment when it comes to evaluations and discipline, except for reasonable accommodations that may be necessary to enable the employee to perform the essential functions of the job. These employees may not be treated more harshly or in any way discriminated against because of their disability, but to evaluate them on a special or lower standard than other employees or to discipline them less harshly is not equal treatment.

DISCIPLINE DOES NOT HAVE TO BE WAIVED

A police officer with insulin-dependent diabetes failed to properly monitor his condition and became disoriented while driving his police cruiser. He was stopped by other officers for speeding while 40 miles outside of his jurisdiction. The officer protested his firing, insisting he was entitled to a second chance as a reasonable accommodation for his disability.

The employer claimed the officer was a threat to public safety. Reasonable accommodation did not include giving the officer a second chance after he had broken his employer's conduct or safety rules, the appeals court determined (*Siefken v. Village of Arlington Heights*, 65 F.3d 664 (7th Cir. 1995)).

Similarly, an employee who was fired for being under the influence of alcohol on the job could not escape discipline by belatedly requesting reasonable accommodation. The ADA does not require an employer to rehire an employee who was discharged for failure to meet its legitimate job requirements even if that failure was disability related, the appeals court held (*Flynn v. Ratheon Co.*, 1996 U.S. App. LEXIS 20837 (1st Cir. 1996) (unpublished)).

The ADA does not require rescinding or waiving discipline even if the employee's disability played a role in causing the conduct that was the subject of the discipline, according to the EEOC in training information provided to its investigators. The employer may have to provide a reasonable accommodation so workplace rules are not broken in the future, however. For example, if an employee is disciplined for tardiness and then reveals that her late arrivals are due to early morning medical treatments, the employer does not have to rescind the discipline, but may have to adjust the employee's work schedule to accommodate her disability.

On the other hand, if the employer was aware that an employee's disability was causing him or her to be late and despite accommodation requests did nothing to aid the employee, it may not impose discipline. Such was the case when a mobility impaired worker was tardy primarily due to the lack of a van-accessible parking place and an assigned work cubicle (*Holly v. Clairson Industries*, 2007 WL 2050769 (11th Cir. 2007)).

Another appeals court suggested that *firing* an employee who broke conduct rules because of a disability may not be permitted. The employee was fired partly because of her violent outbursts. Applying ADA standards to Washington state law, the court held that because the outbursts were caused by the employee's bi-polar disorder, it would have been correct to instruct the jury in her discrimination case that an employer could not fire an employee for poor job performance if the performance was due to a mental disability and reasonable accommodation could have rectified the problem (*Gambini v. Total Renal Care, Inc.*, 2007 U.S. App. LEXIS 5444 (9th Cir. 2007)). (It must be remembered that the 9th Circuit tends to render more employee-friendly rulings. Another appeals court might have seen this case differently.)

Employers may hold employees with disabilities to the same production and performance standards for essential job functions as other similarly situated employees, as long as any required reasonable accommodations that do not impose an undue hardship on the employer's business have been provided. Equal standards also can apply to marginal job functions, unless the employee's disability affects his or her ability to perform those functions, in which case reasonable accommodation may require job restructuring.

An employee who needs an accommodation to perform a job's essential functions should not be evaluated on the ability to perform those functions without the accommodation, the EEOC explained in its Technical Assistance Manual on Title I, and the employee should not be downgraded because an accommodation is needed.

Employers must provide reasonable accommodations, such as an interpreter for an employee with a hearing impairment, to enable employees with disabilities to participate in the evaluation and disciplinary process.

If an employee with a disability is performing poorly, the employer may make medical inquiries to determine whether the disability is causing the poor performance and whether there is an accommodation that would correct the problem. All inquiries must be job related and consistent with business necessity. (See Chapter 4 for more detail on disability inquiries.) If the reason for unsatisfactory performance is the employer's refusal to provide a reasonable accommodation that would not cause an undue hardship, the employer may not discipline or terminate the employee.

Access to Communications

An employee does not have an equal opportunity to participate in the workplace if he or she does not have access to workplace communications. Employers are required to ensure that employees with disabilities have access to information provided to similarly situated employees through meetings, computers, bulletin boards, mailboxes, posters and public address systems, regardless of whether this information is necessary to perform essential job functions, the EEOC said in its guidance on reasonable accommodations and undue hardship.

Numerous reasonable accommodations are available to provide access to all types of communication mediums. Employees with visual impairments have the most difficulty with written communications, such as bulletin boards, mailboxes and posters. Solutions can be as simple as having someone read the information to the visually impaired individual.

Public address systems are inaccessible for individuals with hearing impairments. The solution can be sending a simultaneous e-mail message or a written notice. Removing many communications barriers often requires no more than sensitivity and taking a logical, problem-solving approach.

Access to computers is more complicated and more expensive, but because the use of electronic technology is required for more and more jobs, computer accessibility is often required so the employee can perform essential job functions. Problems confronting employees with disabilities when attempting to use computers include:

• difficulty reading or comprehending text or images;

• inability to use the computer keyboard or mouse;

• inability to see, hear, move or easily understand graphic displays or functions; and

• inability to move or process some types of information.

Accommodations exist to overcome each of these barriers. Screen readers are an add-on that can enable employees with visual impairments to use computers; magnifiers and large screens are others. Keyboards and mice come in various configurations and types. "Sticky keys" permit individuals with agility problems to hit keys one at a time when a command calls for a combination of keys to be pressed simultaneously. Speech synthesizers enable employees with various disabilities to communicate verbally with computers.

Making computer technology in the workplace accessible may require employers, employees with disabilities and vocational rehabilitation agencies to cooperate. Rehabilitation agencies may help share in the costs. Expertise from information technology specialists also can be sought. (See the resource list at the end of this book.)

The ADA does not provide specifications on what constitutes an accessible computer workstation, but it might include basics such as clearance in the furniture for a wheelchair user, screen reader or magnification software, a large-screen monitor, voice recognition software or a sound card. Employers also should make sure that any intranet or Internet pages are accessible by following good design techniques such as carefully chosen colors and clean, simple page layouts.

Access to Training

Most employers offer training so employees can learn new skills and keep old ones current. The ADA's reasonable accommodation requirement extends to employer-sponsored training so employees with disabilities will have an equal opportunity to participate. The obligation extends to in-house training as well as that provided by an outside entity, the EEOC explained in its guidance on reasonable accommodations and undue hardship.

The type of accommodation required depends on the employee's disability and the type of training being offered. Sign language interpreters for employees with hearing impairments and alternative formats such as Braille, large print or audiocassettes for visually impaired workers are examples of the types of accommodations that may be needed. Facilities must be accessible to individuals with mobility impairments.

The EEOC pointed out that both employers and outside trainers (which are public accommodations covered under Title III of the ADA) are individually and separately liable for providing reasonable accommodations to make the training accessible. The fact that one refuses to do so does not relieve the other of liability.

For example, if an employer contracts with a training company to provide training to its staff, one member of which is blind, and the training company refuses to provide written materials in an alternative format, the employer is obligated to provide the reasonable accommodation. It is good practice for employers to specify in their contracts with outside entities which party will be responsible for providing reasonable accommodations. The employer also has an obligation to ensure that training is held at an accessible site.

Employers are responsible for providing reasonable accommodations even for training that is optional, the EEOC said. Training is a benefit and it is discriminatory to not make whatever arrangements are necessary to permit employees with disabilities to participate, as long as the accommodations do not impose an undue hardship on the employer's business.

Access to Services

Employers must provide reasonable accommodations so workers with disabilities can enjoy employer-sponsored services, such as employee assistance programs (EAPs), credit unions, cafeterias, lounges, gymnasiums, auditoriums, transportation and parking. The ability to enjoy many of these services is contingent on access to facilities.

Employer-sponsored EAPs generally involve contractual relationships with outside entities. Employers must be careful when contracting to include a provision concerning reasonable accommodation for employees with disabilities. Just as with outside trainers, the employer remains responsible for accessibility even though the EAP provider is also responsible for assuring that employees with disabilities can fully participate.

Transportation

Employer assistance with transportation may be a reasonable accommodation. For example, in an opinion letter dated April 24, 1998, the EEOC told an employer with multiple worksites that assigning an employee with a disability to a work location near his home might be a reasonable accommodation if the employee had difficulty with commuting and an open position for which he was qualified existed.

If an employer offers some form of transportation for its employees such as shuttle buses, that transportation service must be accessible to individuals with disabilities under the public accommodation provisions of the ADA (28 C.F.R. §36.310; 49 C.F.R. §37.101), although the statute itself specifically addresses only public transportation offered by public entities and by private companies that are in the transportation business (42 U.S.C. §12141 – §12165; §12184).

The U.S. Department of Transportation, which enforces all of the ADA's transportation provisions, has set different requirements for private entities that offer transportation only as an auxiliary service to their main business, than for public transportation services and those offered by companies whose business is providing transportation. The requirements for private, tangential service vary, depending on the nature of the business and the seating capacity of the vehicle.

Companies that buy or lease vehicles seating more than 16 people, including the driver, for use on fixed-route systems must ensure that those vehicles are accessible for individuals with disabilities. Newly acquired or leased vehicles that seat 16 or fewer, including the driver, need not be accessible if the fixed-route system provides equivalent service to both individuals with disabilities and those without in the most integrated setting appropriate (49 C.F.R. §37.101(c)). The service must be equivalent in terms of:

- schedules/headways;

- fares;

- geographic area of service;

- hours and days of service;

- availability of information; and

- constraints based on capacity or service availability (49 C.F.R. §37.105).

Businesses that offer tangential demand-responsive transportation systems are required to have accessible vehicles only under certain circumstances. If the service operates on request, new vans seating more than 16 persons, including the driver, must be accessible, unless the system when viewed in its entirety meets the standards for equivalent service (49 C.F.R. §37.101(d)). Equivalent service for demand-responsive systems means in terms of:

- response time;

- fares;

- geographic area served;

- hours and days of service;

- availability of information;

- constraints on capacity or service availability; and

- restrictions or priorities based on trip purpose (49 C.F.R. §37.105).

Demand-responsive systems with a capacity of fewer than 16 people are not required to ensure that new vehicles are accessible, but are required to ensure that their systems, when viewed in their entirety, meet the equivalent service requirements listed above (49 C.F.R. §37.101(e)).

Parking

Parking as a reasonable accommodation has been the subject of several court cases. Mobility impaired employees want a parking place as close to an accessible entrance of their workplace as possible. In one case, a lawyer suffered a severe leg injury. After she returned to work, permanently disabled, her employer refused to provide her with a parking space near the entrance to its building. She sued under the ADA, claiming it was unlawful for the employer to refuse to provide her the reasonable accommodation she needed.

The employer insisted a parking place was not a reasonable accommodation because it would not enable the employee to perform the essential functions of her job. The ability to get to her office was a job requirement, however. The appeals court ruled that the parking place might be a reasonable accommodation (*Lyons v. Legal Aid Society*, 68 F.3d 1512 (2d Cir. 1995)).

In another case, the employer provided several parking lots, one for visitors, one for employees, and one for visitors and employees, each of which had the required number of parking spaces for individuals with disabilities. A mobility impaired employee insisted that the employer was required to provide her with a space in the lot closest to the building's entrance, which was reserved for county commissioners and officials, because it afforded her the shortest accessible route.

The federal appeals court held that the ADA does not prohibit the employer from having three separate lots as long as accessible parking is provided in each and that it did not have to provide the employee with a reserved space closest to the building (*Kornblau v. Dade County*, 86 F.3d 193 (11th Cir. 1996)).

In a June 29, 1998, opinion letter, the EEOC told an employer that enforcing employee rules concerning handicapped parking in the employer-provided parking lot so that the spaces would be available for workers with disabilities was a required reasonable accommodation.

Whether an employer is required to provide accessible parking for an employee with a disability depends on individual circumstances. Among the issues to examine are whether employee parking is provided or available at all and whether it would impose an undue hardship on the employer's business to provide the employee with a space close to the building's entrance.

Access to Fringe Benefits

If an employer provides fringe benefits, such as retirement and insurance plans, for its employees, it must provide the same benefits to employees with disabilities, regardless of whether those benefits are administered by the employer itself (29 C.F.R. §1630.4).

Health Insurance Plans

Employees with disabilities must be given the same access to health insurance coverage that other employees are accorded (29 C.F.R. Part 1630 App. §1630.5). Moreover, the ADA does not provide a safe harbor for health insurance plans adopted before the law became effective.

This is not to say that pre-existing conditions clauses in employer-sponsored health insurance plans are illegal under the ADA. Policies with these clauses may be offered even if they adversely affect employees with disabilities, as long as the clauses are not subterfuges to evade the purposes of the law, according to the EEOC. (A cautionary note: employers must comply with the Health Insurance Portability and Accountability Act in regard to pre-existing conditions clauses.)

It is permitted under the ADA to provide health insurance policies that limit coverage for certain procedures or treatments to a specified number each year. In its appendix to its regulations the EEOC explained that limiting blood transfusions to five per year for all employees is not discriminatory even though an employee with hemophilia may require more. It would be a violation of the ADA to limit other types of coverage for that specific employee solely on the basis that he or she is a hemophiliac. For example, the health insurance plan could not deny the individual with hemophilia coverage for heart or other surgery, even though it would not have to provide more than the limited number of blood transfusions provided for all employees.

Limits also may be placed on reimbursements for specified procedures or medications, the EEOC said, as long as the limit is applied equally to all employees. For example, health insurance plans may deny coverage for experimental drugs or procedures if the restriction is applied to all insured individuals.

The key to compliance is that benefits plans are uniformly applied to all employees regardless of disability. An employer may not deny insurance to an individual with a disability or subject that employee to different terms or conditions based on the disability alone. An employer cannot fire or refuse to hire an individual because his or her disability is not covered by the employer-provided health insurance plan or because the individual may cause the employer's future health care costs to increase.

Moreover, an employer cannot fire or refuse to hire an individual because the person's family member has a disability that is not covered by the employer's health insurance plan or that may increase the employer's future health care costs (EEOC's Technical Assistance on Title I §7.9).

In its policy statement, Application of the ADA to Health Insurance (6/9/93), the EEOC explained that insurance plans violate the law if terms, provisions or conditions single out a particular disability, a discrete group of disabilities, or disability in general for different coverage. Health insurance plans also violate the law if they single out a procedure

---

REDUCING BENEFITS AFTER CLAIM IS MADE

Reducing or eliminating health care benefits for a specific disability after an employee files a claim violates the ADA, the EEOC determined. A union changed its health insurance plan to exclude payments for AIDS-related treatment after one of its members developed the disease. The union member filed a charge with the commission, claiming the exclusion had a negative impact on his health because he was unable to secure necessary treatment.

The EEOC decided that the union had no viable defense to the discrimination charge and sued under the ADA. The case was subsequently settled for more than $1 million (*Donaghey v. Mason Tenders Dist. Council Trust Fund*, EEOC Charge No. 160-93-0419 (1/28/93)).

or treatment for a particular disability or discrete group of disabilities for non-coverage or coverage that is different from other similar procedures or treatments.

A health plan that does not cover or that limits benefits for kidney disease but not for other conditions is making a disability-based distinction that is probably discriminatory. Likewise, a plan that caps benefits for AIDS at $10,000 while all other illnesses are capped at $100,000 would probably violate the law.

On the other hand, broad distinctions or limits are acceptable if they apply equally to all participants, the EEOC said. Insurance plans that make a distinction between mental and physical conditions, capping benefits for the former at a much lower level than the latter, do not violate the ADA, according to the EEOC's guidance. (Note: Employer-sponsored plans must comply with the Mental Health Parity Act.)

Appeals courts that have ruled on the issue have agreed with the EEOC, although not always for the same reason. In *EEOC v. CNA Ins. Cos.* (96 F.3d 1039 (7th Cir. 1996)), the court let stand a long-term disability plan that limited benefits for mental and nervous disorders to two years but covered other disabilities until age 65, finding that former employees were not covered by the ADA.

In *Parker v. Metropolitan Life. Ins. Co.* (121 F.3d 1006 (6th Cir. 1997), *cert. denied,* 522 U.S. 1084 (1998)), a similar long-term disability plan was upheld when the appeals court ruled that the ADA does not prohibit an insurance company from differentiating between different types of disabilities. The court in *Ford v. Schering-Plough Corp.* (145 F.3d 601 (3d Cir. 1998), *cert. denied,* 119 S. Ct. 850 (1999)) upheld a nearly identical disability plan, ruling that while the former employee was covered by the ADA, the disparity in benefits was not discriminatory because every employee had the opportunity to join the same plan with the same schedule of coverage.

Using logic similar to that of the *Ford* court, the EEOC also stated in its guidance that caps on eye care that are much lower than those for other physical conditions do not violate the law. An eye-care cap applies to all employees, regardless of the condition to be treated or whether the employee has a visual disability or perfect 20/20 vision, the commission explained.

The Supreme Court's statement in *Olmstead v. L.C.* (119 S. Ct. 2176 (1999)) to the effect that it may be discriminatory under the ADA to differentiate between individuals with disabilities as well as between individuals with disabilities and the rest of the population (footnote 10) has had no apparent impact on rulings on disparities in insurance plans.

Retirement Plans

As with health insurance plans, the ADA does not require employers to provide disability retirement plans even if they offer length-of-service retirement plans. If a disability retirement plan is offered, its benefits do not have to be as generous as those of the length-of-service plan.

The following would not violate the law:

- Employees with 20 years of service may retire and receive 50 percent of their highest annual pay while employees who retire under a disability retirement provision receive only 40 percent of their highest annual pay.

- Employees who retire after 20 years of service receive periodic benefit payment increases while those who retire under a disability retirement provision do not.

- Outside earnings of length-of-service retirees are disregarded, but outside earnings of employees who retire under a disability provision offset disability benefit payments.

According to the EEOC in its policy guidance Questions and Answers About Disability and Service Retirement Plans Under the ADA (5/11/95), these benefits plans are not conditioned on whether the retiree is covered by the ADA. Employees who qualify for length-of-service retirement may receive full benefits regardless of whether they have disabilities.

Plans that deny full benefits *because of* disabilities do violate the ADA, however. Examples given by the EEOC include the following:

- Employees who are eligible for both service and disability retirement plans are required to take the less advantageous disability retirement plan.

- Employees with disabilities are eligible for service retirement with 25 years of service, but other employees may receive the same benefit with only 20 years of service.

- Employees who have disabilities when they are hired are eligible for disability retirement after five years of service, while all other employees are eligible for disability retirement after one year.

- Employees covered by the ADA who take disability retirement are eligible to receive 33 percent of their highest annual pay, while employees not covered by the ADA can receive 50 percent.

- Employees with certain types of disabilities such as diabetes are not eligible for disability retirement plan participation.

The ADA specifically states that it does not prohibit or restrict insurance plans from underwriting risks, classifying risks or administering risks based on or not inconsistent with state law. Nor does it prohibit employers or organizations covered by the ADA from establishing, sponsoring, observing or administering the terms of a bona fide benefit plan based on underwriting risks, classifying risks or administering risks that are based on or not inconsistent with state law or not subject to state laws that regulate insurance, as long as these provisions are not used as a subterfuge to evade the purposes of the ADA (42 U.S.C. §12201(c)).

The EEOC said in its guidance on service retirement plans that the reach of this defense is beyond the scope of the guidance, but the burden is on the employer to prove that an allegedly discriminatory plan is sheltered by this section of the law.

Access to Social Functions

Employer-sponsored social activities, such as parties, picnics and sports teams, are benefits of employment that must be accessible to employees with disabilities. As with accommodations to provide accessibility to other employment-related activities, access to social activities often involves removing physical barriers to facilities. Holiday, retirement and other parties should be held in locations that accommodate mobility impaired employees. Picnic sites should be examined before the event to ensure that they are accessible.

Access to other social activities sometimes is limited by attitudes. Employees with disabilities should be solicited to participate in all employer-sponsored events, just as every other employee is. Presuming that an employee would not want to be part of a softball team because his artificial leg would hinder his running is no less discriminatory than presuming a female employee would not want to play "a man's game." Neither attitude is acceptable in the workplace. It is up to the employee to decide whether to participate.

Reasonable accommodation for social functions requires providing equality of opportunity, nothing more or less. Under the ADA, employees with disabilities are entitled to enjoy all of the benefits and privileges of employment and it is up to employers to make that happen by providing reasonable accommodations, if doing so does not impose an undue hardship on their business.

Types of Reasonable Accommodations

6

There are many kinds of reasonable accommodations that can enable an employee with a disability to perform a job's essential functions. The kind of accommodation needed has to be determined on a case-by-case basis, because every individual and every job situation is different.

While specialized equipment or devices may be required in some instances, most accommodations are inexpensive or can be provided by the individual. Sometimes an employer will need to reevaluate the job or company policies to effectively accommodate an employee's disability. Job restructuring is a common way to accommodate an employee or potential employee who can perform some parts of the job but not others, although larger employers may find it easier to do that than smaller ones.

Temporary leave can in some instances provide an accommodation that will enable a worker to return to the job, and a modified work schedule might enable an employee to remain on the job while seeking treatment for a disability. Available light-duty jobs may be given to employees who are no longer able to perform the essential functions of the jobs for which they were hired, although this may create precedents when such jobs have been reserved solely for employees who are injured while working.

Telecommuting may be a reasonable accommodation in some circumstances. Reassignment is another accommodation that can enable employees with disabilities to keep working after they are no longer able to perform the essential functions of the jobs they were hired to do.

The EEOC discussed these accommodations in its various guidelines and Technical Assistance Manual on Title I. The federal courts have issued opinions on these accommodations that do not always agree with the commission's position. This chapter discusses accommodations from both the agency and judicial perspectives.

Equipment and Devices

When most employers think of job accommodations, the first thing that probably comes to mind is specialized equipment. Purchasing equipment or making modifications to existing equipment can provide effective accommodations for many employees with disabilities. While some electronic equipment, such as voice recognition computer systems or computers that can be operated with eye or head movements, is expensive, there are many devices that cost little or nothing. As the EEOC pointed out in its Technical Assistance Manual on Title I, a simple elastic band can enable an employee with cerebral palsy to hold a pencil and perform the essential job function of writing. And that may be all the accommodation that is needed.

There also are many inexpensive assistive devices and modifications that can be made to existing equipment to enable an employee with a disability to safely and effectively perform the essential functions of a particular job. Often the affected employee can suggest ways to make office equipment accessible. The interactive process described in Chapter 3 enables the employer and employee to identify functional abilities and limitations in relation to job needs and find an appropriate solution.

There are sources of technical assistance to identify and locate devices, specialized equipment and equipment modifications for specific jobs and disabilities. One of the most helpful is the Job Accommodation Network (http://www.jan.wvu.edu; 800-526-7234; 877-781-9403 (TTY)), a free consulting service that maintains a database of accommodations employers have made to enable employees with various types of disabilities to perform a wide variety of jobs.

When an employer or employee calls for assistance, a JAN consultant obtains information about the requirements of the job, the worker and the work environment. The consultant then searches the database for solutions and/or may engage other experts to help determine appropriate accommodations. Callers are given information about possible accommodations for their particular situations and may receive names and phone numbers of employers or workers who have made those accommodations. Callers also are provided with lists of helpful information, such as funding resources and tax incentives.

SIX RESPONSES TO EXPENSIVE REQUESTS

When given a request for an expensive accommodation, employers should discern the following facts before making a decision:

- Is the accommodation for the functional limitations of an ADA disability, or something else?
- What is the net cost of the requested accommodation?
- Does the company as a whole (rather than a single department) have the resources to make the accommodation?
- What accommodations have been provided in the past?
- What needs to be changed to enable the individual to do the essential functions of the job?
- Are there cheaper, equally effective alternatives?

Source: Peter Petesch, Esq., partner, Ford & Harrison LLP, Washington, D.C.

Those who make accommodations in their workplaces are asked to share their experiences and the information is added to JAN's database so it can be used to benefit others. About 80 percent of the job accommodations suggested by JAN cost less than $500. Employers are not required to provide an expensive accommodation if a less costly one is just as effective. There are no cost limitations on accommodations in the law, but employers are not required to "gold plate" their accommodations or provide one that would impose an undue hardship on their business.

Other sources of assistance include vocational rehabilitation specialists, occupational therapists and independent living centers. Consultants conduct a job analysis and recommend appropriate accommodations. The resource list at the back of this book gives information about other agencies and organizations.

Various types of low-cost assistive devices are listed at the end of this book. Examples the EEOC provided in its Technical Assistance Manual of equipment and devices that may be reasonable accommodations include:

•   telecommunication devices for the deaf, which make telephones usable by hearing and speech impaired employees;

•   telephone amplifiers;

•   specialized computer software to enlarge print or convert printed documents to spoken words;

•   tactile markings in Braille or raised print on equipment;

•   telephone headsets, large keyboard buttons and adaptive switches for employees with manual disabilities;

•   talking calculators; and

•   speaker phones.

Employers are only obligated to provide equipment that is needed to perform the essential functions of the job the employee has or desires. Equipment the individual uses in everyday life, such as a wheelchair, is not required as a reasonable accommodation, and equipment, modifications or devices that would impose an undue hardship on the employer's business also are not required. Of course an employer may be required to permit the employee to provide his or her own accommodation, such as a guide dog.

Job Restructuring

Job restructuring is listed as a reasonable accommodation in the statute (42 U.S.C. §12111(9)). The EEOC explained that job restructuring includes modifications such as "reallocating or redistributing marginal job functions that an employee is unable to perform because of a disability and altering when and/or how a function, essential or marginal, is performed" (Enforcement Guidance on Reasonable Accommodations and Undue Hardship Under the ADA (10/17/02)).

An employer may even restructure a job rather than provide accommodations so the employee can perform marginal functions. There is "nothing in the statute" that "requires an employer to accommodate the employee so that she may perform any nonessential function that she chooses," an appeals court noted *(Hoffman v. Caterpillar, Inc.*, 256 F.3d 568 (7th Cir. 2001)).

In its Technical Assistance Manual on Title I of the ADA, the EEOC said that job restructuring or modification "enables many qualified individuals with disabilities to perform jobs effectively." The Technical Assistance Manual stated that employers are not required to reallocate essential job functions and the guidance on reasonable accommodation said, "An employer never has to reallocate essential functions as a reasonable accommodation, but can do so if it wishes."

Job restructuring does not mean simply relieving a worker with a disability of those marginal functions that cannot be done even with an accommodation. Employers can exchange the marginal functions of one job for those of one or more others.

The example given in the EEOC's guidance on reasonable accommodation is of an office building cleaning crew. One member of the crew has a prosthetic leg that makes climbing stairs painful. As a result, the employee cannot sweep the building's stairs. He can, however, clean a small kitchen in the employees' lounge, which another worker has been doing. As a reasonable accommodation, the employer can give the marginal duty of sweeping the stairs to the employee who has been cleaning the kitchen, and give the kitchen chore to the employee with the disability.

Altering the way in which job functions, essential or marginal, are performed is another way of job restructuring. Rescheduling when a task is performed, permitting a handwrit-

---

No Exemption From Essential Job Functions

Only qualified individuals with disabilities are covered by the ADA, which states that a qualified individual with a disability is one who, with or without reasonable accommodation, can perform the essential functions of a job. Given that definition, federal courts have agreed with the EEOC that essential job functions do not have to be reassigned as a reasonable accommodation. (See Chapter 2 for more information on essential functions.)

Exemption is not accommodation, one court said. In that case, a school bus driver who could not lift children due to a back condition wanted to be assigned to a bus route in which the need to lift youngsters was minimized. The driver was not a qualified individual with a disability and reassignment was not reasonable, the court said, because the ADA does not require an employer to exempt an employee from an essential function of the job (*Bickers v. Cleveland Bd. of Ed.*, 145 F.3d 846, *rehearing denied*, 1998 U.S. App. LEXIS 24423 (6th Cir. 1998)).

Similarly, another appeals court said reducing an employee's previously assigned duties was not a necessary accommodation. Requiring another person to perform an essential function of a disabled employee's job is not a reasonable accommodation, the court found (*Nunn v. Illinois State Bd. of Education*, 211 Fed. Appx. 502 (7th Cir. 2006) unpublished; see also *Peters v. City of Mauston*, 311 F.3d 835 (7th Cir. 2002)).

Employers are not required to create new positions (*Watson v. Lithonia Lighting*, 304 F.3d 749 (7th Cir. 2002)) or manufacture jobs that will allow an employee to work despite a disability, courts have held (*Jackson v. City of Chicago*, 414 F.3d 806 (7th Cir. 2005)).

---

ten job to be done on a computer and providing a checklist of duties that is reviewed by a supervisor are all reasonable accommodations that can enable employees with disabilities to perform essential job functions.

Technical assistance on restructuring or modifying jobs for individuals with various types of limitations can be obtained from state vocational rehabilitation agencies and other organizations. (See the resource list at the back of this book.)

Interpreters and Assistants

Sometimes accommodation involves providing the expertise or assistance of another person on an as-needed basis. For instance, a person who is hearing impaired may need an interpreter in some situations, such as when discussions of complex subject matter are involved, or a job applicant may need an interpreter to communicate fully during the interview process.

An interpreter should be provided if doing so does not impose an undue hardship, according to the EEOC (EEOC's Technical Assistance on Title I §3.10(9)). Resources available to the employer are considered in determining whether it would be an undue hardship to provide a sign language interpreter, the commission stated.

Another accommodation that might be appropriate is a personal assistant for certain job-related functions, such as a travel attendant on occasional business trips for an employee with a visual impairment. A job coach for a new employee with a mental impairment can give individualized training that the employer would have neither the time nor expertise to do. Job coaches are provided at no cost to the employer by vocational rehabilitation agencies through supported employment programs. (See the resource list at the end of this book.)

Leave

Leave may be a reasonable accommodation in some instances as long as the leave has at least an approximate end date. Providing unpaid leave after accrued leave has been exhausted is a controversial reasonable accommodation. The EEOC lists it as a reasonable accommodation in the appendix to its regulations (29 C.F.R. Part 1630 App. §1630.2(o)). It also discusses leave as an accommodation in its Technical Assistance Manual on Title I of the ADA and in its guidance on reasonable accommodation.

Some federal appeals courts have held that coming to work regularly is an essential function of the job (*Byrne v. Avon Products, Inc.*, 328 F.3d 379 (7th Cir. 2003); *Hypes v. First Commerce Corp.*, 134 F.3d 721 (5th Cir. 1998); *Carr v. Reno*, 23 F.3d 525 (D.C. Cir. 1994)). An employee who is unable to meet the attendance requirements of the job, in spite of accommodations from the employer, is not otherwise qualified under the ADA and thus not entitled to its protections, another appeals court held (*Tyndall v. National Educational Centers*, 31 F.3d 209 (4th Cir. 1994)).

Attendance "is an essential aspect of most jobs and the inability to work for a multi-month period removes a person from the class protected by the ADA," the 7th Circuit insisted. The ADA "only contemplates accommodations that will allow the individual to 'perform the essential function of the employment position. Not working is not a means to perform the job's essential functions," the court added (*Hamm v. Exxon Mobil Corp.*, 2007 WL 1353985 (7th Cir. 2007)).

Another federal appeals court disagreed, holding that the presumption that regular attendance is an essential job requirement is erroneous and that medical leave, even for an indefinite time, can be a reasonable accommodation. The employer should be forced to prove that such leave would cause an undue hardship to escape liability for failing to accommodate under the ADA, the court said (*Cehrs v. Northeast Ohio Alzheimer's Research Center*, 155 F.3d 775 (6th Cir. 1998)).

In a footnote to its guidance on reasonable accommodation, the EEOC took issue with courts that have characterized attendance as an essential job function. "Attendance ... is not an essential function as defined by the ADA because it is not one of the 'fundamental job duties of the employment position,'" the commission insisted, adding that "essential functions are duties to be performed" (footnote 61).

In its Technical Assistance Manual, the EEOC explained that while employers may establish attendance and leave policies that are uniformly applied to all employees, they may not refuse leave needed by a worker with a disability if other employees can take leave. Moreover, the commission said, an employer may be required to make adjustments in its leave policy as a reasonable accommodation. Employers are not obligated to provide additional *paid* leave, the EEOC said, but accommodations may include leave flexibility and unpaid leave.

For example, if an employer has a policy providing two weeks of paid leave for all employees with no other provision for sick leave and no leave at all for the first six months, the policy is not discriminatory per se under the ADA. However, if an employee with a disability needs leave for medical treatment, unpaid leave or advanced leave might be a required reasonable accommodation.

In its guidance, the EEOC expanded on its discussion of leave. "Permitting the use of accrued paid leave, or unpaid leave, is a form of reasonable accommodation when necessitated by an employee's disability." Employers do not have to provide paid leave beyond that which is provided to similarly situated employees, the commission conceded, adding that employers should allow employees with disabilities to exhaust accrued paid leave first, and then grant unpaid leave.

Employees with disabilities may need leave for a variety of reasons, the EEOC noted in its guidance, including:

- obtaining medical treatment or therapy;

- recuperating from an illness or manifestation of the disability;

- obtaining repairs on an assistive device;

- avoiding temporary adverse conditions in the workplace such as a breakdown in the air conditioning;

- training a service animal; or

- receiving training in the use of Braille or sign language.

Employers may not penalize employees for work missed during leave taken as a reasonable accommodation, the commission stated, because doing so would be retaliation and make the leave an ineffective accommodation. If a salesperson took five months of leave as a reasonable accommodation, the employer could not compare the employee's 12-month sales record unfavorably with that of other salespersons, but would have to prorate his or her record.

Similarly, the EEOC explained, an employer that decides to terminate any employee who missed more than four weeks of work in the previous year as part of a reduction in force (RIF) may not count the five weeks of leave an employee with a disability took for treatment of that disability in determining whether to RIF the employee.

The commission contended that a federal appeals court that held to the contrary "failed to consider that the employee needed leave and a modified schedule as reasonable accommodations for his disability, and that the accommodations became meaningless when he was penalized for using them" (*Matthews v. Commonwealth Edison Co.*, 128 F.3d 1194 (7th Cir. 1997)). In that case, an employee missed several months of work following a heart attack and then returned to his job on a part-time basis until his health permitted him to work full-time. The appeals court held that the employer could RIF the worker on the basis of his lower productivity due to his absence.

If leave is granted as a reasonable accommodation to an employee with a disability, the employee's job must be held open for his or her return, unless the employer can show that doing so would impose an undue hardship on its business, according to the EEOC. If the employer cannot hold the employee's position open during the leave period, it must consider whether it has a vacant, equivalent position for which the employee is qualified and reassign the employee to that position.

If no equivalent position is available, the employer must look for a vacant position at a lower level and only if one does not exist would continued leave not be required, the EEOC insisted in its guidance on reasonable accommodation. If the employee accepts a lower level job, the employer can reduce the worker's pay accordingly. (See the section on reassignment in this chapter.)

Some employers have "no fault" leave policies that permit employees to take a specified amount of leave for any reason during a specified time period, most often a calendar year. After the leave is exhausted, employees may take no more, and are terminated if they do so. These policies generally may not be applied to employees with disabilities who need additional leave as an accommodation, the EEOC said. Employers must modify their leave policies, unless they can show that there is another effective accommodation or granting additional leave would cause an undue hardship, the commission stated in its guidance.

If an employer can offer an effective accommodation that eliminates the need for leave, the employee can be required to remain on the job, as long as doing so does not interfere with the worker's medical needs. (The Family and Medical Leave Act may require unpaid leave regardless of other available accommodations.) The employer is obligated to restore the employee's full duties, or to return the employee to his or her original position after the accommodation is no longer needed, the EEOC guidance said.

Amount of Leave

The amount of leave an individual must be given as a reasonable accommodation is fact specific and depends in part on whether the needed time would impose an undue hardship on the employer and whether the employee is qualified under the ADA. There is no bright line test for the maximum amount of leave that can be a reasonable accommodation.

Employers with numerous part-time or seasonal employees might be required to provide lengthy leave and keep the worker's job open (see *Nunes v. Wal-Mart Stores, Inc.*, 164 F.3d 1243 (9th Cir. 1999)). The same can be said for an employee in a job that is easily filled by a temporary worker (see *Garcia-Ayala v. Lederle Parenterals, Inc.*, 212 F.3d 638 (1st Cir. 2000)). When the leave requested under the ADA is the same as under the Family and Medical Leave Act, it is difficult for an employer to prove undue hardship (see *Smith v. Diffee Ford-Lincoln-Mercury*, 298 F.3d 955 (10th Cir. 2002)).

Smaller employers can show undue hardship more easily than large ones when the leave is outside the bounds of the FMLA. A police officer in a small municipality who requested six months of leave created an undue hardship for the employer because it could not reallocate his job duties among its 15 to 22 remaining officers. "An employer is not required to hire additional people or assign tasks to other employees to reallocate essential functions that an employee must perform," the court held (*Epps v. City of Pine Lawn*, 353 F.3d 588 (8th Cir. 2003)).

Indefinite Unpaid Leave

Regardless of how many weeks or months of leave may be reasonable, most courts hold that an employer does not have to provide indefinite leave as an accommodation. Totally indefinite leave with no end in sight is not a reasonable accommodation, which by definition is assistance that enables an employee to presently or in the immediate future do the job (see *Myers v. Hose*, 50 F.3d 278 (4th Cir. 1995)).

"An employer does not have to wait for an indefinite period for an accommodation to achieve its intended effect," the 11th Circuit stated. Reasonable accommodation "is by its terms most logically construed as that which, presently or in the immediate future, enables the employee to perform the essential functions of the job in question, the court said (*Wood v. Green*, 323 F.3d 1309 (11th Cir. 2003)).

The 10th Circuit held much the same way, stating "a request for indefinite leave cannot constitute 'reasonable' accommodation" because it "does not allow the employee to perform the essential functions of the job in the near future" (*Cisneros v. Wilson*, 226 F.3d 1113 (10th Cir. 2000)). In that case the employee argued that her request was for three months, but because neither she nor her doctors provided a specific date for return to work, saying only that it was expected she would be recovered by the end of the third month, the court found that the request was indefinite.

In an earlier case involving a telecommunications company customer service representative with carpal tunnel syndrome, the 10th Circuit noted that the physician's report did not indicate when the employee could be expected to resume her regular duties, and held that the employer "was not required to wait indefinitely" for the worker's recovery (*Hudson v. MCI Telecommunications,* 87 F.3d 1167 (10th Cir. 1996)).

Another court found that "the duty to make reasonable accommodations does not, of course, require an employer to hold an injured employee's position open indefinitely while the employee attempts to recover (*Parker v. Columbia Pictures Industries,* 204 F.3d 326 (2d Cir. 2000)).

In a case in which an employee had already taken 18 months of leave and might need one to three years more, the 6th Circuit ruled that "when the requested accommodation has no reasonable prospect of allowing the individual to work in the identifiable future, it is objectively not an accommodation that the employer should be required to provide." When the employer had already provided substantial leave, "an additional leave period of significant duration with no clear prospects for recovery, is an objectively unreasonable accommodation," the court held (*Walsh v. United Parcel Service,* 201 F.3d 718 (6th Cir. 2000)).

On the other hand, courts recognize that physicians often have difficulty defining exactly how much time an individual will need to be healthy enough to return to work, so some leeway usually is permitted the employee. "Some employees, by the nature of their dis-

---

GUIDELINES FOR LEAVE DECISIONS

The following guidelines can help employers determine whether and how much leave to grant.

- Remember that an extended medical leave, or an extension of an existing leave period, may be a reasonable accommodation if it does not pose an undue hardship on the employer's business.

- Establish a written policy regarding the process of requesting leave, the medical documentation required, the maximum leave allowed and the consequences of failing to abide by the established policy.

- Communicate and administer the established policy uniformly and in a nondiscriminatory manner, without making exceptions.

- Consider obligations under the FMLA, the ADA and state workers' compensation laws before making a decision regarding an employee's request for extended leave as an accommodation.

- Provide the employee with as much leave as allowed under the applicable laws.

- Do not make a decision based on one unanswered request by the employee for medical documentation, but instead provide the employee with a written notice of the consequences of failing to respond within a clear timeframe.

- Document all reasons supporting a decision to decline leave or a leave extension as an accommodation to an employee.

- Be prepared to show, with verifiable proof, that offering an employee an extended leave of absence would be an undue hardship, if that is the reason for the denial of leave.

- In every case, be satisfied that the leave is designed to alleviate the problem so the employee can return to work. The ADA is not a "leave law." It is a "be allowed to work" law.

---

ability, are unable to provide an absolutely assured time for their return to employment" (*Garcia-Ayala v. Lederle Parenterals, Inc.*, 212 F.3d 638 (1st Cir. 2000)).

The approximation may be as vague as "in six to eight weeks" or "in about three months," the EEOC said in its guidance. Because FMLA leave is 12 weeks, a time period of about that length probably would be considered reasonable by most courts, at least for employers large enough to be covered by that law.

Tip for employers: Evaluate a request for leave the same as any other accommodation request. Discuss the matter with the employee and look for options, such as a job transfer, that might accommodate the employee and also suit the company's business needs better.

Family and Medical Leave Act and ADA Leave

Both the Family and Medical Leave Act and the ADA may be implicated when an employee with a disability needs leave. The overlap in the two laws can be confusing, because their coverage and requirements are different. The EEOC advises employers to determine an employee's rights under each statute separately and then consider whether there is any overlap before determining what action to take.

FMLA leave – The FMLA provides eligible employees of covered employers with up to 12 weeks of unpaid leave in a 12-month period. Employees may use FMLA leave for the birth, adoption, or placement in foster care of a son or daughter; for the care of the employee's spouse, son, daughter or parent with a serious health condition; or for the employee's own serious health condition. A serious health condition may *not* and *need not* be a disability under the ADA.

Serious health conditions include illnesses, injuries, impairments, or physical or mental conditions that involve overnight in-patient care in a hospital or continuing treatment by or under the supervision of a health care provider for an incapacity (29 U.S.C. §2611(11)). To qualify as an incapacity subject to continuing treatment, there must be:

- more than three consecutive calendar days' absence from work, school or daily activities and treatment by or under the supervision of a health care provider for two or more times, or one time followed by a regimen of treatment;

- any period of incapacity for pregnancy and prenatal care;

- chronic serious health conditions that continue over an extended period, require periodic visits to a health care provider, and may involve occasional episodes of incapacity (e.g., asthma and diabetes);

- permanent and long-term conditions for which treatment may not be effective (e.g., Alzheimer's, severe stroke or terminal cancer); and

- absences to receive multiple treatments or restorative surgery for a condition that would likely result in more than three calendar days of incapacity if not treated (e.g., chemotherapy or radiation treatment for cancer, or kidney dialysis).

Leave for incapacity due to pregnancy or a chronic serious health condition, such as asthma, is covered even if the employee does not receive treatment from a health care provider during the specific absence. Intermittent leave is permitted when the employee's illness can best be accommodated through an intermittent or reduced work schedule, such as for physical therapy or dialysis.

The FMLA guarantees the right of the employee to return to the same position or an equivalent one. Employers may compel workers to use any accrued paid leave first, and if that is insufficient to cover the entire period, the employee can take unpaid leave. Some states permit employees to choose whether to exhaust available paid leave during an FMLA leave. The law requires the employer to continue the employee's health insurance coverage during the leave, provided the employee pays his or her share of the premiums, which can be no higher than those paid by similarly situated employees who are not on leave.

ADA leave – According to the EEOC's interpretation, under the ADA an employee who needs leave related to a disability is entitled to take it if there is no other effective accommodation and the leave will not cause an undue hardship on the employer's business. It is difficult to think of an ADA disability that would not also be a serious health condition under the FMLA. The employee must be allowed to use accrued paid leave first, and if that is insufficient, unpaid leave. The employee's health insurance benefits must be continued during the period of leave only if the employer does so for other employees on similar leave status.

The ADA requires that the employer hold the employee's job open for the worker to return to unless it can show an undue hardship, and the employee must be permitted to return to the same position if he or she is still qualified, the commission said.

Overlap – As noted, health conditions covered by the FMLA are not necessarily disabilities covered by the ADA. Normal pregnancy, for example, is not an ADA disability, but is covered by the FMLA. Illnesses that last three days or more could include bronchitis, pneumonia or severe flu. None of these would be considered disabilities, assuming the employee recovered. Remember, a "flare-up" of a chronic ADA disability would almost certainly be a "serious health condition" under the FMLA.

However, there are some challenging situations. Asthma, diabetes or some other serious health condition might also be a disability. If so, the employer would have to evaluate the employee's rights under both laws and apply the most generous provisions of each to the situation. The EEOC gives the following examples in its guidance on reasonable accommodation:

Example. An employee with an ADA disability requests 13 weeks of leave for medical treatment related to the disability. The employee is eligible under the FMLA for 12 weeks of leave. The first 12 weeks are both FMLA leave and a reasonable accommodation under the ADA. The employer could deny the 13th week of leave under the FMLA but, according to the EEOC, could not deny it under the ADA unless it would cause an undue hardship.

Example. An employee with an ADA disability takes 10 weeks of FMLA leave and plans to return to work. The employer could put the worker in an equivalent position under the

FMLA, but the ADA requires return to the original job, the EEOC said, warning that unless the employer can show an undue hardship or that the employee is no longer qualified, it must reinstate the worker to the original position.

Example. An employee with an ADA disability took 12 weeks of FMLA leave and then notified his employer he was ready to return to work, but could no longer perform the essential functions of his job or an equivalent position. Under the FMLA, the employer can terminate the worker (29 C.F.R. §825.702(c)(4)), but under the ADA the employer should consider whether the employee could perform the essential functions of the original job or an equivalent one with a reasonable accommodation. If not, the EEOC insisted, the ADA requires the employer to assign the worker to a vacant position for which he is qualified with or without reasonable accommodation, assuming there is no undue hardship in doing so.

As noted above in the section on leave, courts have not always agreed with the EEOC's position. They also do not all agree with the agency on reassignment, as noted in that section later in this chapter.

Modified Schedules and Part-Time Work

Sometimes it is not access or special equipment an employee with a disability needs, it is personal time. For example, an insulin-dependent diabetic must take insulin at set times during the day and as an accommodation needs breaks to perform the task. Or an employee takes medication that makes him or her groggy in the morning, so needs a later starting time as an accommodation. A modified schedule may be a required reasonable accommodation.

A modified schedule may involve adjusting arrival or departure times, providing periodic breaks, altering when certain job functions are performed, allowing an employee to take accrued leave, or providing additional unpaid leave, the EEOC said in its guidance on reasonable accommodation.

Part-time work also may be a reasonable accommodation. The doctor for an employee who had a mental breakdown due to same-sex harassment on the job said returning to work on a part-time basis was essential to the worker's recovery. The court said part-time work must be provided, adding that the employer's duty to accommodate was not exhausted by paid disability leave (*Ralph v. Lucent Technologies*, 135 F.3d 166 (1st Cir. 1998)).

Other courts also have held that part-time work can be a reasonable accommodation, at least for a temporary period and if the employee can perform the essential functions of his or her job while working part time (*Pals v. Schepel Buick & GMC Truck, Inc.*, 220 F.3d 495 (7th Cir. 2000); see also *Parker v. Columbia Pictures Industries*, 204 F.3d 326 (2d Cir. 2000) and *Hatchett v. Philander Smith College*, 251 F.3d 670 (8th Cir. 2001)).

On the other hand, if an employer does not have part-time work "the ADA does not require an employer to create a new part-time position where none previously existed," some courts have ruled (see *Treanor v. MCI Telecommunications Corp.*, 200 F.3d 570 (8th Cir. 2000); *Terrell v. USAir*, 132 F.3d 621 (11th Cir. 1998); *Burch v. Coca-Cola*, 119 F.3d 305 (5th Cir. 1997), *cert. denied*, 118 S. Ct. 871 (1998)).

Shift or Time of Work

The time during which an essential job function is performed may be critical, the commission conceded, but said the employer should carefully assess whether modifying the hours would significantly disrupt operations or whether the functions may be performed at different times with little or no impact. If modifying the employee's schedule would be an undue hardship, the employer must consider reassignment to a vacant position, the guidance stated (see the section on reassignment in this chapter).

The guidance gave the example of a day-care worker who requests to change her hours from 7 a.m.–3 p.m. to 10 a.m.–6 p.m. The day-care center is open from 7 a.m. to 7 p.m. and would have ample coverage at the beginning of the morning if the employee's schedule were changed, so providing the modified schedule would be a reasonable accommodation.

On the other hand, a printing press operator for a morning newspaper must work at night to perform the essential function of getting the paper out early in the morning. The daytime schedule she requested would cause an undue hardship, so the employer should consider whether there is another vacant position available for which she is qualified.

As with many things under the ADA, whether a particular shift is an essential job functions depends on the job itself. The EEOC in its Technical Assistance Manual on Title I said that if a position exists so the employee can work on any of the shifts, a permanent shift position may not be required. In the case of a warehouse technician, for example, a federal appeals court found that a rotating-shift schedule was an essential part of the employee's job (Rehrs v. Iams Co., 486 F.3d 353 (8th Cir. 2007)).

If essential job functions can be performed at different times with little or no impact on the employer's business, a specific shift may be a reasonable accommodation.

FMLA, ADA Interplay in Modified Schedules

Sometimes an employee with a disability who requests a modified or part-time schedule as an accommodation is also covered by the FMLA. The EEOC advised employers to determine the employee's rights under each law separately, consider whether the two laws overlap, and then determine the appropriate action to take.

ATTENDANCE DURING NORMAL HOURS

Several federal appeals courts have ruled that regular attendance during normal business hours is an essential job function. When a teacher was unable to meet attendance requirements in spite of accommodations, including sick leave, a flexible schedule and rest periods during the work day, the court held she was not otherwise qualified for the job (*Tyndall v. National Educational Centers*, 31 F.3d 209 (4th Cir. 1994)).

Another court ruled that an employee with obstructive lung disease whose illness caused extensive tardiness and absenteeism was not qualified because coming to work regularly and being in the office during normal business hours was an essential function of his job as a loan review analyst (*Hypes v. First Commerce Corp.*, 134 F.3d 721 (5th Cir. 1998)).

Under the ADA, the EEOC's position is that an employee who needs a modified or part-time schedule is entitled to one if there is no other effective accommodation and the schedule will not cause an undue hardship on the employer's business. If undue hardship would be caused, the employer should reassign the worker to a vacant position in which the changed schedule would not be a hardship, according to the agency.

If the modification is a part-time schedule, the employee would be entitled only to the benefits, including health insurance, that other part-time employees receive.

Under the FMLA, eligible employees are entitled to take leave intermittently, including on a part-time basis, when medically necessary, until the equivalent of 12 work weeks in a 12-month period have been exhausted. When the leave is foreseeable, the employer may require the worker to temporarily transfer to an alternative position with equivalent pay and benefits for the duration of the leave, if the alternative job better suits the part-time schedule.

If the modification is a part-time schedule, the employee's existing level of health insurance coverage must be maintained during the period of FMLA leave, provided the employee pays the appropriate share of premiums.

An FMLA-eligible employee with an ADA disability who requests a part-time schedule must be granted the leave under the FMLA even if it would cause an undue hardship and there is no vacant position for which the employee is qualified. Moreover, the employer must maintain the employee's group health insurance benefits.

Telecommuting

Working from home with electronic equipment that enables an employee with a disability to telecommute can be a reasonable accommodation, the EEOC said. The commission's guidance, Work at Home/Telework as a Reasonable Accommodation (last modified 10/27/05), stated that an employer does not have to offer telework programs to all employees, but if it does, it must give employees with disabilities an equal opportunity to participate in the program.

Moreover, even if an employer has no telework program, changing "the location where work is performed may fall under the ADA's reasonable accommodation requirement of modifying workplace policies, even if the employer does not allow other employees to telework."

Courts have ruled both for and against telecommuting as a reasonable accommodation. Whether an employee can effectively telecommute depends mainly on the job to be done. Telemarketing, writing or editing might easily be done at home, while jobs requiring in-person interaction with students, clients or customers do not lend themselves to telecommuting.

As one court said, "Except in the unusual case when an employee can effectively perform all work-related duties at home, an employee who does not come to work cannot perform any of his job functions, essential or otherwise" (*Tyndall v. National Educational Centers*,

31 F.3d 209 (4th Cir. 1994)). The employee in *Tyndall* was a part-time business college instructor who could not teach her students from home.

Another federal appeals court explained that the "ADA does not require employers to allow disabled workers to work at home where their productivity inevitably would be greatly reduced" (*Vande Zande v. Wisconsin Dept. of Admin.*, 44 F.3d 538 (7th Cir. 1995)) In that case, a paraplegic clerical worker was held to be not qualified because she could no longer perform her job, even with accommodations. Only about 50 percent of her essential job duties could be performed outside the office and in any event, the court held, an employer is not required to accommodate a disability by allowing the worker to work without supervision at home. "This will no doubt change as communication technology advances," the court said, but that "is the situation today."

An employee who claimed his employer failed to reasonably accommodate him by reassigning him to another job and permitting him to telecommute from home also was determined by a federal appeals court to be not otherwise qualified. The employee, who had injured his back, failed to show that any vacant positions would accommodate his disability, the court said, and the employer was not obligated to create a position under the ADA. Moreover, telecommuting is not a reasonable accommodation except in rare cases when the job can be performed at home without substantial reduction in performance, the court insisted (*Smith v. Ameritech*, 129 F.3d 857 (6th Cir. 1997)).

One appeals court stated that because a great deal is expected from federal employers in the way of accommodation, the Rehabilitation Act of 1973 requires federal agencies to consider work at home in appropriate cases (*Carr v. Reno*, 23 F.3d 525 (D.C. Cir. 1994)). Even in that case, however, the court determined that the employee, who had Meniere's disease and could not get to work regularly because of dizziness and nausea, could not do her job at home and that an essential job function was the ability to appear at work.

While the EEOC insisted that regular attendance could not be an essential job function, many courts have not agreed. Those that hold coming to work is an essential function of the job do not find telecommuting to be a reasonable accommodation.

More recently, and especially in those jurisdictions that do not hold regular attendance is an essential job function, telecommuting has been viewed favorably. Work at home could be an accommodation for a supervisor who supervised a team that was allegedly "self-directed," the employer's handbook anticipated telecommuting for up to five days per week, and the employee had been working at home for part of each week for several months, an appeals court held (*Woodruff v. Peters*, 482 F.3d 521 (D.C. Cir. 2007)).

Another court ruled that "working at home is a reasonable accommodation when the essential functions of the position can be performed at home and a work-at-home arrangement would not cause undue hardship" (*Humphrey v. Memorial Hospitals Assoc.*, 239 F.3d 1128 (9th Cir. 2001)).

Technology and the changes it has brought to the workplace may have passed by the courts and the commission. As more employees work from home offices or while traveling, the notion of telecommuting has been replaced by the notion of the "virtual office." When confronted with a request for a telecommuting accommodation, employers should

---

WHAT TO ASK ABOUT TELECOMMUTING

Not all jobs can be done remotely. When an employee asks about telework, the EEOC advised that answers to the following questions be determined.

1. Can the employer supervise the work-at-home employee adequately?

2. Is the employee hourly or salaried? If hourly, how is the time worked to be monitored?

3. Can the employee be reached when the supervisor desires?

4. Do the employee's duties require the use of certain equipment or tools that cannot be replicated at home?

5. Does the employee's job require face-to-face interaction and coordination of work with other employees?

6. If the employee interacts with colleagues, clients or customers as a regular part of his or her duties, is it necessary for this interaction to be in person, or can it be done telephonically or electronically?

7. Does the employee's job require him or her to have immediate access to documents and/or other information located only in the workplace?

8. Does the company workers' compensation insurance cover injuries to employees while they are working at home?

---

consider how many employees routinely work from locations other than the office, before determining whether a request is "reasonable."

Note that there is a difference between working from a remote location because it is the nature of the job, and working from home as an ADA accommodation. The existence of the former does not make the latter *per se* "reasonable." Other factors discussed above must also be considered.

Employers may choose an accommodation other than telecommuting, as long as it is effective in enabling the worker to perform a job's essential functions, the EEOC said in its guidance. When telecommuting is requested, an employer should consider whether the job could be done at home or another location, assuming there is no accommodation that would enable the employee to do the job at the employer's worksite.

Modified Workplace Policies

Modifications of various existing workplace policies may be necessary to reasonably accommodate an employee with a disability, according to both the ADA and EEOC regulations (42 U.S.C. 12111(9)(B); 29 C.F.R. §1630.2(o)(2)(ii)). Modifications to leave and transfer policies and work hours may be required.

Policies prohibiting animals in the workplace may have to be waived and evacuation policies may need modification to properly protect individuals with disabilities. In its guidance on reasonable accommodation, the EEOC explained that while employers may be required to modify policies for an employee with a disability as a reasonable accommodation, those policies may continue to apply to all other employees.

For example, a policy that prohibits eating at employees' desks may need to be modified for an employee with insulin-dependent diabetes, the commission noted. To keep from

94

going into insulin shock, the employee may need to eat candy or drink fruit juice. That need can arise quickly and the employee might not have time to search for an appropriate sugar-laden snack. Absent undue hardship, modifying the no-eating policy to permit the employee to keep candy or juice in his or her desk and ingest it when needed would be a reasonable accommodation. The employer could, however, still prohibit all other employees from eating at their desks.

Employers may need to examine emergency evacuation and other safety procedures to make sure the needs of individuals with disabilities are met. For example, individuals in wheelchairs cannot use stairs. If elevators cannot be used for emergency evacuation of buildings, the employer would have to make arrangements for employees with mobility impairments, which might include ground floor offices.

Hiring and testing policies may need modification for individuals with disabilities. Just as with all reasonable accommodations, the type of modification depends on the needs of the individual. Flexibility and a willingness to examine the reason behind workplace policies are keys to making reasonable accommodations when needed.

Reassignment

The ADA lists reassignment to a vacant position as a form of reasonable accommodation (42 U.S.C. §12111(9)(B)). Of course reassignment "may not be used to limit, segregate, or otherwise discriminate against an employee with a disability," the EEOC warned. It would violate the law to reassign individuals with disabilities only to undesirable positions or to certain offices or buildings.

In its guidance on reasonable accommodation the EEOC said reassignment "is the reasonable accommodation of last resort and is required only after it has been determined that:

1. there are no effective accommodations that will enable the employee to perform the essential functions of his/her current position; or

2. all other reasonable accommodations would impose an undue hardship."

Reassignment is available only to current employees who, because of their disability, can no longer perform the essential functions of the job they are doing (29 C.F.R. Part 1630 App. §1630.2(o)). Employers do not have an obligation to assign job applicants to a job other than the one for which they are applying.

Probationary employees are entitled to reassignment, the EEOC said in its guidance, "as long as the employee adequately performed the essential functions of the position, with or without reasonable accommodation, before the need for a reassignment arose." The longer the employee has adequately performed the current job, the more likely reassignment will be appropriate. If the probationary employee never adequately performed the original job's essential functions, he or she was not qualified for the original position and is in the same position as an applicant, not entitled to reassignment, the EEOC stated.

Although the commission said reassignment should be provided when reasonable accommodation in the current job would cause undue hardship or when it would not be possible, and despite the language in the statute, federal courts are divided on the issue.

An employee who is unable to perform the essential functions of his or her current position is not a qualified individual with a disability and therefore not eligible for reassignment, some courts reason (see *Schmidt v. Methodist Hosp. of Indiana*, 89 F.3d 342 (7th Cir. 1996)). For these courts, the problem lies in making individuals with disabilities a "super-protected group."

What if a black or Hispanic female single parent had studied and trained on her own to be qualified for a new position and was dutifully waiting her turn, only to be told that a white male with a disability without the training was going to be reassigned to the newly open position? What if the most qualified candidate was another employee with a disability?

Some courts have found that such reassignment would create an unfairness not contemplated or imposed by Congress and concluded that Congress did not write a law that required an employer to choose a less qualified employee for any job. The commission insisted that such concerns were resolved by the law and that these decisions nullify Congress' inclusion of reassignment in the statute.

On the other hand, some courts have acknowledged that reassignment is part of the ADA's statutory scheme, and rule that reassignment to a vacant position can be a reasonable accommodation (*Cravens v. Blue Cross and Blue Shield of Kansas City*, 214 F.3d 1011 (8th Cir. 2000)).

A transfer to a vacant job for which the employee is qualified may prevent the worker from being out of work and the employer from losing a valuable employee, one court pointed out (*Dalton v. Subaru-Isuzu Automotive*, 141 F.3d 667 (7th Cir. 1998)). Another explained that individuals with disabilities are qualified, even if they are unable to perform the essential functions of their present positions, if there are other vacant positions within the company they can perform (*Smith v. Midland Brake*, 180 F.3d 1154 (10th Cir. 1999)).

A third court said that reassignment to a vacant position is a possible accommodation, although "the ADA does not require that [the employer] take action inconsistent with the contractual rights of other workers under a collective bargaining agreement" (*Benson v. Northwest Airlines*, 62 F.3d 1108 (8th Cir. 1995)). (See Chapter 8 for a discussion of seniority rules, collective bargaining agreements and reasonable accommodation.)

Reassignment may be appropriate when an employee becomes disabled, when a disability becomes more severe or when changes or new technology affects the job performance of an employee with a disability, and of course reassignment is appropriate if both the employer and employee agree that it is better than accommodation in the current job (EEOC's Technical Assistance on Title I §3.10(5)).

Competing for New Position

Reassignment does not mean that an employee is permitted to compete for vacant positions, the EEOC insisted in its guidance. It means that if the employee is qualified, he or she gets the job (29 C.F.R. §1630.2(o) Appendix). "Otherwise reassignment would be of little value and would not be implemented as Congress intended," the guidance said. After all, even without the ADA an employee with a disability could have the right to compete for a vacant position.

Reassignment means more than "merely allowing a disabled person to compete equally with the rest of the world for a vacant position" (Smith v. Midland Brake, 180 F.3d 1154 (10th Cir. 1999)). That court also said it is incorrect under the statute to require the employee with a disability to be the best qualified employee for the vacant job. Another court said "reassign" must mean more than allow the employee to apply for a job on the same basis as anyone else. The word implies some active effort on the part of the employer (*Aka v. Washington Hospital Center*, 156 F.3d 1284 (D.C. Cir. 1998); see also *Gile v. United Airlines, Inc.,* 213 F.3d 365 (7th Cir. 2000)).

Not all courts agree. The 7th Circuit ruled that saying a worker with a disability does not have to compete for an open position is "affirmative action with a vengeance" (*EEOC v. Humiston-Keeling*, 227 F.3d 1024 (7th Cir. 2000)). The ADA "does not require an employer to reassign a qualified disabled employee to a vacant position when such a reassignment would violate a legitimate nondiscriminatory policy of the employer to hire the most qualified candidate" the 8th Circuit stated (*Huber v. Wal-Mart Stores, Inc.*, 486 F.3d 480 (8th Cir. 2007)). The 6th Circuit ruled that a nurse who could no longer perform her job's physical tasks was not entitled to preferential treatment in reassignment (*Hedrick v. Western Reserve Care System and Forum Health*, 355 F.3d 444 (6th Cir. 2004)) and the 5th Circuit similarly held that an individual who could no longer perform his job because of a disability was not entitled to priority in hiring or reassignment over those who were not disabled (*Daugherty v. City of El Paso*, 56 F.3d 695 (5th Cir. 1995) *cert. denied*, 516 U.S. 1172 (1996)).

Most courts do agree, however, that reassignment to a job for which the employee is qualified is a reasonable accommodation. "The statute clearly requires that qualified disabled persons be allowed to compete for and accept the available 'positions' that they seek to obtain," the 9th Circuit said, clarifying that assignment to a position an employee "does not desire instead of one he seeks does not comply with the ADA's mandate" (*Cripe v. City of San Jose*, 261 F.3d 877 (9th Cir. 2001)).

Employee Must Be Qualified

To be eligible for reassignment, the employee must be qualified for the new position. To be considered qualified, the employee must:

1. satisfy the legitimate prerequisites for the alternative job; and

2. be able to perform the essential functions of the job with or without reasonable accommodations (*Dalton v. Subaru-Isuzu Automotive*, 141 F.3d 667 (7th Cir. 1998) and EEOC Enforcement Guidance on Reasonable Accommodation and Undue Hardship Under the Americans With Disabilities Act (10/17/02)).

The employer is not required "to abandon its legitimate, nondiscriminatory company policies defining job qualifications, prerequisites and entitlements to intra-company transfers," according to a federal appeals court (*Dalton v. Subaru-Isuzu Automotive,* 141 F.3d 667 (7th Cir. 1998)). The EEOC agreed only in part.

While nondiscriminatory qualifications and legitimate prerequisites do not have to be modified to accommodate employees with disabilities, employers must offer reassignment as a reasonable accommodation even if they do not allow any other employees to transfer from one position to another, the commission stated in its guidance. Just as other policy modifications might have to be made for individuals with disabilities but not other employees, so, too, a no-transfer policy might have to be changed to provide a reasonable accommodation, the EEOC explained.

Employers are not required to assist employees in becoming qualified for a position to which they desire reassignment. For example, an employer does not have to provide special training so the employee can acquire the skills necessary to perform the new job. The employer would, however, have to provide whatever training is normally given to a newly hired or transferred employee.

The EEOC cautioned that the employee does *not* have to be the best qualified for the position to obtain it. Reassignment is a reasonable accommodation and employees with disabilities are entitled to reasonable accommodations under the ADA, the commission reasoned. Therefore, if the employee can no longer perform the essential functions of his or her current job, reassignment to a vacant position for which he or she is qualified is an entitlement, absent undue hardship. At least one court noted that this is "affirmative action with a vengeance," and is not required (*EEOC v. Humiston-Keeling,* 227 F.3d 1024 (7th Cir. 2000)).

Meaning of 'Vacant'

A vacant position is one that is available when the employee asks for a reasonable accommodation or that will become available reasonably soon, the EEOC's guidance states. What is a reasonable amount of time should be determined on a case-by-case basis. If several weeks are involved, the employer may place the employee on paid or unpaid leave or give the employee a temporary light-duty assignment.

An employer does not have to bump an employee from a job or create a new position, the commission emphasized in its regulations and guidance. Courts agree that employers generally do not have to bump another employee from a job to create a vacancy for an employee with a disability (*Lucas v. W.W. Grainger, Inc.,* 257 F.3d 1249 (11th Cir. 2001); *Cravens v. Blue Cross and Blue Shield of Kansas City,* 214 F.3d 1011 (8th Cir. 2000); *Smith v. Midland Brake,* 180 F.3d 1154 (10th Cir. 1999); *Pond v. Michelin,* 183, F.3d 592 (7th Cir. 1999); *Cassidy v. Detroit Edison Co.,* 138 F.3d 629 (6th Cir., 1998)).

Reassignment is not limited to the employee's current office, branch, agency, department, facility, personnel system or geographical area, the EEOC noted. Even if an employer has a policy of prohibiting transfers between divisions, that does not apply to employees protected by the ADA, which contains no such limitations on reassignments. The extent to which an employer must search for a vacant position is an issue of undue hardship, the commission stated. Employees with disabilities are not entitled to benefits such as relocation expenses unless expenses are paid for other employees making voluntary transfers.

The employer is obligated to inform the employee about potential vacant positions for which he or she qualifies, the EEOC's guidance said, because the employer is in the best position to know about vacancies. The commission recommended an interactive process to determine the employee's limitations, qualifications and interests. The employee should assist the employer in identifying appropriate vacancies and the employer should solicit all information necessary to determine whether the employee is qualified for a potential reassignment.

Reassignment must be to a vacant position that is equivalent in terms of pay and status if the employee is qualified, the EEOC stated in its guidance. The offer of an inferior position does not constitute a reasonable accommodation when a position with comparable benefits and salary is available (*Norville v. Staten Island University Hospital*, 196 F.3d 89 (2d Cir. 1999); see also *Dilley v. Supervalu, Inc.*, 296 F.3d 958 (10th Cir. 2002)).

If there is no vacant equivalent position, the employer must reassign the employee to a vacant lower-level position that most closely matches the employee's current position in terms of pay and status and for which he or she is qualified (29 C.F.R. §1630.2(o)(2)(ii)). Unless the employer does so for nondisabled employees, it does not have to maintain the reassigned employee's salary if reassignment is to a lower-level position.

The duty of reassignment does not include giving the employee a promotion. If an employee with a disability desires reassignment to a higher-level vacant position, he or she must compete for it on the same basis as any other employee. Most court's agree that employers do not have to promote an employee with a disability as a reasonable accommodation (see *Hedrick v. Western Reserve Care System and Forum Health*, 355 F.3d 444 (6th Cir. 2004); *White v. York International Corp.*, 45 F.3d 357 (9th Cir. 1995)).

The EEOC advised employers to proceed expeditiously in determining whether appropriate vacancies exist. Once the search results are completed, the employee is informed of the results and either offered a vacant position or informed that no appropriate position exists, the employer has fulfilled its obligation, the agency stated.

Light Duty

A light-duty assignment may be a reasonable accommodation for an injured worker. Light-duty jobs arose from workers' compensation laws and employers' desire to get employees back to work as soon as possible after workplace injuries to reduce liability. These positions are a response to workers' medical restrictions. They place few physical demands on employees and often involved administrative work, such as answering telephones and typing. Light-duty jobs usually are temporary in nature, some with specific time limitations. Their purpose is to enable an employee to recuperate fully while performing compensable tasks before returning to his or her actual job.

> ### JUDICIAL DECISIONS ON LIGHT DUTY
>
> Courts that have ruled on the issue agree with the EEOC that while employees with disabilities who are recuperating from temporary restrictions must be given an equal opportunity to participate in an employer's light-duty program, employers do not have to assign permanently disabled workers to light-duty positions reserved for individuals recovering from industrial injuries (*Dalton v. Subaru-Isuzu Automotive,* 141 F.3d 667 (7th Cir. 1998)).
>
> Employers may take their least strenuous jobs, put them in a pool for temporary light-duty work, and use them so their employees can get back on their feet after a workplace injury, a federal appeals court explained, but the ADA does not require an employer "to reduce the number of bona fide temporary jobs it has set aside ... and convert them to permanent positions for its disabled employees" (*Robinson v. Excel Corp.*, 154 F.3d 685 (7th Cir. 1998)).
>
> In Robinson, the employer had reserved a number of its least physically demanding jobs for rehabilitating injured employees. The employees were placed in those light-duty jobs until they were able to return to their former jobs. They were permitted to perform light-duty work for indefinite and varying lengths of time, but when their medical restrictions were determined to be permanent because their medical condition was not expected to improve, they became ineligible for the light-duty work.
>
> The employer was entitled to reserve a reasonable number of positions for that special purpose, the court said, adding that "it would frustrate the ADA for permanently impaired employees to fill temporary light-duty assignments when those jobs have been set aside specifically for recuperating employees."

Light duty as an accommodation only applies to existing employees who are no longer able to perform the essential functions of the job they hold. Obviously employers do not have to give job applicants light-duty jobs to accommodate their disabilities when they were applying for another job entirely.

Moreover, only injured workers who meet the ADA's definition of a qualified individual with a disability are entitled to the law's protections, regardless of whether they satisfy criteria for receiving workers' compensation benefits. Work-related injuries often result in non-chronic impairments that heal in a short time with little or no long-term or permanent impact. If an injury does not cause a physical or mental impairment severe enough to substantially limit a major life activity, it is not a disability under the ADA (EEOC's Technical Assistance on Title I §9.2).

The ADA does not require employers to create light-duty jobs, although heavy physical tasks that are marginal job functions that an employee with a disability cannot perform may have to be reallocated to a co-worker as part of the reasonable accommodation of job restructuring, the EEOC pointed out in its Technical Assistance Manual on Title I. Creating a totally different job from the one the employee had prior to injury is not required, however.

On the other hand, if a vacant light-duty job for which the injured worker is qualified already exists, it might be a reasonable accommodation to assign the employee to that position. The EEOC explained that if the position was created as a temporary one, reassignment only needs to be temporary.

Qualifications must be gauged in relation to the light-duty job, not the position the worker held prior to injury. Moreover, it may be necessary to provide reasonable accommodations to enable the injured employee to perform the light-duty job's essential functions. The EEOC gives the example of a telephone line repair worker who is seriously injured in a fall and must use a wheelchair for at least nine months. If the office for the vacant administrative position to which the worker is assigned is not wheelchair accessible, the employer may need to place the employee in another office. The employer also might need to modify the employee's work schedule to accommodate physical therapy sessions.

Medical Information About Workplace Injuries

Although medical information may be useful in determining whether an injured worker can work and in what job, as well as what accommodations may be necessary, the EEOC warned employers that they bear the ultimate responsibility for deciding whether the employee is qualified with or without an accommodation. Employers cannot avoid liability by relying on doctors' advice that is not consistent with the ADA's requirements, the commission said in its Technical Assistance Manual.

The EEOC permits some exceptions to the ADA's medical confidentiality provisions when it comes to on-the-job injuries. Information may be submitted to second injury funds or state workers' compensation authorities as required by state laws.

Employers also can obtain information about pre-existing injuries that may be needed to participate in second injury funds. Second injury funds are designed to remove financial disincentives for hiring employees with disabilities. They limit the amount an employer must pay when an employee suffers increased disability from a work-related injury because of a pre-existing condition.

Most second injury funds require employers to certify that they knew about the worker's pre-existing injury at the time of hire. Employers can find out about pre-existing conditions under the ADA as long as they do so by making the necessary medical inquiries after a conditional job offer has been made and the same inquiry is made of all applicants in the same job category.

It must not be forgotten that employers have to keep medical information confidential from the co-workers of an employee with a disability in so far as possible. If a worker who has a disability is given a light-duty assignment, reassignment to another position, leave or some other accommodation, the worker's privacy must be protected, so the disability should not be discussed with others except on a strictly need-to-know basis. Other employees who ask can be told that the employer is meeting its obligations under federal law. A good training program might prevent such questions. (For more information on privacy and training with regard to accommodating, see Chapter 7.)

TIPS ON REASONABLE ACCOMMODATIONS

A reasonable accommodation may consist of one or more of the following:

- reasonable modifications to rules, policies or practices;
- removal of architectural, equipment design, communication or transportation barriers; or
- provision of auxiliary aids and services.

Methods of Accommodation

Ways to accommodate employees with disabilities include the following:

- restructuring jobs;
- reassignment to vacant or soon-to-be-open positions;
- adjusting work schedules;
- flexible leave;
- modifying worksites;
- specialized equipment and assistive devices; and
- visual/hearing assistance.

Accommodations Not Required by ADA

Employers need not do the following:

- provide personal devices, such as eyeglasses and hearing aids;
- provide employee's specific accommodation of choice;
- hire additional personnel to perform essential functions; or
- bump or displace another employee to provide a reasonable accommodation for a person with a disability.

No-Cost Accommodations

The following are some of the workplace accommodations that cost nothing for an employer to provide:

- assign alternative job tasks to comply with physical restrictions;
- reposition equipment, materials and/or supplies;
- relocate worksite; or
- reschedule work hours to accommodate medication or treatment schedule.

Source: Susan Kemp Beardsley, senior employment law counsel, California Chamber of Commerce.

Retaliation and Other Accommodation Issues

7

Some reasonable accommodation issues are not as easy to resolve as others and are more confusing for employers. Just how far does an employer have to go in providing an accommodation? Is more than one accommodation required? If an employee with a disability has a personality conflict with a supervisor, does the employer have to transfer the employee to another supervisor?

What if the employee refuses or forgets to take prescribed medication or indulges in improper conduct? Under the ADA, is the employer required to treat the employee differently than nondisabled workers? If an employer is more generous than the ADA requires, can that be held against it?

The EEOC has answered most of these questions in its Enforcement Guidance on Reasonable Accommodation and Undue Hardship Under the Americans With Disabilities Act (3/1/99, updated 2002) and its regulations on Title I of the ADA.

Some of these issues also have been addressed by federal appeals courts. As a general rule, employees with disabilities must be given an equal opportunity to compete and participate in the workplace, but they are not entitled to special treatment or benefits other employees do not enjoy, except for perhaps modifications of company policies required as reasonable accommodations. Moreover, conduct unrelated to ADA-covered disabilities is not protected by the statute.

Retaliation is prohibited by the ADA, as it is by most civil rights laws. Retaliation claims have doubled since 1992 and presently account for more than a fourth of the EEOC's docket. Even when an employee loses on the underlying discrimination charge, he or she may have a case for retaliation if the employer is not careful, especially after the Supreme Court's 2006 ruling that expanded the grounds for retaliation suits. The section in this chapter on retaliation explains what is considered retaliatory conduct and how to avoid liability.

More Than One Accommodation

The duty to reasonably accommodate an employee with a disability does not necessarily end after a single accommodation has been provided. The employer's obligation is an ongoing one, the EEOC pointed out in its guidance. Sometimes a single accommodation is sufficient; sometimes several are needed. An employee may require one type of accommodation for a while and then need another.

For example, an employee may need leave to recover from surgery related to his or her disability and then part-time work until recovery is complete. That same employee may also need modifications to his or her workplace to accommodate a wheelchair or modifications to office equipment to accommodate a visual or hearing impairment. Employees may have more than one ADA-covered disability, each requiring a different accommodation. However, only those disability-related accommodations that will provide an equal employment opportunity are required, the EEOC explained.

Employers should consider each request for reasonable accommodation and determine the following:

1. whether the accommodation is necessary;

2. if needed, whether the accommodation would be effective; and

3. if effective, whether providing the accommodation would impose an undue hardship on the employer's business.

If a reasonable accommodation proves to be ineffective and the employee remains unable to perform one or more essential job functions, the EEOC advised the employer to consider whether an alternative reasonable accommodation is available. If none is, the employer should reassign the employee to a vacant position for which he or she is qualified, absent undue hardship, the EEOC's guidance on reasonable accommodation stated. If the employee was recently hired and never able to perform the job's essential functions, even with reasonable accommodations, the employee was not qualified and no reassignment is required, the agency said.

Employers should bear in mind that most courts do not agree with the EEOC's position on reassignment as a reasonable accommodation that must be offered as a matter of law.

Personality conflicts with supervisors usually are not related to the employee's disability and an employer does not have to provide the employee with a new supervisor as a reasonable accommodation. The employer should investigate a complaint, however, to make sure the supervisor is not discriminating against or harassing the employee on the basis of the worker's disability. Moreover, although the employer is not required to change supervisors, a modification of supervisory methods may be appropriate, and training on the ADA and appropriate communications with individuals with disabilities is always a good idea.

The example the EEOC provided in its guidance is of a supervisor who frequently calls meetings on a day's notice. An employee whose disability requires frequent physical therapy sessions has missed several meetings because the therapy could not be rescheduled on such short notice. The employee requested that meetings be scheduled two or three days in advance and, assuming doing so would cause no undue hardship, the supervisor must make the reasonable accommodation.

Improper Conduct and Discipline

Employees with disabilities may be held to uniformly applied conduct standards that are job related and consistent with business necessity. Employers do not have to tolerate or excuse violence, threats, stealing or destruction of property from employees with disabilities any more than they do from other employees. Employers may impose the same discipline on an employee with a disability who engages in misconduct as they would on an employee without a disability. (There may be the odd exception. See Chapter 5 for more information on performance evaluations and discipline.)

In its Guidance on the Americans With Disabilities Act and Psychiatric Disabilities (3/25/97), the EEOC explained that employers may discipline individuals with disabilities for violating workplace conduct standards even if the misconduct is the result of the employee's disability. However, imposing discipline for conduct standards that are not job related and consistent with business necessity could violate the ADA.

An example the commission gave is of an employee who works in a warehouse and has no customer contact and little contact with co-workers. The company handbook requires workers to dress neatly and be courteous to fellow employees. Because his disability has worsened, the employee has come to work disheveled and has been rude to co-workers, who have complained.

The dress code and courtesy rules are not job related for the employee's position and consistent with business necessity, the EEOC said, because the employee does not have customer contact and only irregular contact with other employees. Rigid application of the rules with resulting discipline would violate the ADA in this case, the guidance

---

MAINTAINING EFFECTIVE ACCOMMODATIONS

There are some general principles to keep in mind when maintaining accommodations that work not only for the employee, but also for the workplace, according to Linda Carter Batiste, Esq., a consultant and disability law specialist with the Job Accommodation Network, a service of the U.S. Department of Labor's Office of Disability Employment Policy. Those principles are:

1. Remember that accommodations are an ongoing responsibility. People's conditions change and so do job functions. Accommodations might need to change accordingly.

2. Consult with the employee who requested the accommodation. That is the first place to start when searching for options.

3. Use available resources. State departments of vocational rehabilitation, JAN and other organizations are available to help employers find accommodations that work.

4. Brainstorm, weigh options and choose the best option for the situation. It often helps to think creatively about how a job's functions can be done.

5. Follow up, train and monitor. Remember that identifying the accommodation is only the first step. The employee may need training to use new technology and the employer should check back to make sure the chosen accommodation is working.

---

noted. Some employers, on the other hand, have criticized this example, insisting it is an undue hardship not to hold all workers to the same dress and conduct standards.

Illegal Drugs and Alcohol

Employers may prohibit the illegal use of drugs and the use of alcohol in the workplace and may require that employees not be under the influence of drugs or alcohol while at work. Employees may be required to behave in accordance with the requirements of the Drug Free Workplace Act of 1988 (41 U.S.C. §701 *et seq.*) and with regulations issued by the U.S. Department of Defense if they are employed in an industry subject to those regulations.

Employees covered by regulations issued by the U.S. Nuclear Regulatory Commission and the U.S. Department of Transportation can be held to those standards (42 U.S.C. §12114).

Moreover, employers may hold workers who engage in the illegal use of drugs or who are alcoholics to the same qualification standards for employment, job performance and behavior as other employees, even if the unsatisfactory performance or behavior is related to drug use or alcoholism (42 U.S.C. §12114(c)(4)).

Drug tests are not considered medical examinations under the ADA and, therefore, may be given prior to making a job offer or at any time after employment, and employers may make employment decisions based on the results of those tests without violating the law (42 U.S.C. §12114(d)). (See Chapter 4 for more information on drug and alcohol testing.)

Reasonable Accommodation for Past Misconduct

According to the EEOC in its guidances on reasonable accommodation and on psychiatric disabilities, employers are required by the ADA to make reasonable accommodations to enable an otherwise qualified employee with a disability to meet workplace conduct standards that are job related and consistent with business necessity.

Employers do not have to excuse past misconduct, even if it was related to the worker's disability, and do not have to make reasonable accommodations for the future if the punishment for the misconduct was termination. It therefore behooves an employee to ask for a reasonable accommodation before a conduct problem occurs.

Accommodations can include modifications to starting times, breaks and leaves of absence if these will enable an employee to comply with conduct rules. (See Chapter 6 for a discussion of the types of reasonable accommodations that may be required under the ADA.)

Employers are not required to offer last chance agreements to employees whose poor performance or misconduct is the result of alcoholism, according to the EEOC. Last chance agreements often excuse past performance or conduct problems due to alcoholism in exchange for an employee's promise to get substance abuse treatment and refrain from future use of alcohol. Violation of the agreement usually results in termination.

Because the ADA does not require employers to excuse poor performance or violation of conduct rules that are job related and consistent with business necessity, the EEOC said

---

EXAMPLES OF AFTER-DISCIPLINE ACCOMMODATIONS

Example: An employee loses her temper at work and shouts at customers and co-workers. When she is suspended for violating workplace conduct rules, she tells her employer about her psychiatric disability and requests a leave of absence for treatment. The employer is not required to rescind the discipline, but is required to grant the leave of absence, barring undue hardship, the EEOC said in its guidance on psychiatric disabilities. If instead of a suspension the employee had been fired, the employer would not be required to rehire her. See the last example below.

Example: An employee with a disability is often late to work because of the side effects of medication he is taking. His scheduled work hours are 9:00 a.m. to 5:30 p.m., but he often arrives 30 or more minutes late. After he is disciplined for tardiness, he explains his disability to his employer and requests a later work schedule. Assuming the employee can perform the essential functions of his job at the later time without causing undue hardship to the employer's business, the employer must consider the reasonable accommodation. The discipline does not have to be rescinded if the conduct rule – prompt arrival at the scheduled time – is job related and a business necessity, the guidances on reasonable accommodation and psychiatric disabilities explained.

Example: An employee has an altercation with his supervisor and threatens physical harm. When the employee is fired, consistent with company policy, he requests a leave of absence for treatment of his disability. The employer is not required to rescind the termination or to provide the reasonable accommodation, because the conduct rule was job related and a business necessity and the employee is no longer a qualified individual with a disability, the EEOC stated in its guidance on psychiatric disabilities.

---

in its guidance on reasonable accommodation, an employer has no obligation to provide a last chance agreement as an accommodation. Of course an employer may always choose to offer an agreement.

Monitoring Medication

Sometimes employees refuse or forget to take prescribed medications. Employers are not required to monitor employees' medications. The EEOC explained in its guidance on reasonable accommodation that such monitoring does not remove a workplace barrier. Similarly, employers are not responsible for monitoring employees' medical treatments or ensuring that they receive appropriate treatment. An employer may be required to provide an employee with breaks to take medication, access to a refrigerator in which to keep medication or leave to obtain medical treatment, all of which would be reasonable accommodations to enable the employee to perform the essential functions of his or her job.

If an employee is guilty of workplace misconduct because he or she does not take prescribed medication, the employer should focus on the misconduct and make the employee aware of the consequences, the commission advised in its guidance on psychiatric disabilities. The employee is responsible for making decisions about medication and considering the consequences for not taking prescribed drugs.

If an employee cannot perform the essential functions of his or her job or poses a direct threat in the absence of medication, he or she is not a qualified individual with a disability, the EEOC noted in its guidance on reasonable accommodations.

Medications and medical treatment sometimes cause side effects that are more disabling than the underlying condition. These are limitations caused by the disability, the EEOC said in its guidance on reasonable accommodations, and the duty to reasonably accommodate extends to all limitations that are a result of the individual's disability. Thus, an employee whose chemotherapy treatments for cancer cause illness for a day or two afterward may need a modified work schedule, which the employer would have to grant, absent undue hardship.

Refusing Accommodations

Just as it is the employee's choice whether to take medication for a disability, it also is the employee's choice whether to accept a reasonable accommodation. Employers are not required to ask employees if they need accommodations, although an employer should initiate the reasonable accommodation interactive process if it knows the employee has a disability, knows or has reason to believe the employee is having workplace problems because of the disability, or knows or has reason to know that the disability prevents the employee from requesting a reasonable accommodation (see Chapter 3 for more information).

If the employee states that he or she does not need an accommodation, the employer has fulfilled its obligation, according to the EEOC.

While individuals with disabilities are not required to accept accommodations, if an employee refuses an accommodation and as a result cannot perform the essential functions of his or her job, the worker may be considered unqualified (29 C.F.R. §1630.9(d); EEOC's Technical Assistance on Title I §3.8). For example, if an employee with a visual impairment is able to read, he or she would not be required to accept a reader as an accommodation. If the employee could not read accurately unaided, however, and reading was an essential function of the job, he or she would not be qualified for that job if an accommodation were refused.

If an employee has an obvious disability, the employer may ask if a reasonable accommodation is needed. In its guidance on reasonable accommodation, the EEOC used the example of a business luncheon at a restaurant that would include a mobility impaired employee. The employer can ask the employee what accommodations will be needed or if the employee is familiar with the restaurant and knows whether it is accessible.

Publicizing Accommodations

Just as medical information about employees with disabilities must be kept in strictest confidence, employers may not disclose to co-workers that an employee is receiving a reasonable accommodation, because that is tantamount to disclosing that the individual has a disability. The ADA prohibits disclosure of medical information except in certain limited situations:

1. supervisors and managers may be told about physical restrictions and necessary accommodations on a need-to-know basis;

2. first aid and safety personnel may be told, when appropriate, if the employee might require emergency medical treatment or special evacuation procedures; and

3. government officials investigating compliance with the ADA must be given relevant information on request (42 U.S.C. §12112(d)).

The EEOC has interpreted the law to allow employers to disclose medical information in the following circumstances:

*   in accordance with state workers' compensation laws to state workers' compensation offices, second injury funds or workers' compensation insurance carriers; and

*   when necessary for insurance purposes (29 C.F.R. Part 1630 App. §1630.14(b)).

In its guidance on reasonable accommodation, the EEOC advised employers to tell co-workers who ask that it has a policy of assisting any employee who encounters difficulties in the workplace. The employer also should emphasize privacy issues.

The real solution to curious co-workers is for employers to provide training on the ADA, as they should for other federal laws that affect employees in the workplace, such as the Family and Medical Leave Act. Training materials should include information on the employer's reasonable accommodation obligations and the requirement to protect privacy. Information should be included in orientation materials, employee handbooks, notices accompanying pay stubs and posted notices, the EEOC advised.

As long as there is no coercion by an employer, an employee with a disability may of course voluntarily choose to disclose his or her disability and the receipt of any reasonable accommodations.

More Generous Actions

Employers often are more generous than they are required to be by the ADA. Temporarily reallocating essential job functions, searching for alternative positions for an *applicant*, providing indefinite leave, light-duty or part-time work when there normally are no part-time jobs, are just some of the ways employers have accommodated workers with disabilities when they did not have to. Occasionally, an employee attempts to use such good deeds against the employer, such as by insisting a temporary light-duty job be given on a permanent basis and filing suit when the employer refuses, claiming there has been a violation of the ADA.

Most courts refuse to hold an employer liable for its general actions. For example, when a worker tried to force an employer to provide extensive and unpredictable leave because it had on rare occasions permitted extended leave to employees, the court held that it would not punish the employer for its past generosity by deeming its good deeds a concession of the reasonableness standard inherent in the law (*Amadio v. Ford Motor Co.*, 238 F.3d 919 (7th Cir. 2001)).

Good deeds "ought not be punished, and an employer who goes beyond the demands of the law to help a disabled employee incurs no legal obligation to continue to do so," another court ruled. In that case, a laborer attempted to turn a temporary office job into a permanent position. The employer had displaced two other workers from their office duties to give the injured employee the temporary position, but determined it would be an undue hardship to continue the situation on permanent basis (*Lucas v. W.W. Grainger, Inc.*, 257 F.3d 1249 (11th Cir. 2001)).

Similarly, permitting an employee with a disability to avoid doing some of the essential functions of a job on a temporary basis need not be done permanently (*Holbrook v. City of Alpharetta*, 112 F.3d 1522 (11th Cir. 1997); *Laurin v. The Providence Hospital*, 150 F.3d 52 (1st Cir. 1998)). It "would be perverse to discourage employers from accommodating employees with a temporary breathing space during which to seek another position with the employer," the *Laurin* court said.

Along that same line, employers are not required to create positions for employees with disabilities, and doing so temporarily or on rare occasions does not create a permanent obligation (see *Terrell v. USAir*, 132 F.3d 621 (11th Cir. 1998), permitting an employee to work reduced hours on occasion did not make the employer liable for creating a permanent part-time job).

An employer that provides an accommodation that is not required by law to one employee "is not consequently obligated to provide the same accommodation to other disabled employees," the 6th Circuit said, noting it did not want to "deter employers from providing greater accommodations than are required" because doing so would undermine the purposes of the ADA to eradicate discrimination (*Smith v. Ameritech*, 129 F.3d 857 (6th Cir. 1997)).

Retaliation

The purpose of the retaliation provisions in the ADA and other fair employment practices laws is to prevent employers from interfering, through adverse actions, with an employee's attempt to exercise his or her statutory rights.

The ADA prohibits discrimination against an individual for opposing an act or practice that is unlawful under the statute, for making a claim, or for testifying, assisting or participating in an investigation, proceeding or hearing on a claim. It also prohibits coercion, intimidation, threats or interference with anyone for exercising their rights under the law or for aiding or encouraging someone else to exercise their rights (42 U.S.C. 12203 (a) and (b)).

Retaliation suits under the ADA are easier to win than discrimination suits, because they are not restricted to employees who are actually disabled. An employee who reasonably believes, in good faith, that he or she is disabled may charge an employer with retaliation, as can anyone, disabled or not, who advocates compliance with the ADA's mandates or who the employer regarded as disabled and who suffered an adverse action at the employer's hands.

The validity of the underlying discrimination claim is irrelevant. Many juries have absolved an employer of the underlying bias charge or claim of non-compliance with the law, but found it liable for retaliating against the employee for filing the claim.

What Employer Conduct Is Retaliatory?

Until recently, the federal appeals courts were divided on what was required for an action to be considered retaliatory. Some courts held that the actions complained of had to be employment related and, moreover, had to materially change the terms and conditions of the worker's employment. Others required the action to be an ultimate employment decision that involved hiring, granting leave, discharging, promoting or compensating the employee.

At least one circuit court and the EEOC required only that the employee establish adverse treatment based on a retaliatory motive that would be reasonably likely to deter a charging party from engaging in protected activity.

The issue finally went to the U.S. Supreme Court in 2006 in a case brought under Title VII of the 1964 Civil Rights Act. Because the ADA mirrors Title VII's procedural provisions and uses similar language to prohibit retaliation, the case applies to the ADA as well.

What the Supreme Court decided was that retaliation is action that would be material to a reasonable employee and that would likely dissuade that worker from exercising rights under the law. The adverse action does not have to be strictly employment related. An employer can retaliate by taking actions unconnected to the workplace, such as filing false criminal charges against a worker. Another example given by the Court was the FBI failing to investigate death threats against an agent who had complained of discrimination in his workplace.

In the retaliation case before it, an employee who filed a sexual harassment charge with the EEOC was transferred to a dirtier, more physically arduous position. She then was falsely accused of insubordination by her supervisor and suspended without pay for 37 days. An internal investigation cleared her of the supervisor's charge and she was reinstated with back pay, but nevertheless sued, claiming the transfer and the suspension were both in retaliation for her Title VII charge.

The employer argued that reassignment to a different job with the same pay and benefits did not constitute retaliation and that reinstatement with full back pay negated any harm that occurred due to the suspension. Whether reassignment constitutes retaliation depends on the circumstances, the Supreme Court said, ruling that there was ample evidence in the case that the employee's transfer was to a less desirable position. The Court also found that going without pay for 37 days was a serious hardship for an employee even if the salary was ultimately paid (*Burlington Northern & Santa Fe Railway v. White*, 126 S. Ct. 240 (U.S. 2006)).

The Court emphasized that the law does not protect employees from all retaliation, only from retaliation that is injurious or significantly harmful. Trivial harms are not within the provision's scope. The law does not set forth "a general civility code for the American workplace," the Court said. "An employee's decision to report discriminatory behavior cannot immunize that employee from those petty slights or minor annoyances that often take place at work and that all employees experience," the Court wrote.

RETALIATION UNDER NEW STANDARD

The following are some examples where courts found retaliation using the standard adopted by the U.S. Supreme Court.

Contrary to its own policy, the FBI failed to investigate death threats made against an agent who had complained of discrimination (*Rochon v. Gonzales*, 438 F.3d 1211 (D.C. Cir. 2006)).

A former employer accused a scientist, now working as a consultant, of misappropriating trade secrets and threatened legal action, sending a copy of the letter to a client of the scientist's. There was strong evidence that the employer's accusations were untrue. The fact that these actions did not prevent the scientist from securing another job was irrelevant (*Hertz v. Luzenac America, Inc.*, No. 04-CV-01961-LTB-CBS (D. Colo. 2006)).

A high-level government employee was reassigned to another position without diminution in pay or benefits, but was stripped of supervisory duty, lost advancement potential and reported to a lower-level supervisor (*Kalinoski v. Gutierrez*, 435 F. Supp. 2d 55 (D.D.C. 2006)).

An employee did not suffer a reduction in civil service grade, pay or benefits, but experienced "an extraordinary reduction in responsibilities that persisted for years" (*Holcomb v. Powell*, 433 F.3d 889 (D.C. Cir. 2006)).

Supervisors rescinded approval of the flex time for a secretary who relied on it to care for her son, who had Down syndrome (*Washington v. Illinois Dept. of Revenue*, 420 F.3d 658 (7th Cir. 2005)).

An employer decided not to advertise a vacant position competitively, thus precluding the employee from applying (*Cones v. Shalala*, 199 F.3d 512 (D.C. Cir. 2000)).

An employer encouraged the prosecution of baseless criminal charges against a former employee (*Berry v. Stevinson Chevrolet*, 74 F.3d 980 (10th Cir. 1996)).

Determining whether an employer's action was retaliatory depends on the employee's circumstances. The Court discussed changing an employee's work schedule as an example. A changed schedule might make no difference to many workers, but to a mother with school-aged children, it could matter enormously. Even excluding an employee from a weekly training lunch that contributes significantly to his or her professional development could discourage someone from bringing a charge, the Court noted.

Tips for Employers

Employers need to remember that when an employee requests an accommodation or aids another employee in getting an accommodation, that activity may be protected by the ADA. The same is true for an employee who files a claim with the EEOC. Regardless of whether the employee is actually disabled under the law, these activities are protected from retaliation. That means an employer needs to be careful to follow all of its usual policies and practices when dealing with the employee.

Unless it is an absolute business necessity, an employer should not reassign an employee, change his or her work hours or take any other action that could be viewed as negative after a discrimination claim has been made or an accommodation requested, unless the action was asked for by the employee. Supervisors should be warned not to treat the employee differently or take any adverse action that could be construed as retaliation.

For the time being, retaliation may be hard to define precisely, but we all know what it is when we see it, and juries do, too.

Defenses to Providing Accommodations

No accommodation that would cause "an *undue hardship* on the operation of the business of [the employer]" (emphasis added) (42 U.S.C. §12112(5)(A)) is required. Another way of stating it is, an accommodation that would cause an undue hardship on an employer's business is not reasonable.

As with every other definition in the ADA, it is not always easy to determine what is and is not an "undue hardship." Furthermore, the courts and the EEOC do not always agree. Some courts have developed a form of "cost-benefit analysis," that the commission does not recognize. These courts declare that if an accommodation's costs are clearly disproportionate to its benefits, the accommodation is not reasonable and the employer does not have to provide it, regardless of whether doing so would impose an undue hardship.

In 2002, the U.S. Supreme Court held that an accommodation that violates a bona fide seniority policy creates an undue hardship on an employer's business, but there are some caveats, and collective bargaining agreements do not automatically trump the ADA's reasonable accommodation requirement.

In addition to the "undue hardship" defense, employers are not required to provide personal use items such as prosthetic limbs, wheelchairs, glasses and hearing aids that are needed both at and away from the workplace. Personal use amenities, such as refrigerators, are not required unless they are available to all employees. These and other limitations on reasonable accommodations are discussed in Chapter 2.

This chapter examines the factors in the statute and the EEOC's regulations and guidances that can be used to determine whether a proposed accommodation causes an undue hardship. It also discusses the judicially created cost-benefit analysis for determining if an accommodation is reasonable, and the impact of collective bargaining agreements and seniority policies on an employer's duty to provide accommodations.

Undue Hardship

Employers are never required to provide reasonable accommodations that would impose an undue hardship on their businesses, but it is unclear what constitutes an "undue hardship." As with most things under the ADA, determining undue hardship is fact specific and must be done on a case-by-case basis. "[U]ndue hardship must be based on an individualized assessment of current circumstances that show that a specific reasonable accommodation would cause significant difficulty or expense," the EEOC said in its guidance on the subject.

The concept of undue hardship includes accommodations that would be:

- unduly costly;

- extensive;

- substantial;

- disruptive; or

- would fundamentally alter the nature or operation of the employer's business.

The statute and regulations define "undue hardship" as something that creates significant difficulty or expense in relation to the size of the employer's business, the resources available and the nature of the business itself. This is to be considered in light of the following factors:

1. the nature and cost of the accommodation needed;

2. the overall financial resources of the facility or facilities involved in the provision of the reasonable accommodation, the number of persons employed there and the effect on expenses and resources or the impact otherwise of the accommodation on the operation of the facility;

3. the employer's overall financial resources, size with respect to number of employees, and the number, type and location of its facilities; and

4. the employer's type of operation, including the composition, structure and functions of the workforce and the geographic separateness, administrative or fiscal relationship of the facility in question to the employer's total company; and

5. the impact of the accommodation on the operation of the facility making it (42 U.S.C. §12111(10); 29 C.F.R. §1630.2(p)).

If an employer has more than one facility, it is the *overall* company that will be examined to determine undue hardship, unless the affected facility is an entity by itself that has no access to the resources of the larger whole. In its Technical Assistance Manual on Title I of the ADA, the EEOC gave the example of a fast-food franchise. If the franchise is independently owned and the sole financial relationship it has to the national company is the payment of a franchise fee, only the resources of the local facility would be considered in determining whether an accommodation imposes an undue hardship. If the national company has financial and administrative control over the local franchise, the resources of the entire company would be considered.

It is not enough for an employer to *claim* that a requested accommodation would impose an undue hardship. Rather, the employer must present evidence and demonstrate that a hardship would in fact be caused, the EEOC said (29 C.F.R. Part 1630 App. §1630.15(d)). And of course an accommodation that would impose an undue hardship for one employer might not for another, or even for the same employer at a different time.

Cost as Undue Hardship

The commission warns that to prove undue hardship under the ADA, the employer must show substantially more difficulty or expense than would be needed to satisfy the minimal standard for religious accommodation under Title VII of the 1964 Civil Rights Act. To demonstrate that cost poses an undue hardship, the employer would have to show that the cost is undue compared to the employer's budget. Comparing the cost of the accommodation to the salary of the employee with the disability will not suffice for the EEOC (29 C.F.R. Part 1630 App. §1630.15(d)).

The commission pointed out that Congress rejected a proposed amendment that would have established an undue hardship if an accommodation cost more than 10 percent of an employee's salary. The focus for determining undue hardship is on the resources of the employer, the EEOC said in its Technical Assistance Manual on Title I.

Arguing that an accommodation is unduly costly is a tricky defense for an employer. An appeals court agreed with an employer that a modified schedule for a laboratory assistant that would require keeping the lab open extra hours might be an undue hardship because of the significant cost for security personnel and janitors (*Ward v. Massachusetts Health Research Institute*, 209 F.3d 29 (1st Cir. 2000)), but costs for research centers and other nonprofits will be viewed differently than those of for-profit employers. When using the cost defense the employer probably will be required to open its financial records and will find it hard to justify paying for country club memberships but not accommodations. Moreover, most accommodations are not costly. (See the Appendix for examples of low cost accommodations.)

While most courts have found that cost is an important factor in determining the degree of hardship, they agree it is not the only factor. Moreover, an employer cannot rely on cost if tax credits or state aid would significantly lower the price or if the employee with the disability agrees to provide the accommodation or pay for the portion of the cost that constitutes hardship. Undue hardship is based on the *net* cost to the employer.

Adverse Effect on Others as Undue Hardship

In addition to cost, disruption to the workplace or adverse effects on the employer's business can make reasonable accommodations undue hardships. For example, if a receptionist with a disability requests that the office thermostat be set at a temperature that is uncomfortable for other employees, providing the accommodation would impose an undue hardship. If a waiter with a vision impairment requests bright lighting in a restaurant with mood lighting to create a romantic atmosphere, the accommodation would cause an undue hardship.

However, the employer would be required to look at alternatives. A space heater might be a reasonable accommodation for the receptionist and a pen light might provide accommodation for the waiter. (The fact that the specific accommodation requested would cause an undue hardship does not mean the employer can end all discussion of accommodations. The interactive process contemplates a dialogue with back-and-forth discussions between the employee and the employer.)

Accommodations that conflict with other federal laws or regulations that govern an employer's industry may cause an undue hardship. Employers may comply with federal laws and enforcement agencies' rules that impose medical standards and safety requirements, even though they conflict with the ADA. For example, providing a reasonable accommodation that is in violation of the U.S. Department of Transportation's safety regulations would be an undue hardship on a trucking company's business, assuming the business was subject to DOT regulation.

Employees' or customers' fears or prejudices toward an employee with a disability cannot satisfy the employer's undue hardship defense. Neither can showing that providing the accommodation would have a negative impact on the morale of other employees, as long as their ability to perform their jobs is not specifically affected (29 C.F.R. Part 1630 App. §1630.14(d)). Assigning the marginal job functions of an employee with a disability to another employee who can easily handle the extra work might make the second employee grumble, but that would not pose an undue hardship on the employer.

However, an accommodation that would require other employees to work harder or longer hours is unreasonable, one appeals court said (*Mason v. Avaya Communications, Inc.*, 357 F.3d 1114 (10th Cir. 2004)). Employers are not required to make modifications to employees' work hours or job duties if doing so would prevent other workers from performing their jobs. The significant disruption to the employer's operations would constitute an undue hardship, the EEOC said in its guidance on reasonable accommodation.

Indefinite Leave as Undue Hardship

While the EEOC asserts that indefinite leave may be a form of reasonable accommodation, the commission stated in its guidance that leave can be denied if the employer can show that the lack of a fixed date of return would cause an undue hardship. (Most courts have ruled that indefinite leave is not a required accommodation because if the employee cannot work, he or she is not qualified to do any job's essential functions, a requirement of the law. See Chapter 6 for more information on leave as an accommodation.)

Hardship can occur because the employer can neither plan for the employee's return nor permanently fill the position. Even if the employer can grant the leave without undue hardship at the time it is requested, the employer has a right to require that the employee provide periodic updates on his or her condition with potential return dates. Employers may reevaluate after receiving updates whether continued leave imposes an undue hardship, the commission acknowledged.

EFFECTS OF CHANGING WORK SCHEDULES

One form of accommodation employees with disabilities may request is a change in work hours – a later starting time or a part-time schedule. Whether this causes an undue hardship for the employer depends on, among other things, the interaction that employee has with co-workers and the coverage required to provide service to customers. The EEOC provided examples in its guidance on reasonable accommodations.

Example: A crane operator with a disability requests that his work schedule be changed to permit him to start one hour later in the mornings. Three other employees on the construction site cannot do their jobs without the crane operator, so if the employer grants the request, the schedules of the other workers would have to be changed as well. The ADA does not require such a disruption to the employer's operations. The schedule change can be denied, but the employer should discuss other potential accommodations with the employee.

Example: A convenience store clerk requests a part-time schedule to accommodate his multiple sclerosis. The store has two clerks per shift. If one of the two does not work the entire shift, the lone clerk would not be able to adequately serve customers, keep the shelves stocked and maintain security. Because the requested accommodation would cause significant disruption to the employer's operation, the employer can deny the request, but should explore other accommodations that would assist the clerk.

Example: A computer programmer works as part of a team developing new software. The group works together, but each employee also has individual assignments. Through habit, the team work has taken place first thing in the morning. The programmer requests a later starting time to accommodate her disability. Doing so would change the time the team works together and when members work on individual assignments, but would not cause significant disruption to the employer's operations, so the request should be granted.

Pointing out that treatment and recuperation do not always permit exact timetables, the EEOC stated in its guidance on reasonable accommodation that an employer cannot claim undue hardship solely on the basis that the employee can provide only an approximate date of return. However, if an employee who has been granted leave cannot return when expected due to unforeseen complications, the employer is entitled to make a fresh assessment of whether additional leave would cause an undue hardship.

The EEOC also admitted in its guidance that some employees are irreplaceable for any but a short, predetermined period of time. It would cause an undue hardship to grant indefinite leave to an experienced chef at a top restaurant, for example, because of the difficulty of providing a temporary replacement, the commission says.

It must be remembered that some courts have held that employees who are unable to meet attendance requirements, even with accommodations, are not otherwise qualified and that indefinite leave is not required under the ADA (*Tyndall v. National Educational Ctrs.*, 31 F.3d 209 (4th Cir. 1994); *Hudson v. MCI Telecommunications*, 87 F.3d 1167 (10th Cir. 1996)). Other courts have held that attendance is not an essential job function and employers must prove that indefinite leave causes an undue hardship (*Cehrs v. Northeast Ohio Alzheimer's Research Ctr.*, 155 F.3d 775 (6th Cir. 1998)). See Chapter 6 for a more detailed discussion of leave as a reasonable accommodation.

Changes to Another's Property as Undue Hardship

An employer cannot claim undue hardship solely because a reasonable accommodation would require it to make changes to property that is owned by someone else, the EEOC's guidance on reasonable accommodation stated. A lease or other contractual relationship sometimes will give the employer the right to make the necessary changes, and the commission suggested that this is something that should be looked at prior to entering into a lease agreement.

If the contract between the owner and employer requires the owner's consent before changes can be made, or prohibits the necessary changes altogether, the employer should make a good faith effort to obtain the owner's permission or to negotiate an exception to the contract, the EEOC insisted. If the owner refuses, the employer may claim undue hardship. Even then, however, the employer must explore whether another reasonable accommodation exists that would not cause undue hardship.

Of course owners of property that serves as a place of public accommodation have their own obligation under Title III of the ADA to remove structural barriers to provide equal access for individuals with disabilities.

Cost-Benefit Analysis

In an effort to more clearly explain what is required of employers, some federal courts have done a form of cost-benefit analysis of the requested accommodation. This analysis has to do with determining whether an accommodation is reasonable and is done before the issue of undue hardship is addressed, although some of those courts also talk about cost-benefit analysis in relation to showing that an accommodation is an undue hardship.

The ADA's definitions of reasonable accommodation and undue hardship do not include consideration of a cost-benefit analysis and the EEOC has flatly rejected this line of cases in its guidance, but this has not dissuaded those federal appeals courts that have adopted it.

The cost-benefit analysis permits an employer to weigh the *costs* of providing the accommodation against the *benefits* of the accommodation (see, e.g., *Skerski v. Time Warner Cable Co.*, 257 F.3d 273 (3d Cir. 2001); *Cehrs v. Northeast Ohio Alzheimer's Research Center*, 155 F. 3d 775 (6th Cir. 1998)). Unlike undue hardship, cost benefit does not have to do with the employer's resources.

One appeals court explained that "reasonable" is a modifying word that weakens "accommodation" just as reasonable effort means less than the maximum possible effort or reasonable care requires something less than the maximum possible care. While it does not follow that the costs and benefits of altering a workplace to accommodate an employee with a disability "would always have to be quantified, or even that an accommodation would have to be deemed unreasonable if the cost exceeded the benefit however slightly," the court said, "at the very least, the cost could not be disproportionate to the benefit. Even if an employer is so large or wealthy ... that it may not be able to plead 'undue hardship,' it would not be required to expend enormous sums in order to bring about a trivial improvement in the life of a disabled employee" (*Vande Zande v. Wisconsin Dept. of Admin.*, 44 F.3d 538 (7th Cir. 1995)).

The 7th Circuit went on to say that "[i]f the nation's employers have potentially unlimited financial obligations to 43 million disabled persons, the Americans With Disabilities Act will have imposed an indirect tax potentially greater than the national debt. We do not find an intention to bring about such a radical result in either the language of the act or its history. The preamble actually 'markets' the act as a cost saver. ... The savings will be illusory if employers are required to expend many more billions in accommodation than will be saved by enabling disabled people to work."

Another court of appeals divided the issue of reasonableness into two elements. The accommodation must be effective in that it allows the individual with a disability to perform the essential functions of the job in question, just as the EEOC states in its guidance, and it must be reasonable in terms of the burden it places on the employer (*Barth v. Gelb*, 2 F.3d 1180 (D.C. Cir. 1993) *cert. denied*, 511 U.S. 1030 (1994)).

A third appeals court said bluntly, "We would not, for example, require an employer to make a multi-million dollar modification for the benefit of a single individual with a disability, even if the proposed modification would allow that individual to perform the essential functions of a job that she sought. In spite of its effectiveness, the proposed modification would be unreasonable because of its excessive costs. In short, an accommodation is reasonable only if its costs are not clearly disproportionate to the benefits that it will produce" (*Borkowski v. Valley Central Sch. Dist.*, 63 F.3d 131 (2d Cir. 1995)).

As for undue hardship, the *Borkowski* court said an employer must perform a cost-benefit analysis, showing "both that the hardship caused by the proposed accommodation would be undue in light of the enumerated factors [in the statute's definition of undue hardship], and that the proposed accommodation is unreasonable and need not be made [because the cost is too high in relation to the benefits that will result to others]." The court added that all juries will have to do is "a common-sense balancing of the costs and benefits in light of the factors listed in the regulations."

In its guidance on reasonable accommodation, the EEOC insisted a cost-benefit analysis was not supported by either the statute or the ADA's legislative history. "Whether the cost of a reasonable accommodation imposes an undue hardship depends on the employer's resources, not on the individual's salary, position, or status," the commission stated, adding that the House Education and Labor Report (No. 101-485, pt. 2 (1990)) stated that "the fact that an accommodation is used by only one employee should not be used as a negative factor counting in favor of a finding of undue hardship."

As an appeals court pointed out, however, the ADA's legislative history equated undue hardship to undue cost (S. Rep. No. 116 (1989)). Noting that these are terms of relationship, the court read the statute and legislative history to mean undue "in relation to the benefits of the accommodation to the disabled worker as well as to the employer's resources." This gives employers an opportunity to defend against an accommodation on the basis that its costs are excessive in relation either to its benefits or to the employer's financial survival or health, the court concluded (*Vande Zande v. Wisconsin Dept. of Admin.*, 44 F.3d 538 (7th Cir. 1995)).

In a more recent case involving a request for long-term, essentially indefinite, leave, the 6th Circuit found that when "both the time and likelihood of return to work cannot be roughly quantified after a significant period of leave has already been granted, the costs of the requested additional leave outweigh the benefits." The court went on to detail the employer's uncertainty about the composition of its workforce, the absent employee's loss of work skills and probable need for retraining. "When this is balanced against the potential benefit derived from the employee returning to work, which must be significantly discounted by the obvious indeterminacy involved, the cost exceeds the likely benefit," the court concluded (*Walsh v. United Parcel Service*, 201 F.3d 718 (6th Cir. 2000)).

Collective Bargaining Agreements

Labor unions are covered by the ADA and have the same obligation as employers to comply with the law's requirements. Moreover, an employer cannot do through contracting what it cannot do itself, so a union contract that discriminates against individuals with disabilities, such as by imposing physical requirements for jobs that screen out qualified applicants with disabilities, does not protect the employer from discrimination charges.

Nevertheless, the terms of a collective bargaining agreement may have an impact on determining whether an accommodation imposes an undue hardship on the employer, the EEOC stated in its Technical Assistance Manual on Title I. Seniority provisions, for example, may be considered a factor in determining whether reassignment of a less senior employee with a disability would be an undue hardship. The commission suggested that to avoid conflicts over reasonable accommodation, the union and employer include a provision in the collective bargaining agreement that permits the employer to take all actions necessary to comply with the ADA.

Some federal courts of appeals have ruled that collective bargaining agreements trump the ADA. For example, if under a union contract an employee with seniority is entitled to a position over a less senior worker, the position is not a vacant one to which a less senior employee with a disability could be reassigned as a reasonable accommodation (*Eckles v. Consolidated Rail Corp.*, 94 F.3d 1041 (7th Cir. 1996), *cert. denied*, 520 U.S. 1141 (1997)).

Another court agreed that reassignment does not require an employer to violate the rights of the employee who received the job under the selection process outlined in the union contract and departmental policies (*Feliciano v. Rhode Island*, 160 F.3d 780 (1st Cir. 1998)).

Although an employer generally is not required to provide an accommodation that would violate a bona fide seniority system under the terms of a collective bargaining agreement, "it is the *direct* violation of a seniority system that has been held unreasonable," the 10th Circuit ruled. A remote or merely potential violation of a union contract is not sufficient, the court found (*Dilley v. Supervalu, Inc.*, 296 F.3d 958 (10th Cir. 2002)).

BUMPING NOT REQUIRED

Collective bargaining agreements usually give more senior employees bumping rights to protect them from such things as downsizing, creating a "last hired, first fired" rule. The ADA does not require that a less senior employee be bumped from his or her job to make room for a more senior employee with a disability, a federal appeals court ruled.

An employee who worked 12-hour shifts took a nine-month disability leave after she contracted hepatitis C. At the end of her leave, she gave the employer a doctor's letter, stating that she could work no more than eight hours per day. The employee was terminated for failure to return to work and she sued under the ADA, arguing that the employer's collective bargaining agreement gave her the right to bump a less senior employee from a job she could perform.

While the law defines reasonable accommodation as including reassignment to a vacant position, the court held, bumping another employee to create a vacancy is not required (*Pond v. Michelin North America*, 183 F.3d 592 (7th Cir. 1999)). Reassignment, if it is required at all, is to an existing vacancy.

A conflict with a collective bargaining agreement provision that does not contain a bona fide seniority system may not be an undue hardship. In a case involving disabled police officers, the employees did not seek to bypass the seniority system, but rather wanted the opportunity to compete with able-bodied officers by eliminating the rules that barred them from receiving specialized assignments. The employer's contention that modifying the pertinent non-seniority requirements of the union contract would impose an undue hardship was "without merit," the court held. It also ruled that resentment by other employees was not a factor to consider in an undue hardship analysis (*Cripe v. City of San Jose*, 261 F.3d 877 (9th Cir. 2001)).

The EEOC's position is that a collective bargaining agreement dealing with non-seniority issues is relevant, but not determinative. A union employer should determine if it can provide a reasonable accommodation that will remove the workplace barrier without violating its collective bargaining agreement, the EEOC said in its guidance. If there is no such reasonable accommodation, the employer and union should negotiate in good faith a variance to the union contract so the employer may provide a reasonable accommodation, unless the accommodation would unduly burden the expectations of other workers.

Among the relevant factors to assess in determining whether the accommodation would cause an undue hardship are the duration and severity of adverse effects caused by granting the variance and the number of employees whose employment opportunities would be affected by the variance, the commission explained.

At least one appeals court agreed with the EEOC that conflicts with rights under a collective bargaining agreement do not always exempt employers from having to grant a request for a reasonable accommodation. The inquiry must look at the specific accommodation requested and the nature of the business, including the anticipated disruption of the workforce due to upsetting settled expectations created by the union contract, the court said (*Aka v. Washington Hospital Center*, 156 F.3d 1284 (D.C. Cir. 1998)). In other words, back to the case-by-case analysis that the commission has always stressed.

Non-union Seniority Policies

The "relevant seniority system advantages and related difficulties that result from violations of seniority rules, are not limited to collectively bargained systems," the U.S. Supreme Court has ruled (*U.S. Airways, Inc. v. Barnett*, 535 U.S. 391 (2002)). Violating a bona fide seniority system, absent special circumstances that make an exception reasonable, generally will be an undue hardship for an employer. A requested accommodation that conflicts with seniority rules is not reasonable.

In *Barnett*, the employee was a cargo handler who injured his back. He transferred to a less physically demanding mailroom job. The position later became open to seniority-based employee bidding under the airlines' seniority system and more senior employees bid on the job. The employer refused the worker's request to accommodate his disability by permitting him to remain in the mailroom. He lost his job and filed suit under the ADA.

The Supreme Court framed the issue as whether a proposed accommodation that would normally be reasonable is rendered unreasonable because the assignment would violate a seniority system's rules. The Court held that it would. It cautioned that special circumstances might alter the important expectations created by a seniority system. For example, the Court said, a system that is violated regularly or that contains so many exceptions that one more would not matter could make an accommodation that violated it reasonable in a particular case, even though in the *ordinary* case it would not be. The employee has the burden of showing special circumstances that make an exception reasonable, the Court said.

In *Barnett*, the seniority system had been in place for decades and employees relied on it. Any significant alteration would result in undue hardship to both the company and its employees. *Ordinarily* the ADA does not require an employer to assign a disabled employee to a particular position even though another employee is entitled to that position under the employer's established seniority system, the Supreme Court held. Its repeated emphasis on "ordinarily" and its caution that special circumstances could exist that make a violation of a seniority policy reasonable may mean that the D.C. Circuit's ruling in *Aka v. Washington Hospital Center* (156 F.3d 1284 (D.C. Cir. 1998)) is not entirely without merit.

Section II: Accommodations for Religion

Religion and one's personal religious practices have played an important role in this country since before there was a country. Indeed, the history of the European settlement of North America is interwoven with profound notions of freedom of religious expression.

Whether it was the Puritans seeking a place to worship as they wished, William Penn, who sought a refuge for persecuted Quakers, or Peter Stuyvesant in New Amsterdam, admitting a group of Jews searching for a safe haven, religious freedom is a hallmark of the settlement and founding of this nation.

A corollary of valuing religious expression in America is an abiding belief that one's religion is no one else's business, especially not the government's. Indeed, the first words of the Bill of Rights are: "Congress shall make no law respecting an establishment of religion, or prohibiting the free exercise thereof." These words created the doctrine of separation of church and state as one of the founding principles of the American Republic.

This separation has been traditionally interpreted to prohibit the "entanglement" of public power (including the courts) either to support religious expression of any kind or to limit it. Indeed, the courts have been among the most diligent bodies in erecting and preserving the separation of church and state.

Our history on this subject is something of a paradox: strong beliefs about the importance of religious practices on one hand, and, on the other, equally strong principles making sure that religion has no public role. Many people have pointed out the contradictions implicit in a country whose Congress commences with a prayer and whose coinage bears "In God We Trust," but which prohibits the use of public funds to support religious charities dispensing aid on a non-sectarian basis.

Nonetheless, despite the contradictions – or because of them – the debate regarding the size and strength of the "wall" between church and state is one that has been waged since the founding of the country and will continue. There is little debate, however, about the role of religion in the workplace. For the most part, it is not supposed to matter.

That, at least, is the ideal and the road to achieving that ideal is long and never-ending. At one time, discrimination in the workplace against Catholics and Jews was commonplace. If employment was available to employees who practiced these faiths, advancement was not. Many employment doors were simply closed. Religion may not have been "established" in America, but it was not irrelevant, in or out of the workplace.

Times changed and Congress passed the 1964 Civil Rights Act, which prohibited discrimination on the basis of religion at the same time it prohibited bias due to race, national origin and gender. The first chapter in this section, **Chapter 9**, discusses that law and some of its definitions. The Civil Rights Act required some accommodations for employees' sincerely held religious beliefs, as **Chapter 10** discusses.

After Sept. 11, 2001, incidents of religious harassment and occasionally discrimination occurred against Muslims and similar faiths. The Equal Employment Opportunity Commission released new guidance on religious discrimination and accommodation and began pursuing religious discrimination lawsuits. The result has been a new emphasis on accommodations, which is discussed in **Chapter 11**.

The **Appendix** includes the EEOC's regulations, guidance and questions and answers on religious discrimination and accommodation in the workplace.

What Is Religion?

Perhaps because overt religious discrimination appeared to subside by the time of the civil rights revolution, religious discrimination never became the national cause racial discrimination did. However, as with discrimination based on national origin and gender, religion was included in the sweeping law that banned racial discrimination in the workplace, Title VII of the 1964 Civil Rights Act (42 U.S.C. §2000-e *et seq.*).

Under Title VII, factors such as race, religion, gender, color and national origin were not to be considered when making employment-related decisions. The law established the following:

- Employers may not treat employees or applicants less- or more-favorably because of their religious beliefs or practices. For example, an employer may not refuse to hire individuals of a certain religion, may not impose stricter promotion requirements for persons of a certain religion, and may not impose more or different work requirements on an employee because of that employee's religious beliefs or practices.

- Employees cannot be forced to participate – or not participate – in a religious activity as a condition of employment.

- Employers must reasonably accommodate employees' sincerely held religious beliefs or practices, unless doing so would impose an undue hardship on the employer's business. A reasonable religious accommodation is any adjustment to the work environment that will allow the employee to practice his or her religion. Flexible scheduling, voluntary substitutions or job swapping, job reassignments, lateral transfers and modifying workplace practices, policies and/or procedures are examples of how an employer might accommodate an employee's religious beliefs.

- An employer is not required to accommodate an employee's religious beliefs and practices if doing so would impose an undue hardship on the employers' legitimate business interests. An employer can show undue hardship if accommodating an employee's religious practices requires more than ordinary administrative costs, diminishes efficiency in other jobs, infringes on other employees' job rights or benefits, impairs workplace safety, causes co-workers to carry the accommodated employee's share of potentially hazardous or burdensome work, or if the proposed accommodation conflicts with another general law or regulation.

• Employers must permit employees to engage in religious expression if employees are permitted to engage in other personal expression at work, unless the religious expression would impose an undue hardship on the employer's business. Therefore, an employer may not place more restrictions on religious expression than on other forms of expression that have a comparable effect on workplace efficiency.

• Employers must take steps to prevent religious harassment of their employees. An employer can reduce the chance that employees will engage in unlawful religious harassment by implementing an anti-harassment policy and having an effective procedure for reporting, investigating and correcting harassing conduct.

• It is also unlawful to retaliate against an individual for opposing employment practices that discriminate based on religion, or for filing a discrimination charge, testifying or participating in any way in an investigation, proceeding or litigation under Title VII.

The EEOC enforces Title VII. In that role, the commission has issued regulations defining in greater detail the rights and responsibilities of employers and employees with respect to religion in the workplace. (See the **Appendix** for a copy of the regulations.)

To understand the law of religious accommodations in the workplace, it is imperative to reduce the topic to its constituent parts, beginning with "What is a religion?"

As might be expected in a country founded on principles of equality and personal freedom, the law is almost entirely silent on this potentially divisive subject. In a country without an established religion, the very process of defining "religion" could inevitably lead to the "entanglements" the Constitution prohibits.

As a result, the law focuses on the *quality* of one's beliefs, rather than their content. In other words, the courts determined that if one's beliefs were "sincerely held," they could qualify for accommodation.

Sincerely Held Beliefs

The issue of whether one's religious beliefs are sincerely held arose most pointedly in cases involving claims of conscientious objection to military service. The matter ultimately rose to the U.S. Supreme Court. The Court made clear that the "test" was whether one's beliefs were "sincere and meaningful" and occupied a place in the believer's life akin to the role of God in a traditional religious context. The Court also held that such beliefs could be held by those who are not part of traditional religions (*Welsh v. U.S.*, 398 U.S. 333 (1970); see also, *U.S. v. Seeger*, 380 U.S. 163 (1965)). This standard remains in place and has been broadly adopted.

In its regulations, the EEOC makes this same point unambiguously:

> religious practices ... include moral or ethical beliefs as to what is right and wrong which are sincerely held with the strength of traditional religious views (29 C.F.R. §1605.1).

As noted, religious beliefs and/or religious practices need not be tied to a traditional religion, as long as the sincerity of the beliefs mirror those of traditional religionists. For example, an applicant for unemployment compensation was turned down because he refused to work on Sunday. He claimed his religious beliefs dictated this course, although he was *not* a member of a religious group or sect that prohibited work on Sunday (*Frazee v. Illinois Dept. of Employment Security*, 489 U.S. 829 (1989)).

The Court found that Franzee's belief was "sincerely held" and that was sufficient. This precedent has been generally followed (see *Seshadri v. Kadrian*, 130 F.3d 798 (7th cir. 1997) plaintiff in religious discrimination case need not belong to an established church).

The same is true for sincere beliefs regarding atheism (*Young v. Southwestern Savings & Loan Assoc.*, 509 F.2d 140 (5th Cir. 1975) atheist could not be compelled to attend staff meeting that commenced with a prayer). It is also true of sincere beliefs that are not entirely shared by the believer's religion (29 C.F.R. §1605.1; *Carter v. B. Oakley, Inc.*, 849 F. Supp. 673 (E.D. Ark. 1993) wearing beard thought to be required by scriptures, not a religion's doctrine).

Although this definition appears to be without limit, the courts have crafted some limitations by carefully discerning the difference between that which is religious in its very nature and something that could be a cultural accoutrement. For example, a preference for a sari or "African" clothing is not regarded as being a religious practice (*McGlothin v. Jackson Municipal Separate School Dist.*, 829 F. Supp. 853 (S.D. Miss. 1992)). On the other hand, wearing a turban for a Sikh man or a hijab (head scarf) for a Muslim woman likely would be regarded as a religious practice.

Furthermore, ancillary, quasi-religious activities do not receive legal protections. Even a sincere belief in the religious source of one's acts does not suffice to protect (1) an employee who, without permission, leaves work to decorate a church for Christmas celebrations (*Wessling v. Kroger Co.*, 554 F. Supp. 548 (E.D. Mich. 1992)); (2) an organizer of a Ku Klux Klan rally (*Slater v. King Soopers, Inc.*, 809 F. Supp. 809 (D. Colo. 1992)); or (3) a homophobic supervisor (*Bodett v. Coxcom, Inc.*, 366 F.3d 736 (9th Cir 2004)).

What Is Sincerity?

Because there is neither an established religion nor an established definition of religion, it is to be expected that there has been considerable discussion of what constitutes sufficient sincerity to satisfy the courts. In the past, when accommodations were rarely granted, this issue was not of particular importance. As accommodations are now more widely required (see Chapter 11), meeting the criteria for demanding an accommodation has risen in significance.

The cases challenging the sincerity of an employee's beliefs can be roughly divided into those concerning a sudden adherence to religious beliefs, beliefs evolving over time, and selective religious practices. Each case presents its own facts and its own challenges for employers trying to respond in a licit and appropriate manner.

The easiest case to understand is *Bailey v. Associated Press* (2003 WL 22232967 (S.D.N.Y. 2003) unpublished) in which an employee who, for the first time in 14 years, suddenly requested Sundays off for religious observance. He did not couch the request in religious terms, was not an attendee at church services, and cited no religious prohibition against Sunday work.

The issue is also not very complicated when the employee's adherence to asserted religious principles seems to be flexible. For example, an employee objected to paying union dues on the grounds of the beliefs of the Seventh Day Adventists. Contrary to his avowed religion, however, the employee swore oaths before a notary, was divorced and worked five and not six days a week. The court ruled his beliefs were more situational than sincere (*EEOC v. Union Independence … De Puerto Rico*, 279 F.3d 49 (1st Cir. 2002)).

The most difficult cases are those with evolving (usually increasing) religious observance, especially when not related to a conversion to a different faith because of marriage. One employee requested Saturday off even though she had been working on the Sabbath for months after her baptism. She successfully insisted that her religious convictions had grown (*Cooper v. Oak Rubber Co.*, 15 F.3d 1375 (6th Cir. 1994)). This same pattern was followed in a number of instances involving newly-minted "religious resolutions" and/or additional counseling.

Perhaps the most interesting and challenging situation occurred when a previously non-observant employee requested a day off to observe the Jewish holy day of Yom Kippur. During the previous eight years of employment, the employee had never requested time off for religious observance. The employee argued, however, that a number of life events, including the death of a parent and the death of a child, had deepened her religious convictions and that she had observed Yom Kippur for the previous years when it did not conflict with work. Her evolved beliefs finally led her to request time off. The court was convinced of her sincerity and was dismissive of the employer's offer of *another* day off instead (*EEOC v. Ilona of Hungary, Inc.*, 108 F.3d 1569 (7th Cir. 1997)).

In the face of these unclear standards, an employer is not left entirely to a guess. A number of courts have recognized that an employer must be free to make additional inquiries, seek corroborating statements, learn of the religious basis of the requested accommodation and other similar conduct to determine the sincerity of an employee's beliefs (*Burns v. Warwick Valley Central School Dist.*, 166 F. Supp. 2d 881 (S.D.N.Y. 2001); *Bushouse v. Local Union 2209, UAW*, 164 F. Supp. 2d 1066 (N.D. 2001)).

However, this inquiry may not be particularly fruitful. Sincerely held beliefs need not be narrowly tied to or limited by established practices of a religion, traditional or otherwise.

What Accommodations Must Be Made for Religious Practices/Beliefs?

10

Perhaps the most significant interface of law and religion in the work-place takes place when an employee asks the employer to change a policy, schedule or practice to accommodate his or her religion. For a Sabbatarian, it would affect the work week. For some others, it would be time off for prayer; for still others, it could be about attire. Regardless of the nature of the request, requests must follow a pattern. The employee must make known the nature (and, preferably, the source) of the accommodation requested and the employer must assess the request and respond.

If the employer has a good-faith basis for questioning the sincerity of the religious beliefs on which the request is made or about the relationship of the requested accommodation to the employee's professed religion, inquiries can be made and corroboration can be sought. Once satisfied that the request is properly grounded, the employer does not have to accept the precise accommodation requested by the employee. However, the employer cannot refuse to deal with the subject at all. The employer must accommodate a reasonable request that does not cause "undue hardship" for the business (*Ansonia Board of Education v. Philbrook,* 479 U.S. 60 (1986); *TWA, Inc. v. Hardison,* 432 U.S. 63 (1977); 29 C.F.R. §1605.2).

Undue Hardship

Just what constitutes an "undue hardship" has been the focus of the most serious inquiry in the past few years and the area of the greatest shift in the law.

What the Law Was

In the past, one could conclude that any accommodation that required changes to a collective bargaining agreement, inconvenienced other employees and/or increased an employer's costs would be deemed to have caused an "undue hardship." This view rests on U.S. Supreme Court rulings and the EEOC's regulations. The leading case for decades was *TWA, Inc. v. Hardison* (432 U.S. 63 (1977)).

In *Hardison,* there were all the elements of an inevitable collision: a shop that ran all day, every day; a rigid seniority system under a union contract; and a Sabbatarian worker with low seniority. After transferring to a job in which his seniority gave him no flexibility, Hardison asked for Saturdays off. TWA agreed to permit the union to seek a change of work assignments, but the union was not willing to violate the seniority system to accommodate Hardison.

After TWA rejected a proposal that Hardison work only four days a week on the ground that this would impair critical functions in the airline operations, no accommodation could be reached, and Hardison was fired for refusing to work on Saturdays. TWA prevailed in the district court but the appellate court took a different view.

The appeals court ruled that TWA improperly rejected three reasonable alternatives, any one of which would have satisfied its obligation without undue hardship:

1.   within the framework of the seniority system, TWA could have permitted respondent to work a four-day week, utilizing a supervisor or another worker on duty elsewhere, even though this would have caused other shop functions to suffer;

2.   TWA could have filled Hardison's Saturday shift from other available personnel, even though this would have involved premium overtime pay; and

3.   TWA could have arranged a "swap" between Hardison and another employee either for another shift or for the Sabbath days, even though this would have involved a breach of the seniority system.

It was left to the Supreme Court to decide and it did so, emphatically. The Court ruled that TWA made reasonable efforts to accommodate Hardison's religious needs and each of the court of appeals' suggested alternatives would have been an undue hardship within the meaning of the statute as construed by the EEOC guidelines.

Specifically, the Supreme Court held that the seniority system itself represented a significant accommodation to the needs, both religious and secular, of all of TWA's employees. Thus, TWA could not be faulted for having failed to work out a shift or job swap for Hardison.

The Court's reasoning focused on the illegality of elevating a request tied to religious observance above those made for secular reasons.

> It would be anomalous to conclude that by "reasonable accommodation" Congress meant that an employer must deny the shift and job preference of some employees, as well as deprive them of their contractual rights, in order to accommodate or prefer the religious needs of others, and we conclude that Title VII does not require an employer to go that far.

Finally, the *Hardison* Court attempted to define just how much – or how little – an employer would have to bear to accommodate a religious request. The Court concluded that to ask an employer to bear more than a *de minimis* cost to give an employee Saturdays off, for example, would be an undue hardship. Again, the reasoning is critical and rests on not making artificial distinctions among different classes of employees based on religion.

No employer should bear additional costs when no such costs are incurred to give other employees the days off that they want. To do so, wrote the Court, would involve unequal treatment of employees on the basis of their religion.

Basing its position on the one articulated by the Supreme Court in *Hardison,* the EEOC stated that an employer "may assert undue hardship to justify a refusal to accommodate an employee's need to be absent from his or her scheduled duty hours if the employer can demonstrate that the accommodation would require more than a *de minimis* cost."

As a result, there are numerous cases in which employees have been refused a change in shifts or work days to accommodate a religious belief, because doing so would force other employees to work overtime or weekends, on undesirable shifts, or even miss work opportunities (see, *e.g., Beadle v. City of Tampa,* 42 F.3d 633 (11th Cir.), *cert. denied,* 515 U.S. 1152 (1995) no Sabbath observance; *Brown v. Polk Cty.,* 61 F.3d 650 (8th Cir. 1995) secretary need not type boss' Bible study notes; *Lee v. ABF Freight Sys.,* 22 F.3d 1019 (10th Cir. 1994) no requirement to assign another employee to cover an absence for religious reasons; *Weber v. Roadway Express, Inc.,* 199 F.3d 270 (5th Cir. 2000) request by Jehovah's Witness truck driver not to ride overnight with female relief drivers an undue burden on women drivers).

In sum, the standard for employers was very low and the rationale was no special treatment on the basis of religion.

It is also the case that no accommodations need be made that violate a law or regulation. Even the most urgent religious need to wear certain clothing or facial hair must not create a safety hazard for the employee or others. If safety regulations or neutral policies require, for example, that a respirator must be used, a hard hat worn or if only close-fitting garments or a hairnet are permitted, the demands of religion to wear a beard, a burkha, a turban or a hijab can be refused (see *Hover v. Florida Power and Light Co.,* 1994 WL 765369 (S.D. Fla.) unpublished). For the most part, the provisions of a collective bargaining agreement with a labor union also need not be violated to make an accommodation.

Just as clearly, however, an employer must permit an employee to resort to self-help, asking co-workers to swap shifts, trade days off and other similar activities that impose no cost or inconvenience (*Beadle v. Hillsborough County. Sheriff's Dept.,* 29 F.3d 529 (11th Cir. 1994)).

During the period between *Hardison* (1977) and September 2001, it is safe to say that accommodations of religious practices and beliefs in the workplace were not given much legal weight. Although there are always exceptions (see, *e.g., Shpargel v. Stage & Co.,* 914 F. Supp. 1468 (E.D. Mich. 1996) failure to accommodate illicit; others could have covered the employee's duties at no additional cost), the employer's position would prevail if colorably based in reasonable business practices, if arguably rooted in protecting other employee's rights or if modestly couched in controlling unnecessary costs. Chapter 11 discusses the changes that have occurred since Sept. 11, 2001.

Accommodations for Religion Post-9/11

11

In the wake of Sept. 11, 2001, and with a greater awareness of religious beliefs that are different from the Judeo-Christian, a change has taken place without any direction from the U.S. Supreme Court. For the most part, the EEOC has been the leader in the movement to recognize and accommodate religious observance in the workplace in the name of tolerance, *not* equal treatment.

The EEOC issued a new statement regarding accommodation of religion that takes a decidedly more accommodating view than that issued earlier. In its more recent guidance, "Employment Discrimination Based on Religion, Ethnicity, or Country of Origin" (see the Appendix for the full text of the guidance) the commission states:

> Title VII requires an employer to reasonably accommodate the religious practices of an employee or prospective employee, unless doing so would create an undue hardship for the employer. *Some reasonable religious accommodations that employers may be required to provide workers include leave for religious observances, time and/or place to pray, and ability to wear religious garb* (emphasis added).

In light of the austere and unyielding position of the Supreme Court in its *TWA, Inc. v. Hardison* decision (432 U.S. 63 (1977) discussed in Chapter 10), the EEOC's new guidance constitutes a virtual reversal of the law. This change is part of a general movement at the commission regarding accommodations for religious practices and garb.

For the most part, the EEOC now espouses the position that an accommodation that imposes no cost, no safety concerns, or that creates only modest disruption (such as a time and place for prayer at work) should be provided (see EEOC's "Questions and Answers About Employer Responsibilities Concerning the Employment of Muslims, Arabs, South Asians, and Sikhs," in the Appendix).

An employer once could be confident that any request that would cause disruption or require involuntary transfers or assignments would be considered an undue hardship that need not be granted. It is no longer possible to have that confidence.

The EEOC has expanded the views stated in its published documents by pursuing much broader goals in litigation, including a *right* to Sabbath observance, job re-assignment and similar accommodations unthinkable under *Hardison*. It seems clear that the readiness with which courts have adopted many of the commission's views indicates that a significant change is occurring in the country and that the courts are being carried along, rather than leading. It remains to be seen if the Supreme Court agrees with this re-drafting of one of its rulings.

It is perhaps not unexpected that the EEOC would move in this direction. It has a pre-existing model for expansive accommodations in the Americans With Disabilities Act already under its jurisdiction. Indeed, if one is seeking a "road map" to the EEOC's efforts regarding religious accommodations, it is certainly useful to regard the ADA as providing the model.

One of the clearest indications of the current trend to read the ADA into issues involving religious accommodation is found in *Kenner v. Domtar Industries* (2006 WL 662466 (W.D. Ark.) unpublished). In a case involving a shift swap to accommodate a worker's religious needs that was rejected on the grounds that it violated the union contract, the court ruled first that the limitations of the collective bargaining system do *not* limit an employer's obligation to seek to resolve a request for an accommodation. It is hard to imagine a ruling more different from that in *Hardison,* which held that the collectively bargained seniority system was itself a significant accommodation to the needs, both religious and secular, of all the employees. The *Kenner* court then held that the employer was required to engage in *interactive dialogue* with the employee to seek a resolution.

The source of the court's ruling, it said, was to be found in Title VII of the Civil Rights Act of 1964, because the interactive process was "contemplated" in that law. By ruling in this manner, a federal district court brought a notion that had been considered exclusively within the narrow confines of the ADA into the realm of accommodations for all groups protected by Title VII.

Specific Types of Accommodations

Accommodations for employees' religious beliefs in the workplace can take many forms, including modified schedules, leave, modified duties and change in dress and grooming policies.

Modifications of Work Schedules/Leave

In the past, the EEOC stated in its regulations to Title VII that "[a]n employer may assert undue hardship to justify a refusal to accommodate an employee's need to be absent from his or her scheduled duty hours if the employer can demonstrate that the accommodation would require more than a *de minimis* cost" (29 C.F.R. Sec. 1605). The rationale was that requiring more obtrusive accommodations was a form of preferring religion over and above other employee preferences.

As a result, there are numerous cases in which employees were refused a change in shifts or work days to accommodate a religious belief, because doing so would force other employees to work overtime, on weekends or undesirable shifts (see, *e.g., Beadle v. City of Tampa,* 42 F.3d 633 (11th Cir.), *cert. denied,* 515 U.S. 1152 (1995)).

At the same time, an employer must permit an employee to resort to self-help, that is, asking co-workers to swap shifts, trade days off, and other similar activities that impose no cost or inconvenience (*Beadle v. Hillsborough Cty. Sheriff's Dept.,* 29 F.3d 529 (11th Cir. 1994); *Morrissette-Brown v. Mobile Infirmary Medical. Center,* 2006 WL 1999133 (S.D. Ala.) unpublished).

These two approaches formed the balance between an employer's obligations and an employee's rights. There was no doubt that the scales were weighted against providing religious accommodations. Today, the balance has shifted. To put it in terms of the law, it has become significantly more difficult for an employer to show that an accommodation will create an "undue hardship."

In a series of cases, often pursued by the EEOC, the burden has been placed on the employer either to provide an accommodation or an iron-clad reason for denying it. In *EEOC v. Robert Bosch Corp.* (169 Fed. Appx. 942 (6th Cir. 2006) unpublished), for example, an employee in a machine shop asked for Saturdays off for worship. The employer claimed it had a 24/7 operation and the union had a contractual obligation to supply a substitute worker consistent with the rights and privileges in the contract.

The appeals court was not convinced that either the employer or the union had made a good faith effort to reach an accommodation for the employee. Neither the demands of the business nor the presence of the labor agreement were sufficient bases for "undue hardship."

The EEOC was seeking a similar outcome in *EEOC v. Firestone* (2006 WL 2620314 (W.D.N.C.) unpublished). The commission appealed a ruling that a collective bargaining agreement *and* a generous leave policy, flexible holidays and shift-swapping provided sufficient religious accommodation and to do more would an undue hardship. The EEOC asserted that the employee deserved an "absolute" guarantee that her religious practice would be accommodated, not merely the opportunity to use the ample mechanisms made available to her. The appeals court has not yet ruled.

The request for a time and place for prayer made by a number of Muslims appears not to have generated much judicial activity. The EEOC, in its guidance, "Employment Discrimination Based on Religion, Ethnicity, or Country of Origin," advises that "[s]ome reasonable religious accommodations that employers may be required to provide workers include … time and/or place to pray."

In most instances, the lost time is "off-the-clock" and made up. Further, because there is some flexibility in the time for most Muslim prayers during work hours, this request for an accommodation seems to be one that is routinely granted. Complications may occur in the winter when the sunset prayer (Mahgrib) is likely to occur during work hours. An observant Muslim would not be able to adjust the time of this prayer. An employer facing a deadline, a shipping order, or a demanding client has a new issue to confront, akin to that of accommodating a parent who has a right under local law to attend a parent-teacher conference or similar family responsibility.

If the EEOC's guidance is the standard, employers will have to find a way to cope. Many employees, for reasons wholly unrelated to religion, would like to take breaks at any number of times during the day. They are not permitted to do so, even though some *might* even use the time for contemplation, meditation or prayer.

The wisdom of *Hardison* lay in prohibiting these sorts of distinctions and the inevitable conflicts they bring to the workplace. It remains to be seen if the new spirit of accommodation at the EEOC creates a willingness among employers to be understanding, or creates religious tensions among employees.

Modified Duties

Some of the most difficult situations involve an employee's claim that performing all or some of his or her job duties violates sincerely held religious beliefs. Such a claim not only implicates the traditional "undue hardship" analysis, it also calls into question whether an individual's interpretation of a religion's proscriptions are valid. One well-known case involved a pharmacist who claimed that filling prescriptions for birth control pills violated his religious beliefs.

In the past, it is likely that this case would have been dismissed summarily. A state-licensed pharmacist was not thought to be able to choose which customers to serve or which prescriptions to fill. In this instance, the pharmacist insisted that he be allowed not only to refuse to fill contraception prescriptions; he also said he had no obligation to refer patients – including those on the phone – to someone who would. Permitting this accommodation was held to be an undue hardship.

However, the grounds for the court's decision left intact the notion that a less demanding pharmacist *would be* allowed to pick and choose which prescriptions to fill based on his or her interpretation of sincerely held religious beliefs (*Noessen v. Medical Staffing Network, Inc.* (232 Fed. Appx. 581 (7th Cir. 2007)).

The same outcome occurred with less notoriety when a police officer refused to work in a casino, claiming that gambling was against his religion and that by serving at the casino he was being forced to support morally offensive conduct. The court ruled that police officers cannot choose where they are to be assigned, especially in light of the many morally troubled situations in which they may be placed (*Endres v. Indiana State Police,* 349 F.3d 922 (7th Cir. 2003), *cert. denied,* 541 U.S. 969 (2004)).

A moral challenge akin to those raised by conscientious objectors who refuse to be involved in wars was the focus of a case brought by the EEOC (*EEOC v. Dresser-Rand Co.,* 2006 WL 1994792 (W.D.N.Y.) unpublished). The employer was a manufacturer of custom turbines, compressors and other industrial products. The employee, a machine tool operator, claimed that religious beliefs prevented him from working on equipment intended for use in implements of war. He sought an accommodation rather than work on a part intended for use in a U.S. naval submarine.

The employer claimed it offered the employee a transfer to the shipping department, which was rejected, before terminating him. It also asserted that it was not required by law or its collective bargaining agreement to offer the accommodation sought. The EEOC claimed that the employer was a large, diversified manufacturer who could have provided the employee with an accommodation that would not have caused an undue hardship. The court was faced with a number of unresolved factual issues that it determined required it to send the case to trial. Again, what may well have constituted "undue hardship" in the past is no longer an adequate defense.

Dress Code/Grooming Modifications

Although the bulk of the recent cases involved garb arguably worn for religious reasons, this type of accommodation also implicates issues of sincerity and even the nature of religion.

Body piercing was offered as a religious practice that would forestall the application of a uniform company rule against facial jewelry in a 1st Circuit case. Interestingly, although there was evidence in the record that the employee applied for membership to the Church of Body Modification *after* being told to remove her facial jewelry, the court did not delve into the sincerity of her beliefs.

Furthermore, even though the employer received no complaints from customers about its employee's facial jewelry, the court held that Costco was permitted to create and put into place its own concept of a "public image." As a result, it was deemed an undue hardship to carve out a single exception to a companywide rule on an issue that would affect this public image (*Cloutier v. Costco Wholesale Corp.* (390 F.3d 126 (1st Cir. 2004), *cert. denied,* 125 S. Ct. 2940 (2005)).

This case stands in contrast to many others. It appears that in this instance, without saying so and despite stating otherwise, the nature of the practice and its tenuous ties to "religion" served to undermine the employee's claim. In many recent cases, a different rule was created.

Typical of the new attitude toward accommodations for dress is a case in which the employer insisted on standard uniforms for its employees as part of developing its "brand" and its public image. The employee, a Muslim, sought the accommodation of wearing a headscarf (hijab). The company refused, stating that it feared not being able to draw rational distinctions among requests for variations from its standard uniform. The court did not agree. Developing a public image was not a sufficient counterweight to an accommodation for religion, the court held (*EEOC v. Alamo Rent-A-Car,* 432 F. Supp. 1006 (D. Ariz. 2006)). Thus, hijabs are now widely accepted, as are other forms of religious head coverings.

That rule is not universal, however. For example, a police department is given much broader latitude in imposing dress requirements and in limiting any form of religious identification among its officer. A Muslim officer in Philadelphia asked to be permitted to wear a khimar (a cloth that covers the head and neck, at a minimum). She was refused. The court agreed that the police had a compelling public purpose to avoid divisiveness and individuality in the name of its group mission to protect the public. In this instance, wearing a khimar was an undue hardship (*Webb v. City of Philadelphia,* 2007 WL 1866763 (E.D. Pa.) unpublished).

Grooming requirements involving religious accommodation requests have also become more "situational" and raised questions harkening back to the discredited notion of "customer choice." A lube technician was a Rastafarian who claimed his religion required him not to shave or cut his hair. Safety was not an issue here. The employer's new policy requiring employees with customer contact to be clean shaven was.

To accommodate the employee's religious practice, he was moved to an area that he claimed was cold and isolated – but with no customer contact. He objected. Perhaps because the employer made an effort, the court ruled that the employee's insistence on a blanket exemption from the neutral grooming policy was an unreasonable undue hardship (*Brown v. F.L. Roberts & Co.,* 419 F. Supp. 2d 7 (D. Mass. 2006)).

Proselytizing and Religious Expression

Although Congress (and the states) have constitutional concerns regarding limitations on religious expression, the role of the private-sector employer is less clear. If an employer must permit prayer, religious garb and other overtly religious intrusions into the workplace, must proselytizing speech and conduct be allowed? In some cases, the result has depended on how much expression of personal views of any kind is permitted in the workplace. That is, an employer cannot only prohibit religious expression if all sorts of other expression, such as political, is permitted. If there is a rule of thumb, it is the ancient Greek advice – moderation in all things.

It is useful to begin by understanding the truly complicated situations an employer faces in our diverse society. Valued employees and trusted managers are thrown into conflict over deeply felt issues having no relation to work. Asked to choose between the genuine feelings of its employees, many employers are having a difficult time understanding why it is their problem to begin with.

Many recent situations have arisen as the result of unquestionably sincere, but obtrusive, conduct by employees seeking to bring their religion into the workplace using e-mails, meeting rooms and other company property.

Personal e-mails have become such a common element in the workplace that one issue to be resolved is whether the employer can limit only one form of personal e-mails – religious proselytizing – without violating the law. That case has not yet been decided, but there are cases in the labor-management field that indicate that a strict and broad non-solicitation policy is the only one that will survive a challenge by a union seeking to organize employees at work (*Stoddard-Quirk,* 138 NLRB 615 (1962)). Similarly broad rules limiting expression may be required to provide a sound basis for limiting religious expression, particularly proselytizing.

In a recent case, no one questioned Edna Ng's belief that she felt morally compelled to bring her religion to others, including co-workers. There was no overt preaching or grabbing of co-workers to join her in prayer, but she used the company's e-mail system, its computers and meeting rooms in an effort to "save" her colleagues. Twice, she held unauthorized holiday parties in company meeting rooms, inviting her pastor to speak, displaying religious tracts and alerting the employees to the party via the company e-mail. Other employees complained.

Ng's manager counseled her and reminded her of the company's non-harassment policy. The manager advised Ng that she was not to use e-mail for personal messages addressed to large numbers of employees, not to use a large part of the coffee room for non-work purposes and not to present or distribute controversial (religious) materials in the office. He stressed that the employer had to be considerate of the beliefs of all its employees and could not allow Ng to push her beliefs on others who did not welcome her efforts or share her beliefs.

Ng persisted and tried to hold additional meetings. When this was denied, she expanded her proselytizing via e-mail, until, after repeated warnings to stop, she was terminated. She sued under Title VII.

In this instance, the court had little difficulty in holding that the employee had gone too far. The existence of an anti-harassment policy was important and so was the neutrality of the company's policy. To permit Ng's "ministry" would require the employer to permit all others, and this was found to be an "undue hardship."

This same pattern was followed even when a public employer was involved (*Berry v. Dept. of Social Services*, 447 F.3d 642 (9th Cir. 2006). An employee wished to display religious paraphernalia in his cubicle and discuss his evangelical Christian beliefs with clients, colleagues and in workplace prayer meetings. He was told to stop. He sued, claiming a violation of his rights under Title VII.

In this case, the public sector nature of his employment made it more difficult for the employee to prevail. Fearing a breach of the Establishment Clause, the court held that the employer was required to rebut any inference of state sponsorship of Berry's religious views.

Harassment

In many respects, harassment is the "flip side" of accommodation, indicating that some resolution should have been sought and reached before matters reached this extreme circumstance.

Although there has been a renewed interest in this subject, harassment based on religion has been prosecuted by the EEOC for over 35 years. The general American sensitivity concerning the entanglement of the government in religious matters has made it difficult for the commission to articulate with precision just what religious activity – by employer or employee – might be harassing. Nonetheless, the EEOC's regulations on national origin discrimination (29 C.F.R. §1606.8) and the developing case law on sexual harassment have provided useful analogies.

Interestingly, religion-based harassment is an area of the law in which it is as likely as not that the accused is an employee rather than an employer. Regardless of the source, however, aggressive proselytizing or compelled insertion of religion into the workplace is at the core of the complaints.

The duty on employers is that they must take steps to prevent religious harassment of their employees. The EEOC advised that an employer can reduce the chance that employees will engage in unlawful religious harassment by implementing an anti-harassment policy and by having an effective procedure for reporting, investigating and correcting harassing conduct.

As significantly, as with other forms of harassment, a claim of religious harassment can be defended against by noting the existence of anti-harassment policies, employee training and taking prompt and effective action to rectify the situation (*Hafford v. Seidner,* 183 F.3d 506 (6th Cir. 1999)).

In some situations, the facts defy an easy resolution. A senior reliability engineer was a member of a Pentecostal Church. He claimed that he was the subject of mocking and harassment by just about everyone at his workplace – derogatory remarks from his manager, removal of church announcements from the community bulletin board, requests to turn down the religious music on his radio and an order to remove the "Jesus" lanyard he wore for his company ID badge. He claimed this all created a hostile environment and a failure to accommodate his religious beliefs.

The court disagreed, in large part because the "employer as employer" (as opposed to individual employees) could not be found to be involved; the incidents were not repeated, severe or pervasive; and nothing was alleged to have interfered with the employee's ability to do his job (*Jones v. United Space Alliance,* 170 Fed. Appx. 52 (11th Cir. 2006) unpublished).

Although there appears to be a trend toward greater acceptance of religious activity in the workplace, not every employee agrees. When there is a conflict, an employer's intervention can prevent liability.

For example, an employee complained that a co-worker who had experienced a religious conversion was proselytizing her to the point that she was constructively discharged. The employer promptly responded to the employee's complaints, met with and counseled the proselytizer, and claimed that no further incidents occurred. In addition, the employer continued to monitor the situation to assure that no harassment was occurring.

Faced with this, the court determined that no accommodation was required and that no harassment was taking place. The court wrote what could be broadly applied to many of these cases: "Title VII's purpose is not to smooth the rough edges of our daily discourse" (*Powell v. Yellow Book USA, Inc.*, 445 F.3d 1074 (8th Cir. 2006)). An employer once could be confident that any request that would cause disruption or require involuntary transfers or assignments would be considered an undue hardship and need not be granted. It is no longer possible to have that confidence.

Sometimes, of course, the employer causes the problem. That was the case in *Nichols v. Snow* (2006 WL 167708 (M.D. Tenn.) unpublished). The employee did not belong to the same church as his on-the-job instructor and the instructor did not approve of his charge's lifestyle. The employee was chastised for not attending church and for not putting religion in the forefront of his life. The instructor would comment about the employee's moral/religious inadequacies in front of others and appeared not to have done a very good job training the employee. The employee sought relief and was denied. He sued. The employer claimed none of this amounted to a hostile environment. The court disagreed, finding the employer had a duty to assure that its employees did not have to endure religious indoctrination as part of job training.

When the conduct is less overt, courts continue to struggle with the line between religious expression and hostile environment. For example, a Jewish employee claimed he was subjected to "in your face religious behavior" by the evangelical supervisor and his co-religionists at work. He claimed that work was being diverted by his supervisor and he thought a hostile environment was being created by the religious writings left on his desk and the religious songs that his co-workers sang in the office. He asked to be treated with more respect or even indifference. The employer, noting that no one ever tried to convert him or denigrated his religion, refused (*Ennis v. Sonitrol Mgmt. Corp.*, 2006 WL 177173 (S.D.N.Y.) unpublished).

If the *Nichols v. Snow* court had been hearing this case, it would have found a hostile environment. Absent firm controlling precedent, however, each court is free to make its own rules. Here, the court stayed with the existing principle that where religious hostility is claimed, there must be some abusive or coercive behavior. The court also found that the complainant's religion did not prompt any of the conduct. That is to say, it was not motivated by his particular religion, an odd form of permitting wide-spread conduct that would be banned if more focused. As a result, the court ruled that this environment did not reach the level of hostility prohibited by Title VII.

Managers and supervisors who learn about objectionable workplace conduct based on religion are responsible for taking steps to correct the conduct by anyone under their control. Supervisors should relay all complaints to the appropriate manager and the company should investigate the charges. If it is determined that harassment has taken place, disciplinary action should follow to ensure that the harassment does not continue.

Conclusion

The role of religion in American life and at the workplace is in a constant state of "becoming." As a nation of immigrants and as a country that prides itself on its diversity and on its acceptance of people from all over the world, the United States will inevitably be populated by those with a broad variety of religious beliefs and practices, many of which would have been considered "exotic" just a decade ago. In that evolving demographic context, it is certain that responses of governments, courts, employers and individuals will themselves evolve.

Appendix

Examples of Low-Cost Accommodations for Workers With Disabilities

Reasonable accommodations generally are not extensive or expensive. The U.S. General Accounting Office estimated that half of all accommodations cost employers nothing and another 30 percent cost less than $500. The following examples of effective low-cost assistive devices and accommodations are from the EEOC's Technical Assistance Manual on Title I of the ADA and from the Job Accommodation Network, which is listed in the Resources Directory.

Work hours for an employee whose disability made it difficult to commute during rush hours were changed from 8:30 a.m. – 4:30 p.m. to 10 a.m. – 6 p.m. Cost: nothing.

An employee with diabetes was allowed to have breaks so he could take insulin. The break times were made up by a shorter lunch period. Cost: nothing.

A hearing-impaired medical technician was given a timer with an indicator light so he could perform laboratory tests. Cost: $27.

A clerk who had limited use of her hands was given a lazy susan file holder that enabled her to reach all of the materials needed for her job. Cost: $85.

A groundskeeper who had limited use of one arm was provided a detachable extension arm for a rake. The device enabled him to grasp the handle with his impaired hand and control the rake with his functional arm. Cost: $20.

The desk layout was changed from right to left for a visually impaired data entry clerk. Cost: nothing.

A telephone amplifier was provided to a plant worker with a hearing impairment whose hearing aid alone was insufficient to enable him to converse on the telephone. Cost: $24.

A light probe that gives an audible signal when held over an illuminated source enabled a blind receptionist to determine which phone lines were ringing, on hold or in use. Cost: $50 to $100.

A one-handed can opener was provided to a food service worker with one hand who could perform all of her job's essential functions except opening cans. Cost: $35.

A light weight mop and smaller broom enabled an employee with Down's syndrome and congenital heart defects to do his job. Cost: under $40.

A special wrist splint used with a glove designed for skin divers made it possible for a truck driver with carpal tunnel syndrome that limited his wrist movement and caused discomfort in cold weather to drive in extreme weather conditions. Cost: $55.

An insurance salesman with cerebral palsy was given a headset that enabled him to write while talking to clients. Rental cost: $6 per month.

A cardboard form called a "jig" make it possible for an employee with a mental impairment to properly fold jeans as a stock clerk in a retail store. Cost: nothing.

An electro-mechanical assembly crew member with cumulative trauma disorder in his wrist and hand was provided with a rechargeable electric screwdriver. The device worked so well that all workers in similar positions were provided with one. Cost: $65.

Tax Credits and Funding Sources for Disability Accommodations

There are many sources of information about disabilities and reasonable accommodations, including organizations that will give advice on specific types of accommodations for various impairments. Financial assistance for providing reasonable accommodations is also available. The following list is compiled from a variety of sources, including information provided by the EEOC.

Financial Assistance

There are several sources of financial assistance to help employers make accommodations and comply with the ADA's requirements.

Tax Credit for Small Business *(Internal Revenue Code §44)*

Congress established a special tax credit to help smaller employers make accommodations required by the ADA. Eligible small businesses may take a tax credit of up to $5000 per year for accommodations made to comply with the ADA. The credit is available for one-half the cost of eligible access expenditures that are more than $250 but less than $10,250. For example, if the accommodation costs $10,250, an employer could get a tax credit of $5000 or $10,250 minus $250, divided by 2. If the accommodation costs $7000, a tax credit of $3375 would be available.

An eligible small business is one with gross receipts of $1 million or less for the taxable year or 30 or fewer full-time employees.

Eligible expenditures for which the tax credit may be taken include the types of accommodations required under Title I of the ADA as well as accessibility requirements for commercial facilities and places of public accommodation under Title III. To be eligible for the tax credit, changes made to remove barriers or to provide services, materials or equipment must meet technical standards of the ADA Accessibility Guidelines where applicable.

Tax Deduction for Architectural and Transportation Barrier Removal *(Internal Revenue Code §190)*

Any business may take a full tax deduction, up to $15,000 per year, for expenses of removing specified architectural or transportation barriers. Expenses covered include costs of removing barriers created by steps, narrow doors, inaccessible parking spaces, toilet facilities and transportation vehicles. Both the tax credit and the tax deduction are available to eligible small businesses. For example, if a small business makes a qualified expenditure of $24,000, it may take the $5000 tax credit for the initial $10,250 and, if the remaining $13,750 qualifies under Section 190, may deduct that amount from its taxable income.

Information on the Section 44 tax credit and the Section 190 tax deduction can be obtained from a local IRS office or by contacting:
Internal Revenue Service
U.S. Department of the Treasury
Office of Chief Counsel
1111 Constitution Ave. NW,
Washington, DC 20224
202-566-3292 (voice)
800-829-4059 (TDD)
800-829-3676 (publications and forms)
www.irs.ustreas.gov

Work Opportunity Tax Credit

Tax credits also are available under the Work Opportunity Tax Credit Program, which replaced the Targeted Jobs Tax Credit Program. Credits are available to employers who hire, among other groups, individuals with disabilities who are receiving or have recently received welfare. This credit also includes individuals with disabilities who have completed or are completing rehabilitative services from a state-certified agency, an employment network or the U.S. Department of Veterans Affairs.

Employers are eligible to receive up to $2,400 for each new hire, $1,200 for each new summer youth hire and $9,000 for each new long-term family assistance recipient hired over a two-year period.

All new adult employees must work a minimum of 120 or 400 hours and individuals hired as summer youth employees must work at least 90 days, between May 1 and Sept. 15, before an employer is eligible to claim the tax credit.

More information can be obtained from the Department of Labor at http://www.doleta.gov/business/incentives/opptax/. Internal Revenue Service form 8850, the Work Opportunity Tax Credit Pre-Screening Notice and Certification Request, is available at www.irs.gov.

Other Funding Sources

State or local vocational rehabilitation agencies and state commissions for the blind can provide financial assistance for equipment and accommodations for their clients. The U.S. Department of Veterans Affairs also provides financial assistance to disabled veterans for equipment needed to help perform jobs. Some organizations that serve people with particular types of disabilities also provide financial assistance for needed accommodations. Other types of assistance may be available in the community. For example, independent living centers provide transportation service to the workplace for people with disabilities.

Resource Directory for Disability Accommodations

U.S. Equal Employment Opportunity Commission

A key source of information on reasonable accommodations under Title I of the ADA is the federal Equal Employment Opportunity Commission.

Office of Legal Counsel
ADA Policy Division
1801 L St. NW
Washington, DC 20507
800-669-4000
202-663-4900 (voice)
202-663-4494 (TTY)
www.eeoc.gov

Disability and Business Technical Assistance Centers (DBTAC)

800-949-4232 (voice & TTY)
www.dbtac.vcu.edu

Ten regional centers are funded through the U.S. Department of Education. The toll-free number will automatically connect callers to the center that serves their area. Regional centers are:

Region 1 *(Connecticut, Maine, Massachusetts, New Hampshire, Rhode Island, Vermont)*
New England DBTAC
Adaptive Environments Center Inc.
180-200 Portland St., First Floor
Boston, MA 02114
617-695-1225 (voice & TTY)
adainfo@newenglandada.org
www.newenglandada.org

Region 2 *(New Jersey, New York, Puerto Rico, Virgin Islands)*
Northeast DBTAC
Cornell University
Northeast ADA & IT Center
201 ILR Extension
Ithaca, NY 14853
607-255-8660 (voice)
607-255-6686 (TTY)
dbtacnortheast@cornell.edu
www.northeastada.org

Region 3 *(Delaware, District of Columbia, Maryland, Pennsylvania, Virginia, West Virginia)*
Mid-Atlantic DBTAC
TransCen Inc.
451 Hungerford Dr., Suite 700
Rockville, MD 20850
301-217-0124 (voice & TTY)
adainfo@transcen.org
www.adainfo.org

Region 4 *(Alabama, Florida, Georgia, Kentucky, Mississippi, North Carolina, South Carolina, Tennessee)*
Southeast DBTAC
Burton Blatt Institute – Syracruse University
490 10th St. NW
Atlanta, GA 30318
404-385-0636 (voice & TTY)
sedbtacproject@law.syr.edu
www.sedbtac.org

Region 5 *(Illinois, Indiana, Michigan, Minnesota, Ohio, Wisconsin)*
Great Lakes DBTAC
University of Illinois at Chicago
Department of Disability and Human Development
1640 W. Roosevelt Rd.
Chicago, IL 60608
312-413-1407 (voice & TTY)
gldbtac@uic.edu
www.adagreatlakes.org

Region 6 *(Arkansas, Louisiana, New Mexico, Oklahoma, Texas)*
Southwest DBTAC
Independent Living Research Utilization
2323 S. Shepherd Blvd., Suite 1000
Houston, TX 77019
713-520-0232 (voice & TTY)
dlrp@ilru.org
www.dlrp.org

Region 7 *(Iowa, Kansas, Missouri, Nebraska)*
Great Plains DBTAC
University of Missouri at Columbia
100 Corporate Lake Dr.
Columbia, MO 65203
573-882-3600 (voice & TTY)
ada@missouri.edu
www.adaproject.org

Region 8 *(Colorado, Montana, North Dakota, South Dakota, Utah, Wyoming)*
Rocky Mountain DBTAC
Meeting the Challenge Inc.
3630 Sinton Rd., Suite 103
Colorado Springs, CO 80907
719-444-0268 (voice & TTY)
technicalassistance@mtc-inc.com
www.adainformation.org/

Region 9 *(Arizona, California, Hawaii, Nevada, Pacific Basin)*
Pacific ADA and IT Center DBTAC
555 12th St., Suite 1030
Oakland, CA 94607
510-285-5600 (voice & TTY)
adatech@adapacific.org
www.adapacific.org

Region 10 *(Alaska, Idaho, Oregon, Washington)*
Western Washington University
6912 220th St. SW #105
Mountlake Terrace, WA 98043
800-949-4232 (voice & TTY)
dbtaccnw@wwu.edu
www.dbtacnorthwest.org

Other Federal Government Agencies

Other agencies, listed alphabetically, may provide assistance in specific areas.

Access Board
Chairman
1331 F St. NW, Suite 1000
Washington, DC 20004-1111
800-872-2253 (ADA hotline)
800-993-2822 (TTY)
202-272-0080 (general information)
202-272-0082 (TTY)
info@access-board.gov
www.access-board.gov

Environmental Protection Agency
Director, Office of Civil Rights (1201A)
1200 Pennsylvania Ave. NW
Washington, DC 20460
202-564-7272
civilrights@epa.gov
www.epa.gov/ocr

Federal Communications Commission
Office of Workplace Diversity
445 12th St. SW
Washington, DC 20554
88825-5322 (voice)
888-835-5322 (TTY)
fccinfo@fcc.gov
www.fcc.gov/owd

General Services Administration
EEO Officer, Office of Equal Opportunity
1800 F St. NW, Room 5127
Washington, DC 20405
202-501-0767 (voice & TTY)
ocr@gsa.gov
www.gsa.gov/eeo/default.htm

Legal Services Corporation
General Counsel
3333 K St. NW, 3rd Floor
Washington, DC 20007
202-295-1500
info@lsc.gov
www.lsc.gov

National Endowment for the Arts
General Counsel
1100 Pennsylvania Ave. NW, Suite 518
Washington, DC 20506
202-682-5418 (voice)
202-682-5496 (TTY)
www.nea.gov

Director of Civil Rights Office
1100 Pennsylvania Ave. NW, Room 219
Washington, DC 20506
202-682-5454 (voice)
202-682-5695 (TTY)
www.nea.gov/about/civil.html

National Endowment for the Humanities
General Counsel
1100 Pennsylvania Ave. NW, Room 530
Washington, DC 20506
202-606-8322 (voice)
202-606-8282 (TTY)
fencounsel@neh.gov
www.neh.gov

National Science Foundation
Director, Office of Equal Opportunity Programs
4201 Wilson Blvd.
Arlington, VA 22230
703-292-5111 (voice)
703-292-5090 (TTY)
info@nsf.gov
www.nsf.gov/od/oco

U.S. Department of Agriculture
Director, Office of Civil Rights
1400 Independence Ave. SW
Washington, DC 20250
202-720-3808
ascr@usda.gov
www.usda.gov/cr

U.S. Department of Commerce
Director, Office of Civil Rights
1401 Constitution Ave. NW Room 6012
Washington, DC 20230
202-482-0625 (voice)
saramaki@doc.gov
www.osec.doc.gov/ocr

U.S. Department of Defense
Director, Computer/Electronic Accommodations
  Program
5111 Leesburg Pike, Suite 810
Falls Church, VA 22041
703-681-8813 (voice)
703-681-0881 (TTY)
cap@tma.osd.mil
www.tricare.osd.mil/

U.S. Department of Energy
Director, Office of Civil Rights
1000 Independence Ave. SW, Room 5B168
Washington, DC 20585
800-342-5363 (voice)
www.doe.gov

U.S. Department of Health and Human Services
Commissioner, Administration on Developmental
  Disabilities
Mail Stop: HHH 405-D
370 L'Enfant Promenade SW
Washington, DC 20447
202-690-6590
www.acf.hhs.gov/programs/add

**U.S. Department of Housing and Urban
  Development**
Office of General Counsel
451 7th St. SW
Washington, DC 20410
202-708-1112 (voice)
202-708-1455 (TTY)
www.hud.gov

**Director, Office of Program Compliance and
  Disability Rights Support Division**
451 7th St. SW, Room 5240
Washington, DC 20410
800-669-9777 (voice)
www.hud.gov

U.S. Department of the Interior
Director, Office of Civil Rights
1849 C St. NW, Mail Stop 5214
Washington, DC 20240
202-208-5693 (voice)
202-208-5998 (TTY)
Sharon_Eller@ios.doi.gov
www.doi.gov/diversity

U.S. Department of Labor
Director, Office of Disability Employment Policy
200 Constitution Ave. NW
Washington, DC 20210
800-633-7365 (voice)
877-889-5627 (TTY)
civilrightscenter@dol.gov
www.dol.gov/odep

U.S. Department of State
Assistant Secretary for Civil Rights
2201 C St. NW, Room 4216
Washington, DC 20520
202-647-9294
socrweb@state.gov
www.state.gov

U.S. Department of Transportation
Federal Transit Administration
Director, Office of Civil Rights
400 7th St. SW, Room 9100
Washington, DC 20590
888-446-4511
ada.assistance@fta.dot.gov
www.fta.dot.gov/civil_rights.html

U.S. Department of Veterans Affairs
Deputy Assistant Secretary
Office of Resolution Management (08)
1575 I St. NW
Washington, DC 20005
800-827-1000 (voice)
800-829-4833 (TTY)
www.va.gov

Other Government Offices

Job Accommodation Network
West Virginia University
P.O. Box 6080
Morgantown, WV 26506-6080
800-526-7234 (voice)
817-781-9403 (TTY)
800- ADA-WORK (ADA information)
304-293-7186 (voice worldwide)
jan@jan.wvu.edu
http://jan.wvu.edu

National Council on Disability
1331 F St. NW, Suite 850
Washington, DC 20004-1107
202-272-2004 (voice)
202-272-2074 (TTY)
mquigley@ncd.gov
www.ncd.gov

**National Institute on Disability and
  Rehabilitation Research**
400 Maryland Ave. SW
Washington, DC 20202-2572
202-245-7640 (voice & TTY)
www.ed.gov/about/offices/list/osers/nidrr/index.
  html

**National Library Services for the Blind and
  Physically Handicapped**
Library of Congress
Washington, DC 20542
202-707-5100 (voice)
202-707-0744 (TTY)
nls@loc.gov
www.loc.gov/nls

National Trust for Historic Preservation
1785 Massachusetts Ave. NW
Washington, DC 20036
202-588-6000 (voice)
feedbacl@nthp.org
www.nationaltrust.org

Office of Disability Employment Policy
200 Constitution Ave. NW, Room 51303
Washington, DC 20210
866-633-7365 (voice)
866-889-5627 (TTY)
www.dol.gov/odep/index.html

U.S. Department of Education
Rehabilitation Services Administration
400 Maryland Ave. SW
Washington, DC 20202
202-245-7488
www.ed.gov/about/offices/llist/osers/rsa/index.
html

Office of Special Education
400 Maryland Ave. SW
Washington, DC 20202
202-245-7468 (voice)
www.ed.gov/about/offices/list/osers/osep/index.
html

U.S. Department of Housing and Urban Development
Division of Housing for the Elderly and Persons
With Disabilities
Office of Multifamily Housing
451 7th St. SW, Room 6150
Washington, DC 20410
800-877-8339 (TTY)
202-708-2866 (voice)
202-708-9300 (TTY)
www.hud.gov

U.S. House of Representatives
House Committee on Education and Labor
2181 Rayburn House Office Building
Washington, DC 20515
202-225-3725 (voice)
202-226-3116 (TTY)
www.edworkforce.house.gov/

Office of the Clerk, Legislative Resource Center
B106 Cannon House Office Building
2nd and D St. SW
Washington, DC 20515
202-226-5200
www.clerkweb.house.gov
   Contact this office for information on the status of pending congressional legislation.

U.S. Senate
Senate Committee on Health, Education, Labor and
Pensions
428 Dirksen Senate Office Building
Washington, DC 20510
202-224-5375
www.help.senate.gov/

National Organizations
   There are many national organizations that represent people with disabilities. Umbrella groups, such as the National Organization on Disability, may be able to answer general ADA compliance questions. Other organizations, including the American Council of the Blind, the Paralyzed Veterans of America, the National Association of the Deaf, Epilepsy Foundation of America and the AIDS Action Council are sources for information on accommodating specific disabilities.

ABLEDATA
8630 Fenton St., Suite 930
Silver Spring, MD 20910
800-227-0216
301-608-8912 (TTY)
abledata@verizon.net
www.abledata.com

Academic Software Inc.
3504 Tates Creek Rd.
Lexington, KY 40517
859-552-1020
asistaff@acsw.com
www.acsw.com

AIDS Action Council
1730 M St. NW
Washington, DC 20036
202-530-8030
www.aidsaction.org

Alexander Graham Bell Association for the Deaf and Hard of Hearing
3417 Volta Place NW
Washington, DC 20007
202-337-5220 (voice)
202-337-5221 (TTY)
info@agbell.org
www.agbell.org

Alzheimer's Association
225 N. Michigan Ave., Floor 17
Chicago, IL 60611
800-272-3900
866-403-3073 (TTY)
info@alz.org
www.alz.org

American Association for the Advancement of Science
Science, Technology and Disability Project
1200 New York Ave. NW
Washington, DC 20005
202-326-6400
www.aaas.org

American Autoimmune Related Diseases Association
22100 Gratiot Ave.
East Detroit, MI 48021
800-598-4668
586-776-3900
aarda@aol.com
www.aarda.org

American Cancer Society
1599 Clifton Rd. NE
Atlanta, GA 30329
800-227-2345
866-228-4327 (TTY)
www.cancer.org

American Council of the Blind
1155 15th St. NW, Suite 1004
Washington, DC 20005
800-424-8666
202-467-5081
info@acb.org
www.acb.org

American Diabetes Association
1701 N. Beauregard St.
Alexandria, VA 22311
800-342-2383
AskADA@diabetes.org
www.diabetes.org

American Foundation for the Blind
11 Penn Plaza, Suite 300
New York, NY 10011
800-232-5463
afbinfo@afb.net
www.afb.org

American Heart Association
7272 Greenville Ave.
Dallas, TX 75321-4596
800-242-8721
www.americanheart.org

American Institute of Architects
1735 New York Ave. NW
Washington, DC 20006
202-626-7300 (voice)
infocentral@aia.org
www.aia.org

American Kidney Fund
6110 Executive Blvd., Suite 1010
Rockville, MD 20852-3903
800-638-8299
helpline@kidneyfund.org
www.akfinc.org

American Liver Foundation
75 Maiden Lane, Suite 603
New York, NY 10038
800-465-4837
info@liverfoundation.org
www.liverfoundation.org

American National Standards Institute Inc.
25 W. 43rd St., 4th Floor
New York, NY 10036
212-642-4900
info@ansi.org
www.ansi.org

American Occupational Therapy Association
4720 Montgomery Lane
P.O. Box 31220
Bethesda, MD 20824
301-652-2682 (voice)
800-377-8555 (TTY)
www.aota.org

American Social Health Association
P.O. Box 13827
Research Triangle Park, NC 27709
919-361-8400
info@ashastd.org
www.ashastd.org

American Speech, Language and Hearing Association
10801 Rockville Pike
Rockville, MD 20852
800-638-8255 (voice)
301-897-5700 ext. 4157 (TTY)
actioncenter@asha.org
www.asha.org

Arthritis Foundation
P.O. Box 7669
Atlanta, GA 30357
800-283-7800
help@arthritis.org
www.arthritis.org

Association of University Centers on Disabilities
1010 Wayne Ave., Suite 920
Silver Spring, MD 20910
301-588-8252
gclark@aucd.org
www.aucd.org

Association on Higher Education and Disability
107 Commerce Center Dr., Suite 204
Huntersville, NC 28078
704-947-779 (voice & TTY)
AHEAD@ahead.org
www.ahead.org

Asthma and Allergy Foundation of America
1233 20th St. NW, Suite 402
Washington, DC 20036
800-727-8462
info@aafa.org
www.aafa.org

Autism Society of America
7910 Woodmont Ave., Suite 300
Bethesda, MD 20814
800-328-8476
www.autism-society.org

Bazelon Center for Mental Health Law
1101 15th St. NW, Suite 1212
Washington, DC 20005
202-467-5730 (voice)
202-467-4232 (TTY)
info@bazelon.org
www.bazelon.org

Canine Assistants
3160 Francis Rd.
Alpharetta, GA 30004
770-664-7178
info@canineassistants.org
www.canineassistants.org

Canine Companions for Independence
National Headquarters
P.O. Box 446
Santa Rose, CA 95402-0446
800-572-2275 (voice & TTY)
info@cci.org
www.caninecompanions.org

Canine Helpers for the Handicapped
5699 Ridge Rd.
Lockport, NY 14094
716-433-4035 (voice & TTY)
chhdogs@aol.com
http://caninehelpers.netfirms.com

Carnegie Library for the Blind and Physically Handicapped
Leonard C. Staisey Building
4724 Baum Blvd.
Pittsburgh, PA 15213
800-242-0586 (in Pennsylvania)
412-687-2440
lbph@carnegielibrary.org
www.clpgh.org/locations/lbph

Center on Education and Work
School of Education
University of Wisconsin-Madison
1025 W. Johnson St., Room 964
Madison, WI 53706
608-265-6700
800-862-1071
cewmail@education.wisc.edu
www.cew.wisc.edu

Children and Adults With Attention Deficit Disorders
8181 Professional Place, Suite 150
Landover, MD 20785
800-233-4050
301-306-7070
www.chadd.org

Christopher Reeve Paralysis Association
636 Morris Turnpike
Springfield, NJ 07087
800-225-0292
prc@christopherreeve.org
www.christopherreeve.org

Crohn's and Colitis Foundation of America
386 Park Ave. S, 17th Floor
New York, NY 10016
800-932-2423
info@ccfa.org
www.ccfa.org

Council for Exceptional Children
1110 N. Glebe Rd., Suite 300
Arlington, VA 22201
800-224-6820 (voice)
866-915-5000 (TTY)
service@cec.sped.org
www.cec.sped.org

Disability Rights Education and Defense Fund Inc.
2212 6th St.
Berkley, CA 94710
510-644-2555 (voice & TTY)
info@dredf.org
www.dredf.org

Disability Rights Legal Center
919 Albany St.
Los Angeles, CA 90015
213-736-1031 (voice)
213-736-8310 (TTY)
drlc@lls.edu
www.disabilityrightslegalcenter.org

Disabled American Veterans
3725 Alexandria Pike
Cold Spring, KY 41076
859-441-7300
www.dav.org

Epilepsy Foundation
8301 Professional Place
Landover, MD 20785
800-332-1000
www.epilepsyfoundation.org

Forum for State Health Policy Leadership
444 N. Capitol St. NW, Suite 515
Washington, DC 20001
202-624-5400
Donna.folkemer@ncsi.org
www.ncsl.org/health/forum

Gallaudet Interpreting Service
Gallaudet University
Fay House
800 Florida Ave. NE
Washington, DC 20002
202-651-5199 (voice & TTY)
gis@gallaudet.edu
http://gis.gallaudet.edu

HEATH Resource Center
The George Washington University
2134 G St. NW
Washington, DC 20052
202-973-0904 (voice & TTY)
askheath@gwu.edu
www.heath.gwu.edu

Helen Keller National Center
141 Middle Neck Rd.
Sands Point, NY 11050
516-944-8900
HKNCinfo@hknc.com
www.helenkeller.org

Helping Hands
541 Cambridge St.
Boston, MA 02134
617-787-4419
www.helpinghandsmonkeys.org

Human Factors and Ergonomics Society
P.O. Box 1369
Santa Monica, CA 90406
310-394-1811
info@hfes.org
http://hfes.org

Huntington's Disease Society of America
505 8th Ave., Suite 902
New York, NY 10018
800-345-4372
212-242-1968
hdsainfo@hdsa.org
www.hdsa.org

International Dyslexia Association
40 York Rd.
Baltimore, MD 21204
410-296-0232
info@interdys.org
www.interdys.org

Juvenile Diabetes Research Foundation International
120 Wall St., 19th Floor
New York, NY 10005
800-533-2873
info@jdrf.org
www.jdrf.org

Learning Disabilities Association of America
4156 Library Road
Pittsburgh, PA 15234
412-341-1515
info@ldaamerica.org
www.LDAAmerica.org

Leukemia and Lymphoma Society of America
1311 Mamaroneck Ave.
White Plains, NY 10605
800-955-4572
914-949-5213
www.leukemia.org

Lupus Foundation of America
2000 L St. NW, Suite 710
Washington, DC 20036
800-558-0121
info@lupus.org
www.lupus.org

Muscular Dystrophy Association
3300 E. Sunrise Dr.
Tucson, AZ 85718
800-344-4863
mda@mdausa.org
www.mdausa.org

National Amputation Foundation
40 Church St.
Malverne, NY 11565
516-887-3600
amps76@aol.com
www.nationalamputation.org

National Association for the Visually Handicapped
22 W. 21st St., 6th Floor
New York, NY 10010
212-889-3141
navh@navh.org
www.navh.org

National Association of ADA Coordinators
P.O. Box 958
Rancho Mirage, CA 92270
800-722-4232 (voice)
naadac@aol.com
www.jan.wvu.edu/naadac

National Association of the Deaf
8630 Fenton St., Suite 820
Silver Spring, MD 20910
301-587-1788 (voice)
301-587-1789 (TTY)
www.nad.org

National Disability Rights Network
900 2nd St. NE, Suite 211
Washington, DC 20002
202-408-9514 (voice)
202-408-9521 (TTY)
info@ndrn.org
www.ndrn.org

National Black Deaf Advocates
P.O. Box 1126
Asheville, NC 28802
president@nbda.org
www.nbda.org

National Captioning Institute
1900 Gallows Rd., Suite 3000
Vienna, VA 22182
703-917-7600 (voice & TTY)
mail@ncihelpdesk.org
www.ncicap.org

National Center for Disability Services
201 I.U. Willets Rd.
Albertson, NY 11507
516-465-1400
www.ncds.org

National Council on Independent Living
1710 Rhode Island Ave. NW 5th Floor
Washington, DC 20036
877-525-3400 (voice & TTY)
292-207-0334
202-207-0340 (TTY)
ncil@ncil.org
www.ncil.org

National Dissemination Center for Children With Disabilities
P.O. Box 1492
Washington, DC 20013
800-695-0285 (voice & TTY)
nichcy@aed.org
www.nichcy.org

National Down Syndrome Society
666 Broadway
New York, NY 10012
800-221-4602
info@ndss.org
www.ndss.org

National Easter Seal Society
230 W. Monroe St., Suite 1800
Chicago, IL 60606-4802
312-726-6200 (voice)
312-726-4258 (TTY)
www.easter-seals.com

National Federation of the Blind
1800 Johnson St.
Baltimore, MD 21230
410-659-9314
nfb@nfb.org
www.nfb.org

National Health Information Center
P.O. Box 1133
Washington, DC 20013-1133
800-336-4797
301-565-4167
info@nhic.org
www.health.gov/nhic/

National Hemophilia Foundation
116 West 32nd St., 11th Floor
New York, NY 10001
212-328-3700
handi@hemophilia.org
www.hemophilia.org

National Kidney Foundation
30 E. 33rd St., Suite 1100
New York, NY 10016
800-622-9010
www.kidney.org

National Mental Health Association
2000 N. Beauregard St., 6th Floor
Alexandria, VA 22311
800-969-6642 (voice)
800-433-5959 (TTY)
www.nmha.org

National Multiple Sclerosis Society
733 3rd Ave., 3rd Floor
New York, NY 10017
800-344-4867
www.nmss.org

National Organization on Disability
910 16th St. NW, Suite 600
Washington, DC 20006
202-293-5960 (voice)
202-293-5968 (TTY)
ability@nod.org
www.nod.org

National Osteoporosis Foundation
1232 22nd St. NW
Washington, DC 20037
202-223-2226
grassroots@nof.org
www.nof.org

National Parkinson Foundation
Bob Hope Parkinson
Research Center
1501 N.W. 9th Ave.
Miami, FL 33136
800-327-4545
305-243-6666
contact@parkinson.org
www.parkinson.org

National Rehabilitation Association
633 S. Washington St.
Alexandria, VA 22314
703-836-0850 (voice)
703-836-0849 (TTY)
info@nationalrehab.org
www.nationalrehab.org

National Rehabilitation Information Center
8201 Corporate Dr., Suite 600
Landover, MD 20785
800-346-2742 (voice)
301-459-5900 (voice & TTY)
301-459-5984 (TTY)
naricinfo@heitechservices.com
www.naric.com

National Spinal Cord Injury Association
1 Church St., #600
Rockville, MD 20850
800-962-9629
301-214-4006
info@spinalcord.org
www.spinalcord.org

National Technical Institute for the Deaf
Rochester Institute of Technology
52 Lomb Memorial Drive
Rochester, NY 14623
585-475-6400 (voice & TTY)
585-475-6700 (admissions)
ntidmc@rit.edu
www.rit.edu/NTID

One on One Computer Training
P.O. Box 12038
Durham, NC 27709
800-424-8668
www.oootraining.com

Paralyzed Veterans of America
801 18th St. NW
Washington, DC 20006
800-424-8200 (voice)
800-795-4327 (TTY)
info@pva.org
www.pva.org

Recording for the Blind and Dyslexic
20 Roszel Road
Princeton, NJ 08540
866-732-3585
custserv@rfbd.org
www.rfbd.org/

Registry of Interpreters for the Deaf Inc.
333 Commerce St.
Alexandria, VA 22314
703-838-0030 (voice)
703-838-0459 (TTY)
office@rid.org
www.rid.org

Research and Training Center for Access to Rehabilitation and
Economic Opportunity
Howard University
1840 7th St. NW, 2nd Floor
Washington, DC 20001
202-865-8140
www.hurtc.org

Self Help for Hard of Hearing People Inc.
7910 Woodmont Ave., Suite 1200
Bethesda, MD 20814
301-657-2248 (voice & TTY)
www.shhh.org

Spina Bifida Association of America
4590 MacArthur Blvd. NW, Suite 250
Washington, DC 20007
800-621-3141
202-944-3295
sbaa@sbaa.org
www.sbaa.org

TASH
1025 Vermont Ave., 7th Floor
Washington, DC 20005
202-263-5600
btrader@tash.org
www.tash.org/

Telecommunications for the Deaf Inc.
8630 Fenton St., Suite 604
Silver Spring, MD 20910
301-589-3786 (voice)
301-589-3006 (TTY)
info@tdi-online.org
www.tdi-online.org

The ARC
1010 Wayne Ave., Suite 650
Silver Spring, MD 20910
301-565-3842
info@thearc.org
http://thearc.org

Tourette Syndrome Association Inc.
42-40 Bell Blvd., Suite 205
Bayside, NY 11361
718-224-2999
www.tsa-usa.org

Trace Research and Development Center
University of Wisconsin-Madison
2107 Engineering Centers Building
1550 Engineering Dr.
Madison, WI 53706
608-262-6966 (voice)
608-263-5408 (TTY)
info@trace.wisc.edu
http://trace.wisc.edu/

United Cerebral Palsy Association
1660 L St., Suite 700
Washington, DC 20036
800-872-5827
info@ucp.org
www.ucp.org

United Spinal Association
75-20 Astoria Blvd.
Jackson Heights, NY 11370
718-803-3782
info@unitedspinal.org
www.unitedspinal.org

World Institute on Disability
510 16th St., Suite 100
Oakland, CA 94612
510-763-4100 (voice)
510-208-9493 (TTY)
wid@wid.org
www.wid.org

Enforcement Guidance: Reasonable Accommodation and Undue Hardship Under the Americans With Disabilities Act

Introduction

This Enforcement Guidance clarifies the rights and responsibilities of employers and individuals with disabilities regarding reasonable accommodation and undue hardship. Title I of the ADA requires an employer to provide reasonable accommodation to qualified individuals with disabilities who are employees or applicants for employment, except when such accommodation would cause an undue hardship. This Guidance sets forth an employer's legal obligations regarding reasonable accommodation; however, employers may provide more than the law requires.

This Guidance examines what "reasonable accommodation" means and who is entitled to receive it. The Guidance addresses what constitutes a request for reasonable accommodation, the form and substance of the request, and an employer's ability to ask questions and seek documentation after a request has been made.

The Guidance discusses reasonable accommodations applicable to the hiring process and to the benefits and privileges of employment. The Guidance also covers different types of reasonable accommodations related to job performance, including job restructuring, leave, modified or part-time schedules, modified workplace policies, and reassignment. Questions concerning the relationship between the ADA and the Family and Medical Leave Act (FMLA) are examined as they affect leave and modified schedules. Reassignment issues addressed include who is entitled to reassignment and the extent to which an employer must search for a vacant position. The Guidance also examines issues concerning the interplay between reasonable accommodations and conduct rules.

The final section of this Guidance discusses undue hardship, including when requests for schedule modifications and leave may be denied.

General Principles

Reasonable Accommodation

Title I of the Americans With Disabilities Act of 1990 (the "ADA")[1] requires an employer[2] to provide reasonable accommodation to qualified individuals with disabilities who are employees or applicants for employment, unless to do so would cause undue hardship. "In general, an accommodation is any change in the work environment or in the way things are customarily done that enables an individual with a disability to enjoy equal employment opportunities."[3] There are three categories of "reasonable accommodations":

"(i) modifications or adjustments to a job application process that enable a qualified applicant with a disability to be considered for the position such qualified applicant desires; or

(ii) modifications or adjustments to the work environment, or to the manner or circumstances under which the position held or desired is customarily performed, that enable a qualified individual with a disability to perform the essential functions of that position; or

(iii) modifications or adjustments that enable a covered entity's employee with a disability to enjoy equal benefits and privileges of employment as are enjoyed by its other similarly situated employees without disabilities."[4]

---

[1] 42 U.S.C. 12101-12117, 12201-12213 (1994) (codified as amended).

The analysis in this guidance applies to federal sector complaints of nonaffirmative action employment discrimination arising under Section 501 of the Rehabilitation Act of 1973. 29 U.S.C. §791(g) (1994). It also applies to complaints of nonaffirmative action employment discrimination arising under Section 503 and employment discrimination under Section 504 of the Rehabilitation Act. 29 U.S.C. §793(d), §794(d) (1994).

The ADA's requirements regarding reasonable accommodation and undue hardship supercede any state or local disability antidiscrimination laws to the extent that they offer less protection than the ADA. *See* 29 C.F.R. §1630.1(c)(2) (1997).

[2] In addition to employers, the ADA requires employment agencies, labor organizations, and joint labor-management committees to provide reasonable accommodations. *See* 42 U.S.C. §12112(a), (b)(5)(A) (1994).

[3] 29 C.F.R. pt. 1630 app. §1630.2(o) (1997).

[4] 29 C.F.R. §1630.2(o)(1)(i-iii) (1997). The notices that employers and labor unions must post informing applicants, employees, and members of labor organizations of their ADA rights must include a description of the reasonable accommodation requirement. These notices, which must be in an accessible format, are available from the EEOC. *See* the Appendix.

The duty to provide reasonable accommodation is a fundamental statutory requirement because of the nature of discrimination faced by individuals with disabilities. Although many individuals with disabilities can apply for and perform jobs without any reasonable accommodations, there are workplace barriers that keep others from performing jobs which they could do with some form of accommodation. These barriers may be physical obstacles (such as inaccessible facilities or equipment), or they may be procedures or rules (such as rules concerning when work is performed, when breaks are taken, or how essential or marginal functions are performed). Reasonable accommodation removes workplace barriers for individuals with disabilities.

Reasonable accommodation is available to qualified applicants and employees with disabilities.[5] Reasonable accommodations must be provided to qualified employees regardless of whether they work part-time or full-time, or are considered "probationary." Generally, the individual with a disability must inform the employer that an accommodation is needed.[6]

There are a number of possible reasonable accommodations that an employer may have to provide in connection with modifications to the work environment or adjustments in how and when a job is performed. These include:

- making existing facilities accessible;
- job restructuring;
- part-time or modified work schedules;
- acquiring or modifying equipment;
- changing tests, training materials or policies;
- providing qualified readers or interpreters; and
- reassignment to a vacant position.[7]

A modification or adjustment is "reasonable" if it "seems reasonable on its face, i.e., ordinarily or in the run of cases";[8] this means it is "reasonable" if it appears to be "feasible" or "plausible."[9] An accommodation also must be effective in meeting the needs of the individual.[10] In the context of job performance, this means that a reasonable accommodation enables the individual to perform the essential functions of the position. Similarly, a reasonable accommodation enables an applicant with a disability to have an equal opportunity to participate in the application process and to be considered for a job. Finally, a reasonable accommodation allows an employee with a disability an equal opportunity to enjoy the benefits and privileges of employment that employees without disabilities enjoy.

Example A: An employee with a hearing disability must be able to contact the public by telephone. The employee proposes that he use a TTY[11] to call a relay service operator who can then place the telephone call and relay the conversation between the parties. This is "reasonable" because a TTY is a common device used to facilitate communication between hearing and hearing-impaired individuals. Moreover, it would be effective in enabling the employee to perform his job.

Example B: A cashier easily becomes fatigued because of lupus and, as a result, has difficulty making it through her shift. The employee requests a stool because sitting greatly reduces the fatigue. This accommodation is reasonable because it is a common-sense solution to remove a workplace barrier – being required to stand – when the job can be effectively performed sitting down. This "reasonable" accommodation is effective because it addresses the employee's fatigue and enables her to perform her job.

---

[5]All examples used in this document assume that the applicant or employee has an ADA "disability."

Individuals with a relationship or association with a person with a disability are not entitled to receive reasonable accommodations. *See Den Hartog v. Wasatch Academy*, 129 F.3d 1076, 1084 (10th Cir. 1997).

[6]*See* 29 C.F.R. pt. 1630 app. §1630.9 (1997); see also H.R. Rep. No. 101-485, pt. 3, at 39 (1990) [hereinafter House Judiciary Report]; H.R. Rep. No. 101-485, pt. 2, at 65 (1990) [hereinafter House Education and Labor Report]; S. Rep. No. 101-116, at 34 (1989) [hereinafter Senate Report].

For more information concerning requests for a reasonable accommodation, *see* Questions 1-4, *infra*. For a discussion of the limited circumstance under which an employer would be required to ask an individual with a disability whether s/he needed a reasonable accommodation, *see* Question 40, *infra*.

[7]42 U.S.C. 12111(9) (1994); 29 C.F.R. §1630.2(o)(2)(i-ii) (1997).

[8]*US Airways, Inc. v. Barnett*, 535 U.S. 391, 122 S. Ct. 1516, 1523 (2002).

[9]*Id.*

Some courts have said that in determining whether an accommodation is "reasonable," one must look at the costs of the accommodation in relation to its benefits. *See, e.g., Monette v. Electronic Data Sys. Corp.*, 90 F.3d 1173, 1184 n.10 (6th Cir. 1996); *Vande Zande v. Wisconsin Dept. of Admin.*, 44 F.3d 538, 543 (7th Cir. 1995). This "cost/benefit" analysis has no foundation in the statute, regulations, or legislative history of the ADA. See 42 U.S.C. §12111(9), (10) (1994); 29 C.F.R. §1630.2(o), (p) (1997); *see also* Senate Report, *supra* note 6, at 31-35; House Education and Labor Report, *supra* note 6, at 57-58.

[10]*See US Airways, Inc. v. Barnett*, 535 U.S. 391, 122 S. Ct. 1516, 1522 (2002). The Court explained that "in ordinary English the word 'reasonable' does not mean 'effective.' It is the word 'accommodation,' not the word 'reasonable,' that conveys the need for effectiveness." *Id.*

[11]A TTY is a device that permits individuals with hearing and speech impairments to communicate by telephone.

Example C: A cleaning company rotates its staff to different floors on a monthly basis. One crew member has a psychiatric disability. While his mental illness does not affect his ability to perform the various cleaning functions, it does make it difficult to adjust to alterations in his daily routine. The employee has had significant difficulty adjusting to the monthly changes in floor assignments. He asks for a reasonable accommodation and proposes three options: staying on one floor permanently, staying on one floor for two months and then rotating, or allowing a transition period to adjust to a change in floor assignments. These accommodations are reasonable because they appear to be feasible solutions to this employee's problems dealing with changes to his routine. They also appear to be effective because they would enable him to perform his cleaning duties.

There are several modifications or adjustments that are not considered forms of reasonable accommodation.[12] An employer does not have to eliminate an essential function, i.e., a fundamental duty of the position. This is because a person with a disability who is unable to perform the essential functions, with or without reasonable accommodation,[13] is not a "qualified" individual with a disability within the meaning of the ADA. Nor is an employer required to lower production standards – whether qualitative or quantitative[14] – that are applied uniformly to employees with and without disabilities. However, an employer may have to provide reasonable accommodation to enable an employee with a disability to meet the production standard. While an employer is not required to eliminate an essential function or lower a production standard, it may do so if it wishes.

An employer does not have to provide as reasonable accommodations personal use items needed in accomplishing daily activities both on and off the job. Thus, an employer is not required to provide an employee with a prosthetic limb, a wheelchair, eyeglasses, hearing aids, or similar devices if they are also needed off the job. Furthermore, an employer is not required to provide personal use amenities,

such as a hot pot or refrigerator, if those items are not provided to employees without disabilities. However, items that might otherwise be considered personal may be required as reasonable accommodations where they are specifically designed or required to meet job-related rather than personal needs.[15]

Undue Hardship

The only statutory limitation on an employer's obligation to provide "reasonable accommodation" is that no such change or modification is required if it would cause "undue hardship" to the employer.[16] "Undue hardship" means significant difficulty or expense and focuses on the resources and circumstances of the particular employer in relationship to the cost or difficulty of providing a specific accommodation. Undue hardship refers not only to financial difficulty, but to reasonable accommodations that are unduly extensive, substantial, or disruptive, or those that would fundamentally alter the nature or operation of the business.[17] An employer must assess on a case-by-case basis whether a particular reasonable accommodation would cause undue hardship. The ADA's "undue hardship" standard is different from that applied by courts under Title VII of the Civil Rights Act of 1964 for religious accommodation.[18]

Requesting Reasonable Accommodation

1. How must an individual request a reasonable accommodation?

When an individual decides to request accommodation, the individual or his/her representative must let the employer know that s/he needs an adjustment or change at work for a reason related to a medical condition. To request accommodation, an individual may use "plain English"

---

[12]In *US Airways, Inc. v. Barnett*, the Supreme Court held that it was unreasonable, absent "special circumstances," for an employer to provide a reassignment that conflicts with the terms of a seniority system. 535 U.S. 391, 122 S. Ct. 1516, 1524-25 (2002). For a further discussion of this issue, see Question 31, *infra*.

[13]"[W]ith or without reasonable accommodation" includes, if necessary, reassignment to a vacant position. Thus, if an employee is no longer qualified because of a disability to continue in his/her present position, an employer must reassign him/her as a reasonable accommodation. *See* the section on "Reassignment," *infra* pp. 37-38 and n.73.

[14]29 C.F.R. pt. 1630 app. §1630.2(n) (1997).

[15]29 C.F.R. pt. 1630 app. §1630.9 (1997).

[16]*See* 42 U.S.C. §12112 (b)(5)(A) (1994) (it is a form of discrimination to fail to provide a reasonable accommodation "unless such covered entity can demonstrate that the accommodation would impose an undue hardship …"); *see also* 42 U.S.C. §12111(10) (1994) (defining "undue hardship" based on factors assessing cost and difficulty).

The legislative history discusses financial, administrative, and operational limitations on providing reasonable accommodations only in the context of defining "undue hardship." Compare Senate Report, *supra* note 6, at 31-34 with 35-36; House Education and Labor Report, *supra* note 6, at 57-58 with 67-70.

[17]*See* 42 U.S.C. §12111(10) (1994); 29 C.F.R. §1630.2(p) (1997); 29 C.F.R. pt. 1630 app. §1630.2(p) (1997).

[18]*See* 29 C.F.R. pt. 1630 app. §1630.15(d) (1997). *See also Eckles v. Consolidated Rail Corp.*, 94 F.3d 1041, 1048-49 (7th Cir. 1996); *Bryant v. Better Business Bureau of Maryland*, 923 F. Supp. 720, 740 (D. Md. 1996).

---

and need not mention the ADA or use the phrase "reasonable accommodation."[19]

Example A: An employee tells her supervisor, "I'm having trouble getting to work at my scheduled starting time because of medical treatments I'm undergoing." This is a request for a reasonable accommodation.

Example B: An employee tells his supervisor, "I need six weeks off to get treatment for a back problem." This is a request for a reasonable accommodation.

Example C: A new employee, who uses a wheelchair, informs the employer that her wheelchair cannot fit under the desk in her office. This is a request for reasonable accommodation.

Example D: An employee tells his supervisor that he would like a new chair because his present one is uncomfortable. Although this is a request for a change at work, his statement is insufficient to put the employer on notice that he is requesting reasonable accommodation. He does not link his need for the new chair with a medical condition.

While an individual with a disability may request a change due to a medical condition, this request does not necessarily mean that the employer is required to provide the change. A request for reasonable accommodation is the first step

in an informal, interactive process between the individual and the employer. In some instances, before addressing the merits of the accommodation request, the employer needs to determine if the individual's medical condition meets the ADA definition of "disability,"[20] a prerequisite for the individual to be entitled to a reasonable accommodation.

2. May someone other than the individual with a disability request a reasonable accommodation on behalf of the individual?

Yes, a family member, friend, health professional, or other representative may request a reasonable accommodation on behalf of an individual with a disability.[21] Of course, the individual with a disability may refuse to accept an accommodation that is not needed.

Example A: An employee's spouse phones the employee's supervisor on Monday morning to inform her that the employee had a medical emergency due to multiple sclerosis, needed to be hospitalized, and thus requires time off. This discussion constitutes a request for reasonable accommodation.

Example B: An employee has been out of work for six months with a workers' compensation injury. The employee's doctor sends the employer a letter, stating that the employee is released to return to work, but with certain work restrictions. (Alternatively, the letter may state that the employee is released to return to a light duty position.) The letter constitutes a request for reasonable accommodation.

3. Do requests for reasonable accommodation need to be in writing?

No. Requests for reasonable accommodation do not need to be in writing. Individuals may request accommodations in conversation or may use any

---

[19]*See, e.g., Schmidt v. Safeway Inc.*, 864 F. Supp. 991, 997 (D. Or. 1994) ("statute does not require the plaintiff to speak any magic words. … The employee need not mention the ADA or even the term 'accommodation'"). *See also Hendricks-Robinson v. Excel Corp.*, 154 F.3d 685, 694 (7th Cir. 1998) ("[a] request as straightforward as asking for continued employment is a sufficient request for accommodation"); *Bultemeyer v. Ft. Wayne Community Schs.*, 100 F.3d 1281, 1285 (7th Cir. 1996) (an employee with a known psychiatric disability requested reasonable accommodation by stating that he could not do a particular job and by submitting a note from his psychiatrist); *McGinnis v. Wonder Chemical Co.*, 1995 U.S. Dist. LEXIS 18909 (E.D. Pa. 1995) (employer on notice that accommodation had been requested because: (1) employee told supervisor that his pain prevented him from working and (2) employee had requested leave under the Family and Medical Leave Act).

Nothing in the ADA requires an individual to use legal terms or to anticipate all of the possible information an employer may need in order to provide a reasonable accommodation. The ADA avoids a formulistic approach in favor of an interactive discussion between the employer and the individual with a disability, after the individual has requested a change due to a medical condition. Nevertheless, some courts have required that individuals initially provide detailed information in order to trigger the employer's duty to investigate whether reasonable accommodation is required. *See, e.g., Taylor v. Principal Fin. Group, Inc.*, 93 F.3d 155, 165 (5th Cir. 1996); *Miller v. Nat'l Cas. Co.*, 61 F.3d 627, 629-30 (8th Cir. 1995).

[20]*See* Questions 5-7, *infra*, for a further discussion on when an employer may request reasonable documentation about a person's "disability" and the need for reasonable accommodation.

[21]*Cf. Beck v. Univ. of Wis. Bd. of Regents*, 75 F.3d 1130 (7th Cir. 1996); *Schmidt v. Safeway Inc.*, 864 F. Supp. 991, 997 (D. Or. 1994). *But see Miller v. Nat'l Casualty Co.*, 61 F.3d 627, 630 (8th Cir. 1995) (employer had no duty to investigate reasonable accommodation despite the fact that the employee's sister notified the employer that the employee "was mentally falling apart and the family was trying to get her into the hospital").

The employer should be receptive to any relevant information or requests it receives from a third party acting on the individual's behalf because the reasonable accommodation process presumes open communication in order to help the employer make an informed decision. *See* 29 C.F.R. §1630.2(o), §1630.9 (1997); 29 C.F.R. pt. 1630 app. §1630.2(o), §1630.9 (1997).

other mode of communication.[22] An employer may choose to write a memorandum or letter confirming the individual's request. Alternatively, an employer may ask the individual to fill out a form or submit the request in written form, but the employer cannot ignore the initial request. An employer also may request reasonable documentation that the individual has an ADA disability and needs a reasonable accommodation. (See Question 6.)

4. When should an individual with a disability request a reasonable accommodation?

An individual with a disability may request a reasonable accommodation at any time during the application process or during the period of employment. The ADA does not preclude an employee with a disability from requesting a reasonable accommodation because s/he did not ask for one when applying for a job or after receiving a job offer. Rather, an individual with a disability should request a reasonable accommodation when s/he knows that there is a workplace barrier that is preventing him/her, due to a disability, from effectively competing for a position, performing a job, or gaining equal access to a benefit of employment.[23] As a practical matter, it may be in an employee's interest to request a reasonable accommodation before performance suffers or conduct problems occur.

5. What must an employer do after receiving a request for reasonable accommodation?

The employer and the individual with a disability should engage in an informal process to clarify what the individual needs and identify the appro-

priate reasonable accommodation.[24] The employer may ask the individual relevant questions that will enable it to make an informed decision about the request. This includes asking what type of reasonable accommodation is needed.[25]

The exact nature of the dialogue will vary. In many instances, both the disability and the type of accommodation required will be obvious, and thus there may be little or no need to engage in any discussion. In other situations, the employer may need to ask questions concerning the nature of the disability and the individual's functional limitations in order to identify an effective accommodation. While the individual with a disability does not have to be able to specify the precise accommodation, s/he does need to describe the problems posed by the workplace barrier. Additionally, suggestions from the individual with a disability may assist the employer in determining the type of reasonable accommodation to provide. Where the individual or the employer are not familiar with possible accommodations, there are extensive public and private resources to help the employer identify reasonable accommodations once the specific limitations and workplace barriers have been ascertained.[26]

6. May an employer ask an individual for documentation when the individual requests reasonable accommodation?

Yes. When the disability and/or the need for accommodation is not obvious, the employer may ask the individual for reasonable documentation about

---

[22]Although individuals with disabilities are not required to keep records, they may find it useful to document requests for reasonable accommodation in the event there is a dispute about whether or when they requested accommodation. Employers, however, must keep all employment records, including records of requests for reasonable accommodation, for one year from the making of the record or the personnel action involved, whichever occurs later. If a charge is filed, records must be preserved until the charge is resolved. 29 C.F.R. §1602.14 (1997).

[23]*Cf. Masterson v. Yellow Freight Sys., Inc.*, Nos. 98-6126, 98-6025, 1998 WL 856143 (10th Cir. Dec. 11, 1998) (fact that an employee with a disability does not need a reasonable accommodation all the time does not relieve employer from providing an accommodation for the period when he does need one).

[24]*See* 29 C.F.R. §1630.2(o)(3) (1997); 29 C.F.R. pt. 1630 app. §1630.2(o), 1630.9 (1997); *see also Haschmann v. Time Warner Entertainment Co.*, 151 F.3d 591, 601 (7th Cir. 1998); *Dalton v. Subaru-Isuzu*, 141 F.3d 667, 677 (7th Cir. 1998). The appendix to the regulations at §1630.9 provides a detailed discussion of the reasonable accommodation process.

Engaging in an interactive process helps employers to discover and provide reasonable accommodation. Moreover, in situations where an employer fails to provide a reasonable accommodation (and undue hardship would not be a valid defense), evidence that the employer engaged in an interactive process can demonstrate a "good faith" effort which can protect an employer from having to pay punitive and certain compensatory damages. *See* 42 U.S.C. 1981a(a)(3) (1994).

[25]The burden-shifting framework outlined by the Supreme Court in *US Airways, Inc. v. Barnett*, 535 U.S. 391, 122 S. Ct. 1516, 1523 (2002), does not affect the interactive process between an employer and an individual seeking reasonable accommodation. See *infra*, for a further discussion.

[26]*See* 29 C.F.R. pt. 1630 app. §1630.9 (1997). The Appendix to this Guidance provides a list of resources to identify possible accommodations.

his/her disability and functional limitations.[27] The employer is entitled to know that the individual has a covered disability for which s/he needs a reasonable accommodation.

Reasonable documentation means that the employer may require only the documentation that is needed to establish that a person has an ADA disability, and that the disability necessitates a reasonable accommodation. Thus, an employer, in response to a request for reasonable accommodation, cannot ask for documentation that is unrelated to determining the existence of a disability and the necessity for an accommodation. This means that in most situations an employer cannot request a person's complete medical records because they are likely to contain information unrelated to the disability at issue and the need for accommodation. If an individual has more than one disability, an employer can request information pertaining only to the disability that requires a reasonable accommodation.

An employer may require that the documentation about the disability and the functional limitations come from an appropriate health care or rehabilitation professional. The appropriate professional in any particular situation will depend on the disability and the type of functional limitation it imposes. Appropriate professionals include, but are not limited to, doctors (including psychiatrists), psychologists, nurses, physical therapists, occupational therapists, speech therapists, vocational rehabilitation specialists and licensed mental health professionals.

In requesting documentation, employers should specify what types of information they are seeking regarding the disability, its functional limitations, and the need for reasonable accommodation. The individual can be asked to sign a limited release allowing the employer to submit a list of specific questions to the health care or vocational professional.[28]

---

[27]29 C.F.R. pt. 1630 app. §1630.9 (1997); *see also EEOC Enforcement Guidance: Preemployment Disability-Related Questions and Medical Examinations* at 6 (1995) [hereinafter *Preemployment Questions and Medical Examinations*]; *EEOC Enforcement Guidance: The Americans with Disabilities Act and Psychiatric Disabilities* at 22-23 (1997) [hereinafter ADA and Psychiatric Disabilities]. Although the latter Enforcement Guidance focuses on psychiatric disabilities, the legal standard under which an employer may request documentation applies to disabilities generally.

When an employee seeks leave as a reasonable accommodation, an employer's request for documentation about disability and the need for leave may overlap with the certification requirements of the Family and Medical Leave Act (FMLA), 29 C.F.R. §825.305-.306, §825.310-.311 (1997).

[28]Since a doctor cannot disclose information about a patient without his/her permission, an employer must obtain a release from the individual that will permit his/her doctor to answer questions. The release should be clear as to what information will be requested. Employers must maintain the confidentiality of all medical information collected during this process, regardless of where the information comes from. *See* Question 42 and note 111, *infra*.

As an alternative to requesting documentation, an employer may simply discuss with the person the nature of his/her disability and functional limitations. It would be useful for the employer to make clear to the individual why it is requesting information, i.e., to verify the existence of an ADA disability and the need for a reasonable accommodation.

Example A: An employee says to an employer, "I'm having trouble reaching tools because of my shoulder injury." The employer may ask the employee for documentation describing the impairment; the nature, severity, and duration of the impairment; the activity or activities that the impairment limits; and the extent to which the impairment limits the employee's ability to perform the activity or activities (i.e., the employer is seeking information as to whether the employee has an ADA disability).

Example B: A marketing employee has a severe learning disability. He attends numerous meetings to plan marketing strategies. In order to remember what is discussed at these meetings he must take detailed notes but, due to his disability, he has great difficulty writing. The employee tells his supervisor about his disability and requests a laptop computer to use in the meetings. Since neither the disability nor the need for accommodation are obvious, the supervisor may ask the employee for reasonable documentation about his impairment; the nature, severity, and duration of the impairment; the activity or activities that the impairment limits; and the extent to which the impairment limits the employee's ability to perform the activity or activities. The employer also may ask why the disability necessitates use of a laptop computer (or any other type of reasonable accommodation, such as a tape recorder) to help the employee retain the information from the meetings.[29]

Example C: An employee's spouse phones the employee's supervisor on Monday morning to inform her that the employee had a medical emergency due to multiple sclerosis, needed to be hospitalized, and thus requires time off. The supervisor can ask the spouse to send in documentation from the employee's treating physician that confirms that the hospitalization was related to the multiple sclerosis and provides information on how long an absence may be required from work.[30]

If an individual's disability or need for reasonable accommodation is not obvious, and s/he refuses to provide the reasonable documentation requested by the employer, then s/he is not entitled

---

[29]*See* Question 9, *infra*, for information on choosing between two or more effective accommodations.

[30]This employee also might be covered under the Family and Medical Leave Act, and if so, the employer would need to comply with the requirements of that statute.

to reasonable accommodation.[31] On the other hand, failure by the employer to initiate or participate in an informal dialogue with the individual after receiving a request for reasonable accommodation could result in liability for failure to provide a reasonable accommodation.[32]

7. May an employer require an individual to go to a health care professional of the employer's (rather than the employee's) choice for purposes of documenting need for accommodation and disability?

The ADA does not prevent an employer from requiring an individual to go to an appropriate health professional of the employer's choice if the individual provides insufficient information from his/her treating physician (or other health care professional) to substantiate that s/he has an ADA disability and needs a reasonable accommodation. However, if an individual provides insufficient documentation in response to the employer's initial request, the employer should explain why the documentation is insufficient and allow the individual an opportunity to provide the missing information in a timely manner. Documentation is insufficient if it does not specify the existence of an ADA disability and explain the need for reasonable accommodation.[33]

Any medical examination conducted by the employer's health professional must be job-related and consistent with business necessity. This means that the examination must be limited to determining the existence of an ADA disability and the functional limitations that require reasonable accommodation.[34] If an employer requires an employee to go to a health professional of the employer's choice, the employer must pay all costs associated with the visit(s).

8. Are there situations in which an employer cannot ask for documentation in response to a request for reasonable accommodation?

Yes. An employer cannot ask for documentation when: (1) both the disability and the need for reasonable accommodation are obvious, or (2) the individual has already provided the employer with sufficient information to substantiate that s/he has an ADA disability and needs the reasonable accommodation requested.

Example A: An employee brings a note from her treating physician explaining that she has diabetes and that, as a result, she must test her blood sugar several times a day to ensure that her insulin level is safe in order to avoid a hyperglycemic reaction. The note explains that a hyperglycemic reaction can include extreme thirst, heavy breathing, drowsiness, and flushed skin, and eventually would result in unconsciousness. Depending on the results of the blood test, the employee might have to take insulin. The note requests that the employee be allowed three or four 10-minute breaks each day to test her blood, and if necessary, to take insulin. The doctor's note constitutes sufficient documentation that the person has an ADA disability because it describes a substantially limiting impairment and the reasonable accommodation needed as a result. The employer cannot ask for additional documentation.

Example B: One year ago, an employer learned that an employee had bipolar disorder after he requested a reasonable accommodation. The documentation provided at that time from the employee's psychiatrist indicated that this was a permanent condition, which would always involve periods in which the disability would remit and then intensify. The psychiatrist's letter explained that during periods when the condition flared up, the person's manic moods or depressive episodes could be severe enough to create serious problems for the individual in caring for himself or working, and that medication controlled the frequency and severity of these episodes.

Now, one year later, the employee again requests a reasonable accommodation related to his bipolar disorder. Under these facts, the employer may ask for reasonable documentation on the need for the accommodation (if the need is not obvious), but it cannot ask for documentation that the person has an ADA disability. The medical information provided one year ago established the existence of a long-term impairment that substantially limits a major life activity.

Example C: An employee gives her employer a letter from her doctor, stating that the employee has asthma and needs the employer to provide her with an air filter. This letter contains insufficient information as to whether the asthma is an ADA disability because it does not provide any information as to its severity (i.e., whether it substantially limits a major life activity). Furthermore, the letter does not identify precisely what problem exists in the workplace that requires an air filter or any other reasonable accommodation. Therefore, the employer can request additional documentation.

---

[31]*See Templeton v. Neodata Servs., Inc.*, No. 98-1106, 1998 WL 852516 (10th Cir. Dec. 10, 1998); *Beck v. Univ. of Wis. Bd. of Regents*, 75 F.3d 1130, 1134 (7th Cir. 1996); *McAlpin v. National Semiconductor Corp.*, 921 F. Supp. 1518, 1525 (N.D. Tex. 1996).

[32]*See Hendricks-Robinson v. Excel Corp.*, 154 F.3d 685, 700 (7th Cir. 1998).

[33]If an individual provides sufficient documentation to show the existence of an ADA disability and the need for reasonable accommodation, continued efforts by the employer to require that the individual see the employer's health professional could be considered retaliation.

[34]Employers also may consider alternatives like having their health professional consult with the individual's health professional, with the employee's consent.

9. Is an employer required to provide the reasonable accommodation that the individual wants?

The employer may choose among reasonable accommodations as long as the chosen accommodation is effective.[35] Thus, as part of the interactive process, the employer may offer alternative suggestions for reasonable accommodations and discuss their effectiveness in removing the workplace barrier that is impeding the individual with a disability.

If there are two possible reasonable accommodations, and one costs more or is more burdensome than the other, the employer may choose the less expensive or burdensome accommodation as long as it is effective (i.e., it would remove a workplace barrier, thereby providing the individual with an equal opportunity to apply for a position, to perform the essential functions of a position, or to gain equal access to a benefit or privilege of employment). Similarly, when there are two or more effective accommodations, the employer may choose the one that is easier to provide. In either situation, the employer does not have to show that it is an undue hardship to provide the more expensive or more difficult accommodation. If more than one accommodation is effective, "the preference of the individual with a disability should be given primary consideration. However, the employer providing the accommodation has the ultimate discretion to choose between effective accommodations."[36]

Example A: An employee with a severe learning disability has great difficulty reading. His supervisor sends him many detailed memoranda which he often has trouble understanding. However, he has no difficulty understanding oral communication. The employee requests that the employer install a computer with speech output and that his supervisor send all memoranda through electronic mail which the computer can then read to him. The supervisor asks whether a tape recorded message would accomplish the same objective and the employee agrees that it would. Since both accommodations are effective, the employer may choose to provide the supervisor and employee with a tape recorder so that the supervisor can record her memoranda and the employee can listen to them.

Example B: An attorney with a severe vision disability requests that her employer provide someone to read printed materials that she needs to review daily. The attorney explains that a reader enables her to review substantial amounts of written materials in an efficient

manner. Believing that this reasonable accommodation would be too costly, the employer instead provides the attorney with a device that allows her to magnify print so that she can read it herself. The attorney can read print using this device, but with such great difficulty it significantly slows down her ability to review written materials. The magnifying device is ineffective as a reasonable accommodation because it does not provide the attorney with an equal opportunity to attain the same level of performance as her colleagues. Without an equal opportunity to attain the same level of performance, this attorney is denied an equal opportunity to compete for promotions. In this instance, failure to provide the reader, absent undue hardship, would violate the ADA.

10. How quickly must an employer respond to a request for reasonable accommodation?

An employer should respond expeditiously to a request for reasonable accommodation. If the employer and the individual with a disability need to engage in an interactive process, this too should proceed as quickly as possible.[37] Similarly, the employer should act promptly to provide the reasonable accommodation. Unnecessary delays can result in a violation of the ADA.[38]

Example A: An employer provides parking for all employees. An employee who uses a wheelchair requests from his supervisor an accessible parking space, explaining that the spaces are so narrow that there is insufficient room for his van to extend the ramp that allows him to get in and out. The supervisor does not act on the request and does not forward it to someone with authority to respond. The employee makes a second request to the supervisor. Yet, two months after the initial request, nothing has been done. Although the supervisor never definitively denies the request, the lack of action under these circumstances amounts to a denial, and thus violates the ADA.

Example B: An employee who is blind requests adaptive equipment for her computer as a reasonable accommodation. The employer must order this equipment and is informed that it will take three months to receive delivery. No other company sells the adaptive equipment the employee needs. The employer notifies the employee of the results of its investigation and that it has ordered the equipment. Although it will

---

[35]*See* 29 C.F.R. pt. 1630 app. §1630.9 (1997); *see also Stewart v. Happy Herman's Cheshire Bridge, Inc.*, 117 F.3d 1278, 1285-86 (11th Cir. 1997); *Hankins v. The Gap, Inc.*, 84 F.3d 797, 800 (6th Cir. 1996); *Gile v. United Airlines, Inc.*, 95 F.3d 492, 499 (7th Cir. 1996).

[36]29 C.F.R. pt. 1630 app. §1630.9 (1997).

[37]*See Dalton v. Subaru-Isuzu Automotive, Inc.*, 141 F.3d 667, 677 (7th Cir. 1998).

[38]In determining whether there has been an unnecessary delay in responding to a request for reasonable accommodation, relevant factors would include: (1) the reason(s) for the delay, (2) the length of the delay, (3) how much the individual with a disability and the employer each contributed to the delay, (4) what the employer was doing during the delay, and (5) whether the required accommodation was simple or complex to provide.

take three months to receive the equipment, the employer has moved as quickly as it can to obtain it and thus there is no ADA violation resulting from the delay. The employer and employee should determine what can be done so that the employee can perform his/her job as effectively as possible while waiting for the equipment.

11. May an employer require an individual with a disability to accept a reasonable accommodation that s/he does not want?

No. An employer may not require a qualified individual with a disability to accept an accommodation. If, however, an employee needs a reasonable accommodation to perform an essential function or to eliminate a direct threat, and refuses to accept an effective accommodation, s/he may not be qualified to remain in the job.[39]

Reasonable Accommodation and Job Applicants

12. May an employer ask whether a reasonable accommodation is needed when an applicant has not asked for one?

An employer may tell applicants what the hiring process involves (e.g., an interview, timed written test, or job demonstration), and may ask applicants whether they will need a reasonable accommodation for this process.

During the hiring process and before a conditional offer is made, an employer generally may not ask an applicant whether s/he needs a reasonable accommodation for the job, except when the employer knows that an applicant has a disability – either because it is obvious or the applicant has voluntarily disclosed the information – and could reasonably believe that the applicant will need a reasonable accommodation to perform specific job functions. If the applicant replies that s/he needs a reasonable accommodation, the employer may inquire as to what type.[40]

After a conditional offer of employment is extended, an employer may inquire whether applicants will need reasonable accommodations related to anything connected with the job (i.e., job performance or access to benefits/privileges of the job) as long as all entering employees in the same job category are asked this question. Alternatively, an employer may ask a specific applicant if s/he needs a reasonable accommodation if the employer knows that this applicant has a disability – either because it is obvious or the applicant has voluntarily disclosed the information – and could reasonably believe that the applicant will need a reasonable

accommodation. If the applicant replies that s/he needs a reasonable accommodation, the employer may inquire as to what type.[41]

13. Does an employer have to provide a reasonable accommodation to an applicant with a disability even if it believes that it will be unable to provide this individual with a reasonable accommodation on the job?

Yes. An employer must provide a reasonable accommodation to a qualified applicant with a disability that will enable the individual to have an equal opportunity to participate in the application process and to be considered for a job (unless it can show undue hardship). Thus, individuals with disabilities who meet initial requirements to be considered for a job should not be excluded from the application process because the employer speculates, based on a request for reasonable accommodation for the application process, that it will be unable to provide the individual with reasonable accommodation to perform the job. In many instances, employers will be unable to determine whether an individual needs reasonable accommodation to perform a job based solely on a request for accommodation during the application process. And even if an individual will need reasonable accommodation to perform the job, it may not be the same type or degree of accommodation that is needed for the application process. Thus, an employer should assess the need for accommodations for the application process separately from those that may be needed to perform the job.[42]

Example A: An employer is impressed with an applicant's resume and contacts the individual to come in for an interview. The applicant, who is deaf, requests a sign language interpreter for the interview. The employer cancels the interview and refuses to consider further this applicant because it believes it would have to hire a full-time interpreter. The employer has violated the ADA. The employer should have proceeded with the interview, using a sign language interpreter (absent undue hardship), and at the interview inquired to what extent the individual would need a sign language interpreter to perform any essential functions requiring communication with other people.

Example B: An individual who has paraplegia applies for a secretarial position. Because the office has two steps at the entrance, the employer arranges for the applicant to take a typing test, a requirement of the application process, at a different location. The applicant fails

---

[39]*See* 29 C.F.R. pt. 1630 app. §1630.9 (1997); *see also Hankins v. The Gap, Inc.*, 84 F.3d 797, 801 (6th Cir. 1996).

[40]42 U.S.C. §12112(d)(2)(A) (1994); 29 C.F.R. §1630.13(a) (1997). For a thorough discussion of these requirements, *see* Preemployment Questions and Medical Examinations, *supra* note 27, at 6-8.

[41]42 U.S.C. §12112(d)(3) (1994); 29 C.F.R. §1630.14(b) (1997); *see also* Preemployment Questions and Medical Examinations, *supra* note 27, at 20.

[42]*See* Question 12, *supra*, for the circumstances under which an employer may ask an applicant whether s/he will need reasonable accommodation to perform specific job functions.

---

the test. The employer does not have to provide any further reasonable accommodations for this individual because she is no longer qualified to continue with the application process.

Reasonable Accommodation Related to the Benefits and Privileges of Employment[43]

The ADA requires employers to provide reasonable accommodations so that employees with disabilities can enjoy the "benefits and privileges of employment" equal to those enjoyed by similarly-situated employees without disabilities. Benefits and privileges of employment include, but are not limited to, employer-sponsored: (1) training, (2) services (e.g., employee assistance programs (EAP's), credit unions, cafeterias, lounges, gymnasiums, auditoriums, transportation), and (3) parties or other social functions (e.g., parties to celebrate retirements and birthdays, and company outings).[44] If an employee with a disability needs a reasonable accommodation in order to gain access to, and have an equal opportunity to participate in, these benefits and privileges, then the employer must provide the accommodation unless it can show undue hardship.

14. Does an employer have to provide reasonable accommodation to enable an employee with a disability to have equal access to information communicated in the workplace to nondisabled employees?

Yes. Employers provide information to employees through different means, including computers, bulletin boards, mailboxes, posters, and public address systems. Employers must ensure that employees with disabilities have access to information that is provided to other similarly-situated employees without disabilities, regardless of whether they need it to perform their jobs.

Example A: An employee who is blind has adaptive equipment for his computer that integrates him into the network with other employees, thus allowing communication via electronic mail and access to the computer bulletin board. When the employer installs upgraded computer equipment, it must provide new adaptive equipment in order for the employee to be integrated into the new networks, absent undue hardship. Alternative methods of communication (e.g., sending written or telephone messages to the employee instead of electronic mail) are likely to be ineffective substitutes since electronic mail is used by every employee and there is no effective way to ensure that each one will always use alternative measures

to ensure that the blind employee receives the same information that is being transmitted via computer.

Example B: An employer authorizes the Human Resources Director to use a public address system to remind employees about special meetings and to make certain announcements. In order to make this information accessible to a deaf employee, the Human Resources Director arranges to send in advance an electronic mail message to the deaf employee conveying the information that will be broadcast. The Human Resources Director is the only person who uses the public address system; therefore, the employer can ensure that all public address messages are sent, via electronic mail, to the deaf employee. Thus, the employer is providing this employee with equal access to office communications.

15. Must an employer provide reasonable accommodation so that an employee may attend training programs?

Yes. Employers must provide reasonable accommodation (e.g., sign language interpreters; written materials produced in alternative formats, such as Braille, large print, or on audio-cassette) that will provide employees with disabilities with an equal opportunity to participate in employer-sponsored training, absent undue hardship. This obligation extends to in-house training, as well as to training provided by an outside entity. Similarly, the employer has an obligation to provide reasonable accommodation whether the training occurs on the employer's premises or elsewhere.

Example A: XYZ Corp. has signed a contract with Super Trainers, Inc., to provide mediation training at its facility to all of XYZ's Human Resources staff. One staff member is blind and requests that materials be provided in Braille. Super Trainers refuses to provide the materials in Braille. XYZ maintains that it is the responsibility of Super Trainers and sees no reason why it should have to arrange and pay for the Braille copy.

Both XYZ (as an employer covered under Title I of the ADA) and Super Trainers (as a public accommodation covered under Title III of the ADA[45]) have obligations to provide materials in alternative formats. This fact, however, does not excuse either one from their respective obligations. If Super Trainers refuses to provide the Braille version, despite its Title III obligations, XYZ still retains its obligation to provide it as a reasonable accommodation, absent undue hardship.

Employers arranging with an outside entity to provide training may wish to avoid such problems by specifying in the contract who has the respon-

---

[43]The discussions and examples in this section assume that there is only one effective accommodation and that the reasonable accommodation will not cause undue hardship.

[44]*See* 29 C.F.R. pt. 1630 app. §1630.9 (1997).

[45]42 U.S.C. §12181(7), §12182(1)(A), (2)(A)(iii) (1994).

sibility to provide appropriate reasonable accommodations. Similarly, employers should ensure that any offsite training will be held in an accessible facility if they have an employee who, because of a disability, requires such an accommodation.

> *Example B*: XYZ Corp. arranges for one of its employees to provide CPR training. This three-hour program is optional. A deaf employee wishes to take the training and requests a sign language interpreter. XYZ must provide the interpreter because the CPR training is a benefit that XYZ offers all employees, even though it is optional.

Types of Reasonable Accommodations Related To Job Performance[46]

Below are discussed certain types of reasonable accommodations related to job performance.

Job Restructuring

Job restructuring includes modifications such as:
- reallocating or redistributing marginal job functions that an employee is unable to perform because of a disability; and
- altering when and/or how a function, essential or marginal, is performed.[47]

An employer never has to reallocate essential functions as a reasonable accommodation, but can do so if it wishes.

16. If, as a reasonable accommodation, an employer restructures an employee's job to eliminate some marginal functions, may the employer require the employee to take on other marginal functions that s/he can perform?

Yes. An employer may switch the marginal functions of two (or more) employees in order to restructure a job as a reasonable accommodation.

> *Example*: A cleaning crew works in an office building. One member of the crew wears a prosthetic leg which enables him to walk very well, but climbing steps is painful and difficult. Although he can perform his essential functions without problems, he cannot perform the marginal function of sweeping the steps located throughout the building. The marginal functions of a second crew member include cleaning the small kitchen

in the employee's lounge, which is something the first crew member can perform. The employer can switch the marginal functions performed by these two employees.

Leave

Permitting the use of accrued paid leave, or unpaid leave, is a form of reasonable accommodation when necessitated by an employee's disability.[48] An employer does not have to provide paid leave beyond that which is provided to similarly-situated employees. Employers should allow an employee with a disability to exhaust accrued paid leave first and then provide unpaid leave.[49] For example, if employees get 10 days of paid leave, and an employee with a disability needs 15 days of leave, the employer should allow the individual to use 10 days of paid leave and five days of unpaid leave.

An employee with a disability may need leave for a number of reasons related to the disability, including, but not limited to:
- obtaining medical treatment (e.g., surgery, psychotherapy, substance abuse treatment, or dialysis); rehabilitation services; or physical or occupational therapy;
- recuperating from an illness or an episodic manifestation of the disability;
- obtaining repairs on a wheelchair, accessible van, or prosthetic device;
- avoiding temporary adverse conditions in the work environment (for example, an air-conditioning breakdown causing unusually warm temperatures that could seriously harm an employee with multiple sclerosis);
- training a service animal (e.g., a guide dog); or
- receiving training in the use of Braille or to learn sign language.

17. May an employer apply a "no-fault" leave policy, under which employees are automatically terminated after they have been on leave for a certain period of time, to an employee with a disability who needs leave beyond the set period?

No. If an employee with a disability needs additional unpaid leave as a reasonable accommodation, the employer must modify its "no-fault" leave policy to provide the employee with the additional leave, unless it can show that: (1) there is another effective accommodation that would enable the person to perform

---

[46]The discussions and examples in this section assume that there is only one effective accommodation and that the reasonable accommodation will not cause undue hardship.

The types of reasonable accommodations discussed in this section are not exhaustive. For example, employees with disabilities may request reasonable accommodations to modify the work environment, such as changes to the ventilation system or relocation of a work space.

See the Appendix for additional resources to identify other possible reasonable accommodations.

[47]42 U.S.C. 12111(9)(B) (1994); 29 C.F.R. pt. 1630 app. §1630.2(o), §1630.9 (1997); *see Benson v. Northwest Airlines, Inc.*, 62 F.3d 1108, 1112-13 (8th Cir. 1995).

[48]29 C.F.R. pt. 1630 app. §1630.2(o) (1997). *See Cehrs v. Northeast Ohio Alzheimer's*, 155 F.3d 775, 782 (6th Cir. 1998).

An employee who needs leave, or a part-time or modified schedule, as a reasonable accommodation also may be entitled to leave under the Family and Medical Leave Act. *See* Questions 21 and 23, *infra*.

[49]*See A Technical Assistance Manual on the Employment Provisions (Title I) of the Americans With Disabilities Act*, at 3.10(4) [hereinafter TAM].

the essential functions of his/her position, or (2) granting additional leave would cause an undue hardship. Modifying workplace policies, including leave policies, is a form of reasonable accommodation.[50]

18. Does an employer have to hold open an employee's job as a reasonable accommodation?

Yes. An employee with a disability who is granted leave as a reasonable accommodation is entitled to return to his/her same position unless the employer demonstrates that holding open the position would impose an undue hardship.[51]

If an employer cannot hold a position open during the entire leave period without incurring undue hardship, the employer must consider whether it has a vacant, equivalent position for which the employee is qualified and to which the employee can be reassigned to continue his/her leave for a specific period of time and then, at the conclusion of the leave, can be returned to this new position.[52]

Example: An employee needs eight months of leave for treatment and recuperation related to a disability. The employer grants the request, but after four months the employer determines that it can no longer hold open the position for the remaining four months without incurring undue hardship. The employer must consider whether it has a vacant, equivalent position to which the employee can be reassigned for the remaining four months of leave, at the end of which time the employee would return to work in that new position. If an equivalent position is not available, the employer must look for a vacant position at a lower level. Continued leave is not required as a reasonable accommodation if a vacant position at a lower level is also unavailable.

19. Can an employer penalize an employee for work missed during leave taken as a reasonable accommodation?

No. To do so would be retaliation for the employee's use of a reasonable accommodation to which

s/he is entitled under the law.[53] Moreover, such punishment would make the leave an ineffective accommodation, thus making an employer liable for failing to provide a reasonable accommodation.[54]

Example A: A salesperson took five months of leave as a reasonable accommodation. The company compares the sales records of all salespeople over a one-year period, and any employee whose sales fall more than 25 percent below the median sales performance of all employees is automatically terminated. The employer terminates the salesperson because she had fallen below the required performance standard. The company did not consider that the reason for her lower sales performance was her five-month leave of absence; nor did it assess her productivity during the period she did work (i.e., prorate her productivity).

Penalizing the salesperson in this manner constitutes retaliation and a denial of reasonable accommodation.

Example B: Company X is having a reduction-in-force. The company decides that any employee who has missed more than four weeks in the past year will be terminated. An employee took five weeks of leave for treatment of his disability. The company cannot count those five weeks in determining whether to terminate this employee.[55]

20. When an employee requests leave as a reasonable accommodation, may an employer provide an accommodation that requires him/her to remain on the job instead?

Yes, if the employer's reasonable accommodation would be effective and eliminate the need for leave.[56] An employer need not provide an employee's preferred accommodation as long as the employer provides an effective accommodation.[57] Accordingly, in lieu of providing leave, an employer may provide a reasonable accommodation that requires an employee to

---

[50] 42 U.S.C. §12111(9)(B) (1994); 29 C.F.R. §1630.2(o)(2)(ii) (1997). *See US Airways Inc. v. Barnett*, 535 U.S. 391, 122 S. Ct. 1516, 1521 (2002). *See also* Question 24, *infra*. While undue hardship cannot be based solely on the existence of a no-fault leave policy, the employer may be able to show undue hardship based on an individualized assessment showing the disruption to the employer's operations if additional leave is granted beyond the period allowed by the policy. In determining whether undue hardship exists, the employer should consider how much additional leave is needed (*e.g.*, two weeks, six months, one year?).

[51] *See Schmidt v. Safeway Inc.*, 864 F. Supp. 991, 996-97 (D. Or. 1994); *Corbett v. National Products Co.*, 1995 U.S. Dist. LEXIS 3949 (E.D. Pa. 1995).

[52] *See EEOC Enforcement Guidance: Workers' Compensation and the ADA* at 16 [hereinafter *Workers' Compensation and the ADA*]. *See also infra*, for information on reassignment as a reasonable accommodation.

[53] *Cf. Kiel v. Select Artificials*, 142 F.3d 1077, 1080 (8th Cir. 1998).

[54] *See Criado v. IBM*, 145 F.3d 437, 444-45 (1st Cir. 1998).

[55] But *see Matthews v. Commonwealth Edison Co.*, 128 F.3d 1194, 1197-98 (7th Cir. 1997) (an employee who, because of a heart attack, missed several months of work and returned on a part-time basis until health permitted him to work full-time, could be terminated during a RIF based on his lower productivity). In reaching this decision, the Seventh Circuit failed to consider that the employee needed leave and a modified schedule as reasonable accommodations for his disability, and that the accommodations became meaningless when he was penalized for using them.

[56] If an employee, however, qualifies for leave under the Family and Medical Leave Act, an employer may not require him/her to remain on the job with an adjustment in lieu of taking leave. *See* 29 C.F.R. §825.702(d)(1) (1997).

[57] *See* Question 9, *supra*.

remain on the job (e.g., reallocation of marginal functions or temporary transfer) as long as it does not interfere with the employee's ability to address his/her medical needs. The employer is obligated, however, to restore the employee's full duties or to return the employee to his/her original position once s/he no longer needs the reasonable accommodation.

Example A: An employee with emphysema requests 10 weeks of leave for surgery and recuperation related to his disability. In discussing this request with the employer, the employee states that he could return to work after seven weeks if, during his first three weeks back, he could work part-time and eliminate two marginal functions that require lots of walking. If the employer provides these accommodations, then it can require the employee to return to work after seven weeks.

Example B: An employee's disability is getting more severe and her doctor recommends surgery to counteract some of the effects. After receiving the employee's request for leave for the surgery, the employer proposes that it provide certain equipment which it believes will mitigate the effects of the disability and delay the need for leave to get surgery. The employer's proposed accommodation is not effective because it interferes with the employee's ability to get medical treatment.

21. How should an employer handle leave for an employee covered by both the ADA and the Family and Medical Leave Act (FMLA)?[58]

An employer should determine an employee's rights under each statute separately, and then consider whether the two statutes overlap regarding the appropriate actions to take.[59]

Under the ADA, an employee who needs leave related to his/her disability is entitled to such leave if there is no other effective accommodation and the leave will not cause undue hardship. An employer must allow the individual to use any accrued paid leave first, but, if that is insufficient to cover the entire period, then the employer should grant unpaid leave. An employer must continue an employee's health insurance benefits during his/her leave period only if it does so for other employees in a similar leave status. As for the employee's position, the ADA requires that the employer hold it open while the employee is on leave unless it can show

that doing so causes undue hardship. When the employee is ready to return to work, the employer must allow the individual to return to the same position (assuming that there was no undue hardship in holding it open) if the employee is still qualified (i.e., the employee can perform the essential functions of the position with or without reasonable accommodation).

If it is an undue hardship under the ADA to hold open an employee's position during a period of leave, or an employee is no longer qualified to return to his/her original position, then the employer must reassign the employee (absent undue hardship) to a vacant position for which s/he is qualified.

Under the FMLA, an eligible employee is entitled to a maximum of 12 weeks of leave per 12 month period. The FMLA guarantees the right of the employee to return to the same position or to an equivalent one.[60] An employer must allow the individual to use any accrued paid leave first, but if that is insufficient to cover the entire period, then the employer should grant unpaid leave. The FMLA requires an employer to continue the employee's health insurance coverage during the leave period, provided the employee pays his/her share of the premiums.

Example A: An employee with an ADA disability needs 13 weeks of leave for treatment related to the disability. The employee is eligible under the FMLA for 12 weeks of leave (the maximum available), so this period of leave constitutes both FMLA leave and a reasonable accommodation. Under the FMLA, the employer could deny the employee the thirteenth week of leave. But, because the employee is also covered under the ADA, the employer cannot deny the request for the thirteenth week of leave unless it can show undue hardship. The employer may consider the impact on its operations caused by the initial 12-week absence, along with other undue hardship factors.[61]

Example B: An employee with an ADA disability has taken 10 weeks of FMLA leave and is preparing to return to work. The employer wants to put her in an equivalent position rather than her original one. Although this is permissible under the FMLA, the ADA requires that the employer return the employee to her original position. Unless the employer can show that this would cause an undue hardship, or that the employee is no longer qualified for her original position (with or without reasonable accommodation), the employer must reinstate the employee to her original position.

---

[58]For more detailed information on issues raised by the interplay between these statutes, refer to the FMLA/ADA Fact Sheet listed in the Appendix.

[59]Employers should remember that many employees eligible for FMLA leave will not be entitled to leave as a reasonable accommodation under the ADA, either because they do not meet the ADA's definition of disability or, if they do have an ADA disability, the need for leave is unrelated to that disability.

[60]29 C.F.R. §825.214(a), §825.215 (1997).

[61]For further information on the undue hardship factors, *see infra*.

Example C: An employee with an ADA disability has taken 12 weeks of FMLA leave. He notifies his employer that he is ready to return to work, but he no longer is able to perform the essential functions of his position or an equivalent position. Under the FMLA, the employer could terminate his employment,[62] but under the ADA the employer must consider whether the employee could perform the essential functions with reasonable accommodation (e.g., additional leave, part-time schedule, job restructuring, or use of specialized equipment). If not, the ADA requires the employer to reassign the employee if there is a vacant position available for which he is qualified, with or without reasonable accommodation, and there is no undue hardship.

Modified or Part-Time Schedule

22. Must an employer allow an employee with a disability to work a modified or part-time schedule as a reasonable accommodation, absent undue hardship?

Yes.[63] A modified schedule may involve adjusting arrival or departure times, providing periodic breaks, altering when certain functions are performed, allowing an employee to use accrued paid leave, or providing additional unpaid leave. An employer must provide a modified or part-time schedule when required as a reasonable accommodation, absent undue hardship, even if it does not provide such schedules for other employees.[64]

Example A: An employee with HIV infection must take medication on a strict schedule. The medication causes extreme nausea about one hour after ingestion, and generally lasts about 45 minutes. The employee asks that he be allowed to take a daily 45-minute break when the nausea occurs. The employer must grant this request absent undue hardship.

For certain positions, the time during which an essential function is performed may be critical. This could affect whether an employer can grant a request to modify an employee's schedule.[65] Employers should carefully assess whether modifying the hours could significantly disrupt their operations – that is, cause undue hardship – or whether the essential functions may be performed at different times with little or no impact on the operations or the ability of other employees to perform their jobs.

If modifying an employee's schedule poses an undue hardship, an employer must consider reassignment to a vacant position that would enable the employee to work during the hours requested.[66]

Example B: A day care worker requests that she be allowed to change her hours from 7:00 a.m.-3:00 p.m. to 10:00 a.m.-6:00 p.m. because of her disability. The day care center is open from 7:00 a.m.-7:00 p.m. and it will still have sufficient coverage at the beginning of the morning if it grants the change in hours. In this situation, the employer must provide the reasonable accommodation.

Example C: An employee works for a morning newspaper, operating the printing presses which run between 10 p.m. and 3 a.m. Due to her disability, she needs to work in the daytime. The essential function of her position, operating the printing presses, requires that she work at night because the newspaper cannot be printed during the daytime hours. Since the employer cannot modify her hours, it must consider whether it can reassign her to a different position.

23. How should an employer handle requests for modified or part-time schedules for an employee covered by both the ADA and the Family and Medical Leave Act (FMLA)?[67]

---

[62] 29 C.F.R. §825.702(c)(4) (1997).

[63] 42 U.S.C. §12111(9)(B) (1994); *see Ralph v. Lucent Technologies, Inc.*, 135 F.3d 166, 172 (1st Cir. 1998) (a modified schedule is a form of reasonable accommodation).

[64] *See US Airways Inc. v. Barnett*, 535 U.S. 391, 122 S. Ct. 1516, 1521 (2002).

[65] Certain courts have characterized attendance as an "essential function." *See, e.g., Carr v. Reno*, 23 F.3d 525, 530 (D.C. Cir. 1994); *Jackson v. Department of Veterans Admin.*, 22 F.3d 277, 278-79 (11th Cir. 1994). Attendance, however, is not an essential function as defined by the ADA because it is not one of "the fundamental job duties of the employment position." 29 C.F.R. 1630.2(n)(1) (1997) (emphasis added). As the regulations make clear, essential functions are duties to be performed. 29 C.F.R. 1630.2(n)(2) (1997). *See Haschmann v. Time Warner Entertainment Co.*, 151 F.3d 591, 602 (7th Cir. 1998); *Cehrs v. Northeast Ohio Alzheimer's*, 155 F.3d 775, 782-83 (6th Cir. 1998).

On the other hand, attendance is relevant to job performance and employers need not grant all requests for a modified schedule. To the contrary, if the time during which an essential function is performed is integral to its successful completion, then an employer may deny a request to modify an employee's schedule as an undue hardship.

[66] Employers covered under the Family and Medical Leave Act (FMLA) should determine whether any denial of leave or a modified schedule is also permissible under that law. *See* 29 C.F.R. §825.203 (1997).

[67] For more detailed information on issues raised by the interplay between these statutes, refer to the FMLA/ADA Fact Sheet listed in the Appendix.

An employer should determine an employee's rights under each statute separately, and then consider whether the two statutes overlap regarding the appropriate actions to take.

Under the ADA, an employee who needs a modified or part-time schedule because of his/her disability is entitled to such a schedule if there is no other effective accommodation and it will not cause undue hardship. If there is undue hardship, the employer must reassign the employee if there is a vacant position for which s/he is qualified and which would allow the employer to grant the modified or part-time schedule (absent undue hardship).[68] An employee receiving a part-time schedule as a reasonable accommodation is entitled only to the benefits, including health insurance, that other part-time employees receive. Thus, if nondisabled part-time workers are not provided with health insurance, then the employer does not have to provide such coverage to an employee with a disability who is given a part-time schedule as a reasonable accommodation.

Under the FMLA, an eligible employee is entitled to take leave intermittently or on a part-time basis, when medically necessary, until s/he has used up the equivalent of 12 workweeks in a 12-month period. When such leave is foreseeable based on planned medical treatment, an employer may require the employee to temporarily transfer (for the duration of the leave) to an available alternative position, with equivalent pay and benefits, for which the employee is qualified and which better suits his/her reduced hours.[69] An employer always must maintain the employee's existing level of coverage under a group health plan during the period of FMLA leave, provided the employee pays his/her share of the premium.[70]

> *Example*: An employee with an ADA disability requests that she be excused from work one day a week for the next six months because of her disability. If this employee is eligible for a modified schedule under the FMLA, the employer must provide the requested leave under that statute if it is medically necessary, even if the leave would be an undue hardship under the ADA.

Modified Workplace Policies

24. Is it a reasonable accommodation to modify a workplace policy?

Yes. It is a reasonable accommodation to modify a workplace policy when necessitated by an individual's disability-related limitations,[71] absent undue hardship. But, reasonable accommodation only requires that the employer modify the policy for an employee who requires such action because of a disability; therefore, the employer may continue to apply the policy to all other employees.

> *Example*: An employer has a policy prohibiting employees from eating or drinking at their workstations. An employee with insulin-dependent diabetes explains to her employer that she may occasionally take too much insulin and, in order to avoid going into insulin shock, she must immediately eat a candy bar or drink fruit juice. The employee requests permission to keep such food at her workstation and to eat or drink when her insulin level necessitates. The employer must modify its policy to grant this request, absent undue hardship. Similarly, an employer might have to modify a policy to allow an employee with a disability to bring in a small refrigerator, or to use the employer's refrigerator, to store medication that must be taken during working hours.

Granting an employee time off from work or an adjusted work schedule as a reasonable accommodation may involve modifying leave or attendance procedures or policies. For example, it would be a reasonable accommodation to modify a policy requiring employees to schedule vacation time in advance if an otherwise qualified individual with a disability needed to use accrued vacation time on an unscheduled basis because of disability-related medical problems, barring undue hardship.[72] Furthermore, an employer may be required to provide additional leave to an employee with a disability as a reasonable accommodation in spite of a "no-fault" leave policy, unless the provision of such leave would impose an undue hardship.[73]

In some instances, an employer's refusal to modify a workplace policy, such as a leave or attendance policy, could constitute disparate treatment as well as a failure to provide a reasonable accommodation. For example, an employer may have a policy requiring employees to notify supervisors before 9:00 a.m. if they are unable to report to work. If an employer would excuse an employee from complying with this policy because of emergency hospitalization due to a car

---

[68]*See infra* for more information on reassignment, including under what circumstances an employer and employee may voluntarily agree that a transfer is preferable to having the employee remain in his/her current position.

[69]29 C.F.R. §825.204 (1997); *see also* special rules governing intermittent leave for instructional employees at §825.601, §825.602.

[70]29 C.F.R. §825.209, §825.210 (1997).

[71]42 U.S.C. §12111(9)(B) (1994); 29 C.F.R. §1630.2(o)(2)(ii) (1997).

[72]*See Dutton v. Johnson County Bd. of Comm'rs*, 868 F. Supp. 1260, 1264-65 (D. Kan. 1994).

[73]*See* 29 C.F.R. pt. 1630 app. §1630.15(b), (c) (1997). *See also* Question 17, *supra*.

accident, then the employer must do the same thing when the emergency hospitalization is due to a disability.[74]

Reassignment[75]

The ADA specifically lists "reassignment to a vacant position" as a form of reasonable accommodation.[76] This type of reasonable accommodation must be provided to an employee who, because of a disability, can no longer perform the essential functions of his/her current position, with or without reasonable accommodation, unless the employer can show that it would be an undue hardship.[77]

An employee must be "qualified" for the new position. An employee is "qualified" for a position if s/he: (1) satisfies the requisite skill, experience, education, and other job-related requirements of the position, and (2) can perform the essential functions of the new position, with or without reasonable accommodation.[78] The employee does not need to be the best qualified individual for the position in order to obtain it as a reassignment.

There is no obligation for the employer to assist the individual to become qualified. Thus, the employer does not have to provide training so that the employee acquires necessary skills to take a job.[79] The employer, however, would have to provide an employee with a disability who is being reassigned with any training that is normally provided to anyone hired for or transferred to the position.

Example A: An employer is considering reassigning an employee with a disability to a position which requires the ability to speak Spanish in order to perform an essential function. The employee never learned Spanish and wants the employer to send him to a course to learn Spanish. The employer is not required to provide this training as part of the obligation to make a reassignment. Therefore, the employee is not qualified for this position.

Example B: An employer is considering reassigning an employee with a disability to a position in which she will contract for goods and services. The employee is qualified for the position. The employer has its own specialized rules regarding contracting that necessitate training all individuals hired for these positions. In this situation, the employer must provide the employee with this specialized training.

Before considering reassignment as a reasonable accommodation, employers should first consider those accommodations that would enable an employee to remain in his/her current position. Reassignment is the reasonable accommodation of last resort and is required only after it has been determined that: (1) there are no effective accommodations that will enable the employee to perform the essential functions of his/her current position, or (2) all other reasonable accommodations would impose an undue hardship.[80] However, if both the employer and the employee voluntarily agree that transfer is preferable to remaining in the current position with some form of reasonable accommodation, then the employer may transfer the employee.

"Vacant" means that the position is available when the employee asks for reasonable accommodation, or that the employer knows that it will become available within a reasonable amount of time. A "reasonable amount of time" should be determined on a case-by-case basis considering relevant facts, such as whether the employer, based on experience, can anticipate that an appropriate position will become vacant within a short period

---

[74]*But cf. Miller v. Nat'l Casualty Co.*, 61 F.3d 627, 629-30 (8th Cir. 1995) (court refuses to find that employee's sister had requested reasonable accommodation despite the fact that the sister informed the employer that the employee was having a medical crisis necessitating emergency hospitalization).

[75]For information on how reassignment may apply to employers who provide light duty positions, see Workers' Compensation and the ADA, *supra* note 52.

[76]42 U.S.C. §12111(9)(B) (1994); 29 C.F.R. §1630.2(o)(2)(ii) (1997). *See Benson v. Northwest Airlines, Inc.*, 62 F.3d 1108, 1114 (8th Cir. 1995); *Monette v. Electronic Data Sys. Corp.*, 90 F.3d 1173, 1187 (6th Cir. 1996); *Gile v. United Airlines, Inc.*, 95 F.3d 492, 498 (7th Cir. 1996).

Reassignment is available only to employees, not to applicants. 29 C.F.R. pt. 1630 app. §1630.2(o) (1997).

[77]29 C.F.R. pt. 1630 app. §1630.2(o) (1997); *see Haysman v. Food Lion, Inc.*, 893 F. Supp. 1092, 1104 (S.D. Ga. 1995).

Some courts have found that an employee who is unable to perform the essential functions of his/her current position is unqualified to receive a reassignment. *See, e.g., Schmidt v. Methodist Hosp. of Indiana, Inc.*, 89 F.3d 342, 345 (7th Cir. 1996); *Pangalos v. Prudential Ins. Co. of Am.*, 1996 U.S. Dist. LEXIS 15749 (E.D. Pa. 1996). These decisions, however, nullify Congress' inclusion of reassignment in the ADA. An employee requires a reassignment only if s/he is unable to continue performing the essential functions of his/her current position, with or without reasonable accommodation. Thus, an employer must provide reassignment either when reasonable accommodation in an employee's current job would cause undue hardship or when it would not be possible. *See Aka v. Washington Hosp. Ctr.*,156 F.3d 1284, 1300-01 (D.C. Cir. 1998); *Dalton v. Subaru-Isuzu Automotive, Inc.*, 141 F.3d 667, 678 (7th Cir. 1998); *see also ADA and Psychiatric Disabilities, supra* note 27, Workers' Compensation and the ADA, *supra* note 52.

[78]29 C.F.R. §1630.2(m) (1997); 29 C.F.R. pt. 1630 app. §1630.2(m), 1630.2(o) (1997). *See Stone v. Mount Vernon*, 118 F.3d 92, 100-01 (2d Cir. 1997).

[79]*See Quintana v. Sound Distribution Corp.*, 1997 U.S. Dist. LEXIS 934 (S.D.N.Y. 1997).

[80]*See* 29 C.F.R. pt. 1630 app. §1630.2(o) (1997); Senate Report, *supra* note 6; House Education and Labor Report, *supra* note 6.

of time.[81] A position is considered vacant even if an employer has posted a notice or announcement seeking applications for that position. The employer does not have to bump an employee from a job in order to create a vacancy; nor does it have to create a new position.[82]

> *Example C*: An employer is seeking a reassignment for an employee with a disability. There are no vacant positions today, but the employer has just learned that another employee resigned and that that position will become vacant in four weeks. The impending vacancy is equivalent to the position currently held by the employee with a disability. If the employee is qualified for that position, the employer must offer it to him.

> *Example D*: An employer is seeking a reassignment for an employee with a disability. There are no vacant positions today, but the employer has just learned that an employee in an equivalent position plans to retire in six months. Although the employer knows that the employee with a disability is qualified for this position, the employer does not have to offer this position to her because six months is beyond a "reasonable amount of time." (If, six months from now, the employer decides to advertise the position, it must allow the individual to apply for that position and give the application the consideration it deserves.)

The employer must reassign the individual to a vacant position that is equivalent in terms of pay, status, or other relevant factors (e.g., benefits, geographical location) if the employee is qualified for the position. If there is no vacant equivalent position, the employer must reassign the employee to a vacant lower level position for which the individual is qualified. Assuming there is more than one vacancy for which the employee is qualified, the employer must place the individual in the position that comes closest to the employee's current position in terms of pay, status, etc.[83] If it is unclear which position comes closest, the employer should consult with the employee about his/her preference before determining the position to which the employee will be reassigned. Reassignment does not include giving an employee a promotion. Thus, an employee must compete for any vacant position that would constitute a promotion.

25. Is a probationary employee entitled to reassignment?

Employers cannot deny a reassignment to an employee solely because s/he is designated as "probationary." An employee with a disability is eligible for reassignment to a new position, regardless of whether s/he is considered "probationary," as long as the employee adequately performed the essential functions of the position, with or without reasonable accommodation, before the need for a reassignment arose.

The longer the period of time in which an employee has adequately performed the essential functions, with or without reasonable accommodation, the more likely it is that reassignment is appropriate if the employee becomes unable to continue performing the essential functions of the current position due to a disability. If, however, the probationary employee has never adequately performed the essential functions, with or without reasonable accommodation, then s/he is not entitled to reassignment because s/he was never "qualified" for the original position. In this situation, the employee is similar to an applicant who applies for a job for which s/he is not qualified, and then requests reassignment. Applicants are not entitled to reassignment.

> *Example A*: An employer designates all new employees as "probationary" for one year. An employee has been working successfully for nine months when she becomes disabled in a car accident. The employee, due to her disability, is unable to continue performing the essential functions of her current position, with or without reasonable accommodation, and seeks a reassignment. She is entitled to a reassignment if there is a vacant position for which she is qualified and it would not pose an undue hardship.

> *Example B*: A probationary employee has been working two weeks, but has been unable to perform the essential functions of the job because of his disability. There are no reasonable accommodations that would permit the individual to perform the essential functions of the position, so the individual requests a reassignment. The employer does not have to provide a reassignment (even if there is a vacant position) because, as it turns out, the individual was never qualified – i.e., the individual was never able to perform the essential functions of the position, with or without reasonable accommodation, for which he was hired.

26. Must an employer offer reassignment as a reasonable accommodation if it does not allow any of its employees to transfer from one position to another?

Yes. The ADA requires employers to provide reasonable accommodations to individuals with disabilities, including reassignment, even though they are not available to others. Therefore, an employer who does not normally transfer em-

---

[81]For suggestions on what the employee can do while waiting for a position to become vacant within a reasonable amount of time, *see* note 89, *infra*.

[82]*See* 29 C.F.R. pt. 1630 app. §1630.2(o) (1997); *see also White v. York Int'l Corp.*, 45 F.3d 357, 362 (10th Cir. 1995).

[83]*See* 29 C.F.R. pt. 1630 app. §1630.2(o) (1997).

ployees would still have to reassign an employee with a disability, unless it could show that the reassignment caused an undue hardship. And, if an employer has a policy prohibiting transfers, it would have to modify that policy in order to reassign an employee with a disability, unless it could show undue hardship.[84]

27. Is an employer's obligation to offer reassignment to a vacant position limited to those vacancies within an employee's office, branch, agency, department, facility, personnel system (if the employer has more than a single personnel system), or geographical area?

No. This is true even if the employer has a policy prohibiting transfers from one office, branch, agency, department, facility, personnel system, or geographical area to another. The ADA contains no language limiting the obligation to reassign only to positions within an office, branch, agency, etc.[85] Rather, the extent to which an employer must search for a vacant position will be an issue of undue hardship.[86] If an employee is being reassigned to a different geographical area, the employee must pay for any relocation expenses unless the employer routinely pays such expenses when granting voluntary transfers to other employees.

28. Does an employer have to notify an employee with a disability about vacant positions, or is it the employee's responsibility to learn what jobs are vacant?

The employer is in the best position to know which jobs are vacant or will become vacant within a reasonable period of time.[87] In order to narrow the search for potential vacancies, the employer, as part of the interactive process, should ask the employee about his/her qualifications and interests. Based on this information, the employer is obligated to inform an employee about vacant positions for which s/he may be eligible as a reassignment. However, an employee should assist the employer in identifying appropriate vacancies to the extent that the employee has access to information about them. If the employer does not know whether the employee is qualified for a specific position, the employer can discuss with the employee his/her qualifications.[88]

An employer should proceed as expeditiously as possible in determining whether there are appropriate vacancies. The length of this process will vary depending on how quickly an employer can search for and identify whether an appropriate vacant position exists. For a very small employer, this process may take one day; for other employers this process may take several

---

[84]*See US Airways Inc. v. Barnett,* 535 U.S. 391, 122 S. Ct. 1516, 1521, 1524 (2002). *See also Aka v. Washington Hosp. Ctr.,* 156 F.3d 1284, 1304-05 (D.C. Cir. 1998); *United States v. Denver,* 943 F. Supp. 1304, 1312 (D. Colo. 1996). *See also* Question 24, *supra.*

[85]42 U.S.C. §12111(9)(B) (1994); 29 C.F.R. §1630.2(o)(2)(ii) (1997); *see Hendricks-Robinson v. Excel Corp.,* 154 F.3d 685, 695 (7th Cir. 1998); *see generally Dalton v. Subaru-Isuzu Automotive, Inc.,* 141 F.3d 667, 677-78 (7th Cir. 1998).

[86]*See Gile v. United Airlines, Inc.,* 95 F.3d 492, 499 (7th Cir. 1996); *see generally United States v. Denver,* 943 F. Supp. 1304, 1311-13 (D. Colo. 1996).

Some courts have limited the obligation to provide a reassignment to positions within the same department or facility in which the employee currently works, except when the employer's standard practice is to provide inter-department or inter-facility transfers for all employees. *See, e.g., Emrick v. Libbey-Owens-Ford Co.,* 875 F. Supp. 393, 398 (E.D. Tex. 1995). However, the ADA requires modification of workplace policies, such as transfer policies, as a form of reasonable accommodation. *See* Question 24, *supra.* Therefore, policies limiting transfers cannot be a per se bar to reassigning someone outside his/her department or facility. Furthermore, the ADA requires employers to provide reasonable accommodations, including reassignment, regardless of whether such accommodations are routinely granted to nondisabled employees. *See* Question 26, *supra.*

[87]*See Hendricks-Robinson v. Excel Corp.,* 154 F.3d 685, 695-96, 697-98 (7th Cir. 1998) (employer cannot mislead disabled employees who need reassignment about full range of vacant positions; nor can it post vacant positions for such a short period of time that disabled employees on medical leave have no realistic chance to learn about them); *Mengine v. Runyon,* 114 F.3d 415, 420 (3d Cir. 1997) (an employer has a duty to make reasonable efforts to assist an employee in identifying a vacancy because an employee will not have the ability or resources to identify a vacant position absent participation by the employer); *Woodman v. Runyon,* 132 F.3d 1330, 1344 (10th Cir. 1997) (federal employers are far better placed than employees to investigate in good faith the availability of vacant positions).

[88]*See Dalton v. Subaru-Isuzu Automotive, Inc.,* 141 F.3d 667, 678 (7th Cir. 1998) (employer must first identify full range of alternative positions and then determine which ones employee qualified to perform, with or without reasonable accommodation); *Hendricks-Robinson v. Excel Corp.,* 154 F.3d 685, 700 (7th Cir. 1998) (employer's methodology to determine if reassignment is appropriate does not constitute the "interactive process" contemplated by the ADA if it is directive rather than interactive); *Mengine v. Runyon,* 114 F.3d 415, 419-20 (3d Cir. 1997) (once an employer has identified possible vacancies, an employee has a duty to identify which one he is capable of performing).

---

weeks.[89] When an employer has completed its search, identified whether there are any vacancies (including any positions that will become vacant in a reasonable amount of time), notified the employee of the results, and either offered an appropriate vacancy to the employee or informed him/her that no appropriate vacancies are available, the employer will have fulfilled its obligation.

29. Does reassignment mean that the employee is permitted to compete for a vacant position?

No. Reassignment means that the employee gets the vacant position if s/he is qualified for it. Otherwise, reassignment would be of little value and would not be implemented as Congress intended.[90]

30. If an employee is reassigned to a lower level position, must an employer maintain his/her salary from the higher level position?

No, unless the employer transfers employees without disabilities to lower level positions and maintains their original salaries.[91]

---

[89]If it will take several weeks to determine whether an appropriate vacant position exists, the employer and employee should discuss the employee's status during that period. There are different possibilities depending on the circumstances, but they may include: use of accumulated paid leave, use of unpaid leave, or a temporary assignment to a light duty position. Employers also may choose to take actions that go beyond the ADA's requirements, such as eliminating an essential function of the employee's current position, to enable an employee to continue working while a reassignment is sought.

[90]42 U.S.C. §12111(9)(b) (1994); 29 C.F.R. pt. §1630 app. 1630.2(o) (1997). *See* Senate Report, *supra* note 6, at 31 ("If an employee, because of disability, can no longer perform the essential functions of the job that she or he has held, a transfer to another vacant job for which the person is qualified may prevent the employee from being out of work and the employer from losing a valuable worker."). *See Wood v. County of Alameda*, 1995 U.S. Dist. LEXIS 17514 (N.D. Cal. 1995) (when employee could no longer perform job because of disability, she was entitled to reassignment to a vacant position, not simply an opportunity to "compete"); *cf. Aka v. Washington Hosp. Ctr.*, 156 F.3d 1284, 1304-05 (D.C. Cir. 1998) (the court, in interpreting a collective bargaining agreement provision authorizing reassignment of disabled employees, states that "[a]n employee who is allowed to compete for jobs precisely like any other applicant has not been "reassigned"); *United States v. Denver*, 943 F. Supp. 1304, 1310-11 (D. Colo. 1996) (the ADA requires employers to move beyond traditional analysis and consider reassignment as a method of enabling a disabled worker to do a job).

Some courts have suggested that reassignment means simply an opportunity to compete for a vacant position. *See, e.g., Daugherty v. City of El Paso*, 56 F.3d 695, 700 (5th Cir. 1995). Such an interpretation nullifies the clear statutory language stating that reassignment is a form of reasonable accommodation. Even without the ADA, an employee with a disability may have the right to compete for a vacant position.

[91]29 C.F.R. pt. 1630 app. §1630.2(o) (1997).

31. Must an employer provide a reassignment if it would violate a seniority system?

Generally, it will be "unreasonable" to reassign an employee with a disability if doing so would violate the rules of a seniority system.[92] This is true both for collectively bargained seniority systems and those unilaterally imposed by management. Seniority systems governing job placement give employees expectations of consistent, uniform treatment – expectations that would be undermined if employers had to make the type of individualized, case-by-case assessment required by the reasonable accommodation process.[93]

However, if there are "special circumstances" that "undermine the employees' expectations of consistent, uniform treatment," it may be a "reasonable accommodation," absent undue hardship, to reassign an employee despite the existence of a seniority system. For example, "special circumstances" may exist where an employer retains the right to alter the seniority system unilaterally, and has exercised that right fairly frequently, thereby lowering employee expectations in the seniority system.[94] In this circumstance, one more exception (i.e., providing the reassignment to an employee with a disability) may not make a difference.[95] Alternatively, a seniority system may contain exceptions, such that one more exception is unlikely to matter.[96] Another possibility is that a seniority system might contain procedures for making exceptions, thus suggesting to employees that seniority does not automatically guarantee access to a specific job.

Other Reasonable Accommodation Issues[97]

32. If an employer has provided one reasonable accommodation, does it have to provide additional

---

[92]*See US Airways, Inc. v. Barnett*, 535 U.S. 391, 122 S. Ct. 1516, 1524-25 (2002).

[93]*Id.*

[94]*Id.* at 1525. In a lawsuit, the plaintiff/employee bears the burden of proof to show the existence of "special circumstances" that warrant a jury's finding that a reassignment is "reasonable" despite the presence of a seniority system. If an employee can show "special circumstances," then the burden shifts to the employer to show why the reassignment would pose an undue hardship. See *id.*

[95]*Id.*

[96]*Id.* The Supreme Court made clear that these two were examples of "special circumstances" and that they did not constitute an exhaustive list of examples. Furthermore, Justice Stevens, in a concurring opinion, raised additional issues that could be relevant to show special circumstances that would make it reasonable for an employer to make an exception to its seniority system. See *id.* at 1526.

[97]The discussions and examples in this section assume that there is only one effective accommodation and that the reasonable accommodation will not cause an undue hardship.

reasonable accommodations requested by an individual with a disability?

The duty to provide reasonable accommodation is an ongoing one.[98] Certain individuals require only one reasonable accommodation, while others may need more than one. Still others may need one reasonable accommodation for a period of time, and then at a later date, require another type of reasonable accommodation. If an individual requests multiple reasonable accommodations, s/he is entitled only to those accommodations that are necessitated by a disability and that will provide an equal employment opportunity.

An employer must consider each request for reasonable accommodation and determine: (1) whether the accommodation is needed, (2) if needed, whether the accommodation would be effective, and (3) if effective, whether providing the reasonable accommodation would impose an undue hardship. If a reasonable accommodation turns out to be ineffective and the employee with a disability remains unable to perform an essential function, the employer must consider whether there would be an alternative reasonable accommodation that would not pose an undue hardship. If there is no alternative accommodation, then the employer must attempt to reassign the employee to a vacant position for which s/he is qualified, unless to do so would cause an undue hardship.

33. Does an employer have to change a person's supervisor as a form of reasonable accommodation?

No. An employer does not have to provide an employee with a new supervisor as a reasonable accommodation. Nothing in the ADA, however, prohibits an employer from doing so. Furthermore, although an employer is not required to change supervisors, the ADA may require that supervisory methods be altered as a form of reasonable accommodation.[99] Also, an employee with a disability is protected from disability-based discrimination by a supervisor, including disability-based harassment.

Example: A supervisor frequently schedules team meetings on a day's notice – often notifying staff in the afternoon that a meeting will be held on the following morning. An employee with a disability has missed several meetings because they have conflicted with previously-scheduled physical therapy sessions. The employee asks that the supervisor give her two to three days' notice of team meetings so that, if necessary, she can reschedule the physical therapy sessions. Assuming no undue hardship

would result, the supervisor must make this reasonable accommodation.

34. Does an employer have to allow an employee with a disability to work at home as a reasonable accommodation?

An employer must modify its policy concerning where work is performed if such a change is needed as a reasonable accommodation, but only if this accommodation would be effective and would not cause an undue hardship.[100] Whether this accommodation is effective will depend on whether the essential functions of the position can be performed at home. There are certain jobs in which the essential functions can only be performed at the work site – e.g., food server, cashier in a store. For such jobs, allowing an employee to work at home is not effective because it does not enable an employee to perform his/her essential functions. Certain considerations may be critical in determining whether a job can be effectively performed at home, including (but not limited to) the employer's ability to adequately supervise the employee and the employee's need to work with certain equipment or tools that cannot be replicated at home. In contrast, employees may be able to perform the essential functions of certain types of jobs at home (e.g., telemarketer, proofreader).[101] For these types of jobs, an employer may deny a request to work at home if it can show that another accommodation would be effective or if working at home will cause undue hardship.

35. Must an employer withhold discipline or termination of an employee who, because of a disability, violated a conduct rule that is job-related for the position in question and consistent with business necessity?

No. An employer never has to excuse a violation of a uniformly applied conduct rule that is job-related and consistent with business necessity. This means, for example, that an employer never has

---

[98]*See Ralph v. Lucent Technologies, Inc.*, 135 F.3d 166, 171 (1st Cir. 1998).

[99]For a discussion on ways to modify supervisory methods, *see* ADA and Psychiatric Disabilities, *supra* note 27.

[100]*See* 29 C.F.R. §1630.2(o)(1)(ii), (2)(ii) (1997) (modifications or adjustments to the manner or circumstances under which the position held or desired is customarily performed that enable a qualified individual with a disability to perform the essential functions).

[101]Courts have differed regarding whether "work-at-home" can be a reasonable accommodation. *Compare Langon v. Department of Health and Human Servs.*, 959 F.2d 1053, 1060 (D.C. Cir. 1992); *Anzalone v. Allstate Insurance Co.*, 1995 U.S. Dist. LEXIS 588 (E.D. La. 1995); *Carr v. Reno*, 23 F.3d 525, 530 (D.D.C. 1994), with *Vande Zande v. Wisconsin Dep't of Admin.*, 44 F.3d 538, 545 (7th Cir. 1995). Courts that have rejected working at home as a reasonable accommodation focus on evidence that personal contact, interaction, and coordination are needed for a specific position. *See, e.g., Whillock v. Delta Air Lines*, 926 F. Supp. 1555, 1564 (N.D. Ga. 1995), *aff'd*, 86 F.3d 1171 (11th Cir. 1996); *Misek-Falkoff v. IBM Corp.*, 854 F. Supp. 215, 227-28 (S.D.N.Y. 1994), *aff'd*, 60 F.3d 811 (2d Cir. 1995).

to tolerate or excuse violence, threats of violence, stealing, or destruction of property. An employer may discipline an employee with a disability for engaging in such misconduct if it would impose the same discipline on an employee without a disability.

36. Must an employer provide a reasonable accommodation for an employee with a disability who violated a conduct rule that is job-related for the position in question and consistent with business necessity?

An employer must make reasonable accommodation to enable an otherwise qualified employee with a disability to meet such a conduct standard in the future, barring undue hardship, except where the punishment for the violation is termination.[102] Since reasonable accommodation is always prospective, an employer is not required to excuse past misconduct even if it is the result of the individual's disability.[103] Possible reasonable accommodations could include adjustments to starting times, specified breaks, and leave if these accommodations will enable an employee to comply with conduct rules.[104]

Example: An employee with major depression is often late for work because of medication side-effects that make him extremely groggy in the morning. His scheduled hours are 9:00 a.m. to 5:30 p.m., but he arrives at 9:00, 9:30, 10:00, or even 10:30 on any given day. His job responsibilities involve telephone contact with the company's traveling sales representatives, who depend on him to answer urgent marketing questions and expedite special orders. The employer disciplines him for tardiness, stating that continued failure

to arrive promptly during the next month will result in termination of his employment. The individual then explains that he was late because of a disability and needs to work on a later schedule. In this situation, the employer may discipline the employee because he violated a conduct standard addressing tardiness that is job-related for the position in question and consistent with business necessity. The employer, however, must consider reasonable accommodation, barring undue hardship, to enable this individual to meet this standard in the future. For example, if this individual can serve the company's sales representatives by regularly working a schedule of 10:00 a.m. to 6:30 p.m., a reasonable accommodation would be to modify his schedule so that he is not required to report for work until 10:00 a.m.

37. Is it a reasonable accommodation to make sure that an employee takes medication as prescribed?

No. Medication monitoring is not a reasonable accommodation. Employers have no obligation to monitor medication because doing so does not remove a workplace barrier. Similarly, an employer has no responsibility to monitor an employee's medical treatment or ensure that s/he is receiving appropriate treatment because such treatment does not involve modifying workplace barriers.[105]

It may be a form of reasonable accommodation, however, to give an employee a break in order that s/he may take medication, or to grant leave so that an employee may obtain treatment.

38. Is an employer relieved of its obligation to provide reasonable accommodation for an employee with a disability who fails to take medication, to obtain medical treatment, or to use an assistive device (such as a hearing aid)?

No. The ADA requires an employer to provide reasonable accommodation to remove workplace barriers, regardless of what effect medication, other medical treatment, or assistive devices may have on an employee's ability to perform the job.[106]

However, if an employee with a disability, with or without reasonable accommodation, cannot perform the essential functions of the position or poses a direct threat in the absence of medication, treatment, or an assistive device, then s/he is unqualified.

---

[102]*See* 29 C.F.R. §1630.15(d) (1997).

[103]*See Siefken v. Arlington Heights*, 65 F.3d 664, 666 (7th Cir. 1995). Therefore, it may be in the employee's interest to request a reasonable accommodation before performance suffers or conduct problems occur. For more information on conduct standards, including when they are job-related and consistent with business necessity, *see* ADA and Psychiatric Disabilities, *supra* note 27.

An employer does not have to offer a "firm choice" or a "last chance agreement" to an employee who performs poorly or who has engaged in misconduct because of alcoholism. "Firm choice" or "last chance agreements" involve excusing past performance or conduct problems resulting from alcoholism in exchange for an employee's receiving substance abuse treatment and refraining from further use of alcohol. Violation of such an agreement generally warrants termination. Since the ADA does not require employers to excuse poor performance or violation of conduct standards that are job-related and consistent with business necessity, an employer has no obligation to provide "firm choice" or a "last chance agreement" as a reasonable accommodation. *See Johnson v. Babbitt*, EEOC Docket No. 03940100 (March 28, 1996). However, an employer may choose to offer an employee a "firm choice" or a "last chance agreement."

[104]*See* ADA and Psychiatric Disabilities, *supra* note 27.

[105]*See Robertson v. The Neuromedical Ctr.*, 161 F.3d 292, 296 (5th Cir. 1998); *see also* ADA and Psychiatric Disabilities, *supra* note 27.

[106]While from an employer's perspective it may appear that an employee is "failing" to use medication or follow a certain treatment, such questions can be complex. There are many reasons why a person would choose to forgo treatment, including expense and serious side effects.

39. Must an employer provide a reasonable accommodation that is needed because of the side effects of medication or treatment related to the disability, or because of symptoms or other medical conditions resulting from the underlying disability?

Yes. The side effects caused by the medication that an employee must take because of the disability are limitations resulting from the disability. Reasonable accommodation extends to all limitations resulting from a disability.

Example A: An employee with cancer undergoes chemotherapy twice a week, which causes her to be quite ill afterwards. The employee requests a modified schedule – leave for the two days a week of chemotherapy. The treatment will last six weeks. Unless it can show undue hardship, the employer must grant this request.

Similarly, any symptoms or related medical conditions resulting from the disability that cause limitations may also require reasonable accommodation.[107]

Example B: An employee, as a result of insulin-dependent diabetes, has developed background retinopathy (a vision impairment). The employee, who already has provided documentation showing his diabetes is a disability, requests a device to enlarge the text on his computer screen. The employer can request documentation that the retinopathy is related to the diabetes but the employee does not have to show that the retinopathy is an independent disability under the ADA. Since the retinopathy is a consequence of the diabetes (an ADA disability), the request must be granted unless undue hardship can be shown.

40. Must an employer ask whether a reasonable accommodation is needed when an employee has not asked for one?

Generally, no. As a general rule, the individual with a disability – who has the most knowledge about the need for reasonable accommodation – must inform the employer that an accommodation is needed.[108]

However, an employer should initiate the reasonable accommodation interactive process[109] without being asked if the employer: (1) knows that the employee has a disability, (2) knows, or has reason to know, that the employee is experiencing workplace problems because of the disability, and (3) knows, or has reason to know, that the disability prevents the employee from requesting a reasonable accommodation. If the individual with a disability states that s/he does not need a reasonable accommodation, the employer will have fulfilled its obligation.

Example: An employee with mental retardation delivers messages at a law firm. He frequently mixes up messages for "R. Miller" and "T. Miller." The employer knows about the disability, suspects that the performance problem is a result of the disability, and knows that this employee is unable to ask for a reasonable accommodation because of his mental retardation. The employer asks the employee about mixing up the two names and asks if it would be helpful to spell the first name of each person. When the employee says that would be better, the employer, as a reasonable accommodation, instructs the receptionist to write the full first name when messages are left for one of the Messrs. Miller.

41. May an employer ask whether a reasonable accommodation is needed when an employee with a disability has not asked for one?

An employer may ask an employee with a known disability whether s/he needs a reasonable accommodation when it reasonably believes that the employee may need an accommodation. For example, an employer could ask a deaf employee who is being

---

[107]*See Vande Zande v. Wisconsin Dep't of Admin.*, 44 F.3d 538, 544 (7th Cir. 1995).

[108] *See* 29 C.F.R. pt. 1630 app. §1630.9 (1997); *see also* House Judiciary Report, *supra* note 6, at 39; House Education and Labor Report, *supra* note 6, at 65; Senate Report, *supra* note 6, at 34.

See, e.g., Taylor v. Principal Fin. Group, Inc., 93 F.3d 155, 165 (5th Cir. 1996); *Tips v. Regents of Texas Tech Univ.*, 921 F. Supp. 1515, 1518 (N.D. Tex. 1996); *Cheatwood v. Roanoke Indus.*, 891 F. Supp. 1528, 1538 (N.D. Ala. 1995); *Mears v. Gulfstream Aerospace Corp.*, 905 F. Supp. 1075, 1080 (S.D. Ga. 1995), *aff'd*, 87 F.3d 1331 (11th Cir. 1996). *But see Schmidt v. Safeway Inc.*, 864 F. Supp. 991, 997 (D. Or. 1994) (employer had obligation to provide reasonable accommodation because it knew of the employee's alcohol problem and had reason to believe that an accommodation would permit the employee to perform the job).

An employer may not assert that it never received a request for reasonable accommodation, as a defense to a claim of failure to provide reasonable accommodation, if it actively discouraged an individual from making such a request.

For more information about an individual requesting reasonable accommodation, *see* Questions 1-4, *supra*.

[109]*See* Question 5, *supra*, for information on the interactive process.

sent on a business trip if s/he needs reasonable accommodation. Or, if an employer is scheduling a luncheon at a restaurant and is uncertain about what questions it should ask to ensure that the restaurant is accessible for an employee who uses a wheel-chair, the employer may first ask the employee. An employer also may ask an employee with a disability who is having performance or conduct problems if s/he needs reasonable accommodation.[110]

42. May an employer tell other employees that an individual is receiving a reasonable accommodation when employees ask questions about a coworker with a disability?

No. An employer may not disclose that an employee is receiving a reasonable accommodation because this usually amounts to a disclosure that the individual has a disability. The ADA specifically prohibits the disclosure of medical information except in certain limited situations, which do not include disclosure to coworkers.[111]

An employer may certainly respond to a question from an employee about why a coworker is receiving what is perceived as "different" or "special" treatment by emphasizing its policy of assisting any employee who encounters difficulties in the workplace. The employer also may find it helpful to point out that many of the workplace issues encountered by employees are personal, and that, in these circumstances, it is the employer's policy to respect employee privacy. An employer may be able to make this point effectively by reassuring the employee asking the question that his/her privacy would similarly be respected if s/he found it necessary to ask the employer for some kind of workplace change for personal reasons.

Since responding to specific coworker questions may be difficult, employers might find it helpful before such questions are raised to provide all employees with information about various laws that require employers to meet certain employee needs (e.g., the ADA and the Family and Medical Leave Act), while also requiring them to protect the privacy of employees. In providing general ADA information to employees, an employer may wish to highlight the obligation to provide reasonable accommodation, including the interactive process and different types of reasonable accommodations, and the statute's confidentiality protections. Such information could be delivered in orientation materials, employee handbooks, notices accompanying paystubs, and posted flyers. Employers may wish to explore these and other alternatives with unions because they too are bound by the ADA's confidentiality provisions. Union meetings and bulletin boards may be further avenues for such educational efforts.

As long as there is no coercion by an employer, an employee with a disability may voluntarily choose to disclose to coworkers his/her disability and/or the fact that s/he is receiving a reasonable accommodation.

Undue Hardship Issues[112]

An employer does not have to provide a reasonable accommodation that would cause an "undue hardship" to the employer. Generalized conclusions will not suffice to support a claim of undue hardship. Instead, undue hardship must be based on an individualized assessment of current circumstances that show that a specific reasonable accommodation would cause significant difficulty or expense.[113] A determination of undue hardship should be based on several factors, including:

- the nature and cost of the accommodation needed;
- the overall financial resources of the facility making the reasonable accommodation; the number of persons employed at this facility; and the effect on expenses and resources of the facility;
- the overall financial resources, size, number of employees, and type and location of facilities of the employer (if the facility involved in the reasonable accommodation is part of a larger entity);
- the type of operation of the employer, including the structure and functions of the workforce, the geographic separateness, and the administrative or fiscal relationship of

---

[110]29 C.F.R. pt. 1630 app. §1630.9 (1997).

[111]42 U.S.C. §12112(d)(3)(B), (d)(4)(C) (1994); 29 C.F.R. §1630.14(b)(1) (1997). The limited exceptions to the ADA confidentiality requirements are:

(1) supervisors and managers may be told about necessary restrictions on the work or duties of the employee and about necessary accommodations; (2) first aid and safety personnel may be told if the disability might require emergency treatment; and (3) government officials investigating compliance with the ADA must be given relevant information on request. In addition, the Commission has interpreted the ADA to allow employers to disclose medical information in the following circumstances: (1) in accordance with state workers' compensation laws, employers may disclose information to state workers' compensation offices, state second injury funds, or workers' compensation insurance carriers; and (2) employers are permitted to use medical information for insurance purposes. *See* 29 C.F.R. pt. 1630 app. §1630.14(b) (1997); Preemployment Questions and Medical Examinations, *supra* note 27; *Workers' Compensation and the ADA, supra* note 52.

---

[112]The discussions and examples in this section assume that there is only one effective accommodation.

[113]*See* 29 C.F.R. pt. 1630 app. §1630.15(d) (1996); *see also Stone v. Mount Vernon*, 118 F.3d 92, 101 (2d Cir. 1997) (an employer who has not hired any persons with disabilities cannot claim undue hardship based on speculation that if it were to hire several people with disabilities it may not have sufficient staff to perform certain tasks); *Bryant v. Better Business Bureau of Greater Maryland*, 923 F. Supp. 720, 735 (D. Md. 1996).

the facility involved in making the accommodation to the employer; and

- the impact of the accommodation on the operation of the facility.[114]

The ADA's legislative history indicates that Congress wanted employers to consider all possible sources of outside funding when assessing whether a particular accommodation would be too costly.[115] Undue hardship is determined based on the net cost to the employer. Thus, an employer should determine whether funding is available from an outside source, such as a state rehabilitation agency, to pay for all or part of the accommodation. In addition, the employer should determine whether it is eligible for certain tax credits or deductions to offset the cost of the accommodation.[116] Also, to the extent that a portion of the cost of an accommodation causes undue hardship, the employer should ask the individual with a disability if s/he will pay the difference.

If an employer determines that one particular reasonable accommodation will cause undue hardship, but a second type of reasonable accommodation will be effective and will not cause an undue hardship, then the employer must provide the second accommodation.

An employer cannot claim undue hardship based on employees' (or customers') fears or prejudices toward the individual's disability.[117] Nor can undue hardship be based on the fact that provision of a reasonable accommodation might have a negative impact on the morale of other employees. Employers, however, may be able to show undue hardship where provision of a reasonable accommodation would be unduly disruptive to other employees's ability to work.

Example A: An employee with breast cancer is undergoing chemotherapy. As a consequence of the treatment, the employee is subject to fatigue and finds it difficult to keep up with her regular workload. So that she may focus her reduced energy on performing her essential functions, the employer transfers three of her marginal functions to another employee for the duration of the chemotherapy treatments. The second employee is unhappy at being given extra assignments, but the employer determines that the employee can absorb the new assignments with little effect on his ability to perform his own assignments in a timely manner. Since the employer cannot show significant

disruption to its operation, there is no undue hardship.[118]

Example B: A convenience store clerk with multiple sclerosis requests that he be allowed to go from working full-time to part-time as a reasonable accommodation because of his disability. The store assigns two clerks per shift, and if the first clerk's hours are reduced, the second clerk's workload will increase significantly beyond his ability to handle his responsibilities. The store determines that such an arrangement will result in inadequate coverage to serve customers in a timely manner, keep the shelves stocked, and maintain store security. Thus, the employer can show undue hardship based on the significant disruption to its operations and, therefore, can refuse to reduce the employee's hours. The employer, however, should explore whether any other reasonable accommodation will assist the store clerk without causing undue hardship.

43. Must an employer modify the work hours of an employee with a disability if doing so would prevent other employees from performing their jobs?

No. If the result of modifying one employee's work hours (or granting leave) is to prevent other employees from doing their jobs, then the significant disruption to the operations of the employer constitutes an undue hardship.

Example A: A crane operator, due to his disability, requests an adjustment in his work schedule so that he starts work at 8:00 a.m. rather than 7:00 a.m., and finishes one hour later in the evening. The crane operator works with three other employees who cannot perform their jobs without the crane operator. As a result, if the employer grants this requested accommodation, it would have to require the other three workers to adjust their hours, find other work for them to do from 7:00 to 8:00, or have the workers do nothing. The ADA does not require the employer to take any of these actions because they all significantly disrupt the operations of the business. Thus, the employer can deny the requested accommodation, but should discuss with the employee if there are other possible accommodations that would not result in undue hardship.

Example B: A computer programmer works with a group of people to develop new software. There are certain tasks that the entire group must perform together, but each person also has individual assignments. It is through habit, not necessity, that they have often worked together first thing in the morning.

---

[114]*See* 42 U.S.C. §12111(10)(B) (1994); 29 C.F.R. §1630.2(p)(2) (1997); 29 C.F.R. pt. 1630 app. §1630.2(p) (1997); TAM, *supra* note 49, at 3.9.

[115]*See* Senate Report, *supra* note 6, at 36; House Education and Labor Report, supra note 6, at 69. *See also* 29 C.F.R. pt. 1630 app. §1630.2(p) (1997).

[116]*See* the Appendix on how to obtain information about the tax credit and deductions.

[117]*See* 29 C.F.R. pt. 1630 app. §1630.15(d) (1997).

---

[118]Failure to transfer marginal functions because of its negative impact on the morale of other employees also could constitute disparate treatment when similar morale problems do not stop an employer from reassigning tasks in other situations.

The programmer, due to her disability, requests an adjustment in her work schedule so that she works from 10:00 a.m.-7:00 p.m. rather than 9:00 a.m.-6:00 p.m. In this situation, the employer could grant the adjustment in hours because it would not significantly disrupt the operations of the business. The effect of the reasonable accommodation would be to alter when the group worked together and when they performed their individual assignments.

44. Can an employer deny a request for leave when an employee cannot provide a fixed date of return?

Providing leave to an employee who is unable to provide a fixed date of return is a form of reasonable accommodation. However, if an employer is able to show that the lack of a fixed return date causes an undue hardship, then it can deny the leave. In certain circumstances, undue hardship will derive from the disruption to the operations of the entity that occurs because the employer can neither plan for the employee's return nor permanently fill the position. If an employee cannot provide a fixed date of return, and an employer determines that it can grant such leave at that time without causing undue hardship, the employer has the right to require, as part of the interactive process, that the employee provide periodic updates on his/her condition and possible date of return. After receiving these updates, employers may reevaluate whether continued leave constitutes an undue hardship.

In certain situations, an employee may be able to provide only an approximate date of return. Treatment and recuperation do not always permit exact timetables. Thus, an employer cannot claim undue hardship solely because an employee can provide only an approximate date of return.[119] In such situations, or in situations in which a return date must be postponed because of unforeseen medical developments, employees should stay in regular communication with their employers to inform them of their progress and discuss, if necessary, the need for continued leave beyond what might have been granted originally.[120]

Example A: An experienced chef at a top restaurant requests leave for treatment of her disability but cannot provide a fixed date of return. The restaurant can show that this request constitutes undue hardship because of the difficulty of replacing, even temporarily, a chef of this caliber. Moreover, it leaves the employer unable to determine how long it must hold open the position or to plan for the chef's absence. Therefore, the restaurant can deny the request for leave as a reasonable accommodation.

Example B: An employee requests eight weeks of leave for surgery for his disability. The employer grants the request. During surgery, serious complications arise that require a lengthier period of recuperation than originally anticipated, as well as additional surgery. The employee contacts the employer after three weeks of leave to ask for an additional ten to fourteen weeks of leave (i.e., a total of 18 to 22 weeks of leave). The employer must assess whether granting additional leave causes an undue hardship.

45. Does a cost-benefit analysis determine whether a reasonable accommodation will cause undue hardship?

No. A cost-benefit analysis assesses the cost of a reasonable accommodation in relation to the perceived benefit to the employer and the employee. Neither the statute nor the legislative history supports a cost-benefit analysis to determine whether a specific accommodation causes an undue hardship.[121] Whether the cost of a reasonable accommodation imposes an undue hardship depends on the employer's resources, not on the individual's salary, position, or status (e.g., full-time versus part-time, salary versus hourly wage, permanent versus temporary).

46. Can an employer claim undue hardship solely because a reasonable accommodation would require it to make changes to property owned by someone else?

No, an employer cannot claim undue hardship solely because a reasonable accommodation would require it to make changes to property owned by someone else. In some situations, an employer will have the right under a lease or other contractual relationship with the property owner to make the type of changes that are needed. If this is the case, the employer should make the changes, assuming no other factors exist that would make the changes too difficult or costly. If the contractual relationship between the employer and property owner requires the owner's consent to the kinds of changes that are required, or prohibits them from being made, then the employer must make good

[121]The ADA's definition of undue hardship does not include any consideration of a cost-benefit analysis. *See* 42 U.S.C. §12111(10) (1994); *see also* House Education and Labor Report, *supra* note 6, at 69 ("[T]he committee wishes to make clear that the fact that an accommodation is used by only one employee should not be used as a negative factor counting in favor of a finding of undue hardship.").

Furthermore, the House of Representatives rejected a cost-benefit approach by defeating an amendment which would have presumed undue hardship if a reasonable accommodation cost more than 10 percent of the employee's annual salary. *See* 136 Cong. Rec. H2475 (1990), *see also* House Judiciary Report, *supra* note 6, at 41; 29 C.F.R. pt. 1630 app. §1630.15(d) (1997).

Despite the statutory language and legislative history, some courts have applied a cost-benefit analysis. *See, e.g., Monette v. Electronic Data Sys. Corp.*, 90 F.3d 1173, 1184 n.10 (6th Cir. 1996); *Vande Zande v. Wisconsin Dep't of Admin.*, 44 F.3d 538, 543 (7th Cir. 1995).

---

[119]*See Haschmann v. Time Warner Entertainment Co.*, 151 F.3d 591, 600-02 (7th Cir. 1998).

[120]*See Criado v. IBM*, 145 F.3d 437, 444-45 (1st Cir. 1998).

faith efforts either to obtain the owner's permission or to negotiate an exception to the terms of the contract. If the owner refuses to allow the employer to make the modifications, the employer may claim undue hardship. Even in this situation, however, the employer must still provide another reasonable accommodation, if one exists, that would not cause undue hardship.

> *Example A*: X Corp., a travel agency, leases space in a building owned by Z Co. One of X Corp.'s employees becomes disabled and needs to use a wheelchair. The employee requests as a reasonable accommodation that several room dividers be moved to make his work space easily accessible. X Corp.'s lease specifically allows it to make these kinds of physical changes, and they are otherwise easy and inexpensive to make. The fact that X Corp. does not own the property does not create an undue hardship and therefore it must make the requested accommodation.

> *Example B*: Same as Example A, except that X Corp.'s lease requires it to seek Z Co.'s permission before making any physical changes that would involve reconfiguring office space. X Corp. requests that Z Co. allow it to make the changes, but Z Co. denies the request. X Corp. can claim that making the physical changes would constitute an undue hardship. However, it must provide any other type of reasonable accommodation that would not involve making physical changes to the facility, such as finding a different location within the office that would be accessible to the employee.

An employer should remember its obligation to make a reasonable accommodation when it is negotiating contracts with property owners.[122] Similarly, a property owner should carefully assess a request from an employer to make physical changes that are needed as a reasonable accommodation because failure to permit the modification might constitute "interference" with the rights of an employee with a disability.[123] In addition, other ADA provisions may require the property owner to make the modifications.[124]

---

[122][122]*See* 42 U.S.C. §12112(b)(2) (1994); 29 C.F.R. §1630.6 (1997) (prohibiting an employer from participating in a contractual relationship that has the effect of subjecting qualified applicants or employees with disabilities to discrimination).

[123]*See* 42 U.S.C. §12203(b) (1994); 29 C.F.R. §1630.12(b) (1997).

[124] For example, under Title III of the ADA a private entity that owns a building in which goods and services are offered to the public has an obligation, subject to certain limitations, to remove architectural barriers so that people with disabilities have equal access to these goods and services. 42 U.S.C. §12182(b)(2)(A)(iv) (1994). Thus, the requested modification may be something that the property owner should have done to comply with Title III.

Burdens of Proof

In *US Airways, Inc. v. Barnett*, 535 U.S. 391, 122 S. Ct. 1516 (2002), the Supreme Court laid out the burdens of proof for an individual with a disability (plaintiff) and an employer (defendant) in an ADA lawsuit alleging failure to provide reasonable accommodation. The "plaintiff/employee (to defeat a defendant/employer's motion for summary judgment) need only show that an 'accommodation' seems reasonable on its face, i.e., ordinarily or in the run of cases."[125] Once the plaintiff has shown that the accommodation s/he needs is "reasonable," the burden shifts to the defendant/employer to provide case-specific evidence proving that reasonable accommodation would cause an undue hardship in the particular circumstances.[126]

The Supreme Court's burden-shifting framework does not affect the interactive process triggered by an individual's request for accommodation.[127] An employer should still engage in this informal dialogue to obtain relevant information needed to make an informed decision.

Instructions for Investigators

When assessing whether a Respondent has violated the ADA by denying a reasonable accommodation to a Charging Party, investigators should consider the following:

- Is the Charging Party "otherwise qualified" (i.e., is the Charging Party qualified for the job except that, because of disability, s/he needs a reasonable accommodation to perform the position's essential functions)?
- Did the Charging Party, or a representative, request a reasonable accommodation (i.e., did the Charging Party let the employer know that s/he needed an adjustment or change at work for a reason related to a medical condition)? [see Questions 1-4]
  - Did the Respondent request documentation of the Charging Party's disability and/or functional limitations? If yes, was the documentation provided? Did the Respondent have a legitimate reason for requesting documentation? [see Questions 6-8]
  - What specific type of reasonable accommodation, if any, did the Charging Party request?
  - Was there a nexus between the reasonable accommodation requested and the functional limitations resulting from the Charging Party's disability? [see Question 6]

---

[125]*US Airways, Inc. v. Barnett*, 535 U.S. 391, 122 S. Ct. 1516, 1523 (2002).

[126] *Id.*

[127]*See* Questions 5-10 for a discussion of the interactive process.

- Was the need for reasonable accommodation related to the use of medication, side effects from treatment, or symptoms related to a disability? [see Questions 36-38]
- For what purpose did the Charging Party request a reasonable accommodation:
  - for the application process? [see Questions 12-13]
  - in connection with aspects of job performance? [see Questions 16-24, 32-33]
  - in order to enjoy the benefits and privileges of employment? [see Questions 14-15]
- Should the Respondent have initiated the interactive process, or provided a reasonable accommodation, even if the Charging Party did not ask for an accommodation? [see Questions 11, 39]
- What did the Respondent do in response to the Charging Party's request for reasonable accommodation (i.e., did the Respondent engage in an interactive process with the Charging Party and if so, describe both the Respondent's and the Charging Party's actions/statements during this process)? [see Questions 5-11]
- If the Charging Party asked the Respondent for a particular reasonable accommodation, and the Respondent provided a different accommodation, why did the Respondent provide a different reasonable accommodation than the one requested by the Charging Party? Why does the Respondent believe that the reasonable accommodation it provided was effective in eliminating the workplace barrier at issue, thus providing the Charging Party with an equal employment opportunity? Why does the Charging Party believe that the reasonable accommodation provided by the Respondent was ineffective? [see Question 9]
- What type of reasonable accommodation could the Respondent have provided that would have been effective in eliminating the workplace barrier at issue, thus providing the Charging Party with an equal employment opportunity?
- Does the charge involve allegations concerning reasonable accommodation and violations of any conduct rules? [see Questions 34-35]
- If the Charging Party alleges that the Respondent failed to provide a reassignment as a reasonable accommodation [see generally Questions 25-30 and accompanying text]:
  - did the Respondent and the Charging Party first discuss other forms of reasonable accommodation that would enable the Charging Party to remain in his/her current position before discussing reassignment?
  - did the Respondent have any vacant positions? [see Question 27]
  - did the Respondent notify the Charging Party about possible vacant positions? [see Question 28]
  - was the Charging Party qualified for a vacant position?
  - if there was more than one vacant position, did the Respondent place the Charging Party in the one that was most closely equivalent to the Charging Party's original position?
  - if the reassignment would conflict with a seniority system, are there "special circumstances" that would make it "reasonable" to reassign the Charging Party? [see Question 31]
- If the Respondent is claiming undue hardship [see generally Questions 42-46 and accompanying text]:
  - what evidence has the Respondent produced showing that providing a specific reasonable accommodation would entail significant difficulty or expense?
  - if a modified schedule or leave is the reasonable accommodation, is undue hardship based on the impact on the ability of other employees to do their jobs? [see Question 42]
  - if leave is the reasonable accommodation, is undue hardship based on the amount of leave requested? [see Question 43]
  - if there are "special circumstances" that would make it "reasonable" to reassign the Charging Party, despite the apparent conflict with a seniority system, would it nonetheless be an undue hardship to make the reassignment? [see Question 31]
  - is undue hardship based on the fact that providing the reasonable accommodation requires changes to property owned by an entity other than the Respondent? [see Question 46]
  - if the Respondent claims that a particular reasonable accommodation would result in undue hardship, is there another reasonable accommodation that Respondent could have provided that would not have resulted in undue hardship?
- Based on the evidence obtained in answers to the questions above, is the Charging Party a qualified individual with a disability (i.e., can the Charging Party perform the essential functions of the position with or without reasonable accommodation)?

Employment Discrimination Based on Religion, Ethnicity, or Country of Origin

Anger at those responsible for the tragic events of September 11 should not be misdirected against innocent individuals because of their religion, ethnicity, or country of origin. Employers and labor unions have a special role in guarding against unlawful workplace discrimination.

Title VII of the Civil Rights Act of 1964 prohibits workplace discrimination based on religion, national origin, race, color, or sex. At this time, employers and unions should be particularly sensitive to potential discrimination or harassment against individuals who are – or are perceived to be – Muslim, Arab, Afghani, Middle Eastern or South Asian (Pakistani, Indian, etc.).

The law's prohibitions include harassment or any other employment action based on any of the following:

- *Affiliation*: Harassing or otherwise discriminating because an individual is affiliated with a particular religious or ethnic group. For example, harassing an individual because she is Arab or practices Islam, or paying an employee less because she is Middle Eastern.
- *Physical or cultural traits and clothing:* Harassing or otherwise discriminating because of physical, cultural, or linguistic characteristics, such as accent or dress associated with a particular religion, ethnicity, or country of origin. For example, harassing a woman wearing a hijab (a body covering and/or head-scarf worn by some Muslims), or not hiring a man with a dark complexion and an accent believed to be Arab.
- *Perception*: Harassing or otherwise discriminating because of the perception or belief that a person is a member of a particular racial, national origin, or religious group whether or not that perception is correct. For example, failing to hire an Hispanic person because the hiring official believed that he was from Pakistan, or harassing a Sikh man wearing a turban because the harasser thought he was Muslim.
- *Association*: Harassing or otherwise discriminating because of an individual's association with a person or organization of a particular religion or ethnicity. For example,

harassing an employee whose husband is from Afghanistan, or refusing to promote an employee because he attends a Mosque.

Harassment

Employers must provide a workplace that is free of harassment based on national origin, ethnicity, or religion. They may be liable not only for harassment by supervisors, but also by coworkers or by non-employees under their control. Employers should clearly communicate to all employees – through a written policy or other appropriate mechanism – that harassment such as ethnic slurs or other verbal or physical conduct directed toward any racial, ethnic, or religious group is prohibited and that employees must respect the rights of their coworkers. An employer also should have effective and clearly communicated policies and procedures for addressing complaints of harassment and should train managers on how to identify and respond effectively to harassment even in the absence of a complaint.

Religious Accommodation

Title VII requires an employer to reasonably accommodate the religious practices of an employee or prospective employee, unless doing so would create an undue hardship for the employer. Some reasonable religious accommodations that employers may be required to provide workers include leave for religious observances, time and/or place to pray, and ability to wear religious garb.

Filing a Charge

Anyone who believes that s/he has been subjected to discrimination in violation of Title VII may file a charge with the nearest field office of the Equal Employment Opportunity Commission. Persons who file a charge, oppose unlawful employment discrimination, participate in employment discrimination proceedings, or otherwise assert their rights under the laws enforced by the Commission are protected against retaliation. An EEOC charge must be filed within 180 days – or 300 if the state has a fair employment practices agency – of the date of the disputed conduct. Field offices are located throughout the United States. To be connected to the appropriate office, call 1-800-669-4000. EEOC's TTY number is 1-800-800-3302.

Questions and Answers About Employer Responsibilities Concerning the Employment of Muslims, Arabs, South Asians, and Sikhs

Since the attacks of September 11, 2001, the Equal Employment Opportunity Commission (EEOC) and state and local fair employment practices agencies have recorded a significant increase in the number of charges alleging discrimination based on religion and/or national origin. Many of the charges have been filed by individuals who are or are perceived to be Muslim, Arab, South Asian, or Sikh. These charges most commonly allege harassment and discharge.

While employers have an ongoing responsibility to address workplace discrimination, reaction to the events of September 11, 2001 may demand increased efforts to prevent discrimination. This fact sheet answers questions about what steps an employer can take to meet these responsibilities. The Commission has also prepared a companion fact sheet that answers questions about employee rights. For additional information, visit the EEOC's website at http://www.eeoc.gov.

Introduction

Title VII of the Civil Rights Act of 1964 prohibits workplace discrimination based on religion, ethnicity, country of origin, race and color. Such discrimination is prohibited in any aspect of employment, including recruitment, hiring, promotion, benefits, training, job duties, and termination. Workplace harassment is also prohibited by Title VII. In addition, an employer must provide a reasonable accommodation for religious practices unless doing so would result in undue hardship. The law prohibits retaliation against an individual because s/he has engaged in protected activity, which includes filing a charge, testifying, assisting, or participating in any manner in an investigation, or opposing a discriminatory practice. Employers with 15 or more employees are required to comply with Title VII. Title VII also prohibits discrimination by most unions and employment agencies.

Hiring and Other Employment Decisions

Narinder, a South Asian man who wears a Sikh turban, applies for a position as a cashier at XYZ Discount Goods. XYZ fears Narinder's religious attire will make customers uncomfortable. What should XYZ do?

XYZ should not deny Narinder the job due to notions of customer preferences about religious attire. That would be unlawful. It would be the same as refusing to hire Narinder because he is a Sikh.

XYZ Discount Goods should also consider proactive measures for preventing discrimination in hiring and other employment decisions. XYZ could remind its managers and employees that discrimination based on religion or national origin is not tolerated by the company in any aspect of employment, including hiring. XYZ could also adopt objective standards for selecting new employees. It is important to hire people based on their qualifications rather than on perceptions about their religion, race or national origin.

Harassment

Muhammad, who is Arab American, works for XYZ Motors, a large used car business. Muhammad meets with his manager and complains that Bill, one of his coworkers, regularly calls him names like "camel jockey," "the local terrorist," and "the ayatollah," and has intentionally embarrassed him in front of customers by claiming that he is incompetent. How should the supervisor respond?

Managers and supervisors who learn about objectionable workplace conduct based on religion or national origin are responsible for taking steps to correct the conduct by anyone under their control. Muhammad's manager should relay Muhammad's complaint to the appropriate manager if he does not supervise Bill. If XYZ Motors then determines that Bill has harassed Muhammad, it should take disciplinary action against Bill that is significant enough to ensure that the harassment does not continue.

Workplace harassment and its costs are often preventable. Clear and effective policies prohibiting ethnic and religious slurs, and related offensive conduct, are needed. Confidential complaint mechanisms for promptly reporting harassment are critical, and these policies should be written to encourage victims and witnesses to come forward. When harassment is reported, the focus should be on action to end the harassment and correct its effects on the complaining employee.

Religious Accommodation

Three of the 10 Muslim employees in XYZ's 30-person template design division approach their supervisor and ask that they be allowed to use a conference room in an adjacent building for prayer. Until making the request, those employees prayed at their work stations. What should XYZ do?

XYZ should work closely with the employees to find an appropriate accommodation that meets their religious needs without causing an undue hardship for XYZ. Whether a reasonable accommodation would impose undue hardship and therefore not be required depends on the particulars of the business and the requested accommodation.

When the room is needed for business purposes, XYZ can deny its use for personal religious purposes. However, allowing the employees to use the conference room for prayers likely would not impose an undue hardship on XYZ in many other circumstances.

Similarly, prayer often can be performed during breaks, so that providing sufficient time during work hours for prayer would not result in an undue hardship. If going to another building for prayer takes longer than the allotted break periods, the employees still can be accommodated if the nature of the template design division's work makes flexible scheduling feasible. XYZ can require employees to make up any work time missed for religious observance.

In evaluating undue hardship, XYZ should consider only whether it can accommodate the three employees who made the request. If XYZ can accommodate three employees, it should do so. Because individual religious practices vary among members of the same religion, XYZ should not deny the requested accommodation based on speculation that the other Muslim employees may seek the same accommodation. If other employees subsequently request the same accommodation and granting it to all of the requesters would cause undue hardship, XYZ can make an appropriate adjustment at that time. For example, if accommodating five employees would not cause an undue hardship but accommodating six would impose such hardship, the sixth request could be denied.

Like employees of other religions, Muslim employees may need accommodations such as time off for religious holidays or exceptions to dress and grooming codes.

Temporary Assignments

Susan is an experienced clerical worker who wears a hijab (head scarf) in conformance with her Muslim beliefs. XYZ Temps places Susan in a long-term assignment with one of its clients. The client contacts XYZ and requests that it notify Susan that she must remove her hijab while working at the front desk, or that XYZ assign another person to Susan's position. According to the client, Susan's religious attire violates its dress code and presents the "wrong image." Should XYZ comply with its client's request?

XYZ Temps may not comply with this client request without violating Title VII. The client would also violate Title VII if it made Susan remove her hijab or changed her duties to keep her out of public view. Therefore, XYZ should strongly advise against this course of action. Notions about customer preference real or perceived do not establish undue hardship, so the client should make an exception to its dress code to let Susan wear her hijab during front desk duty as a religious accommodation. If the client does not withdraw the request, XYZ should place Susan in another assignment at the same rate of pay and decline to assign another worker to the client.

Background Investigations

Anwar, who was born in Egypt, applies for a position as a security guard with XYZ Corp., which contracts to provide security services at government office buildings. Can XYZ require Muhammad to undergo a background investigation before he is hired?

XYZ may require Anwar to undergo the same pre-employment security checks that apply to other applicants for the same position. As with its other employment practices, XYZ may not perform background investigations or other screening procedures in a discriminatory manner.

In addition, XYZ may require a security clearance pursuant to a federal statute or Executive Order. Security clearance determinations for positions subject to national security requirements under a federal statute or an Executive Order are not subject to review under the equal employment opportunity statutes.

Where to Go for Guidance

The EEOC is available to provide you with useful information on how to address workplace problems relating to discrimination based on religion, national origin, race or color. We conduct various types of training, and we can help you find a format that is right for you.

Small businesses are faced with unique challenges in promoting effective workplace policies that prevent discrimination. Our Small Business Liaisons are located in each of our District, Local and Area offices to assist you in compliance with EEO laws.

You should feel free to contact EEOC with questions about effective workplace policies that can help prevent discrimination. We are also available to answer more specialized questions. Please call 1-800-669-4000 (TTY 1-800-669-6820), or send inquiries to:

Equal Employment Opportunity Commission
Office of Legal Counsel
1801 L Street, NW, Suite 6000
Washington, D.C. 20507

Table of Cases

Index

For specific case law, check the table of cases.

M

major life activities, substantial limitation of

definition and types of major life activities, 12–14

definition and types of substantial limitation, 14–18

medical examinations and disabilities accommodation, 49–50

after conditional job offer, 57–58

alcohol and drug tests, 56, 59–62

during employment, 58–59

physical agility tests, 56

prior to employment offer, 56–57

for promotions, 56

requests for accommodation, in connection with, 59

medical information about workplace injuries, 101

medical insurance plans, access of disabled employees to, 73–75

medication, monitoring use of, 1–7–108, 103

mental impairments

conduct/misconduct of employees, discipline for and accommodation of, 105–107

defining disability and, 7–8

monitoring prescription medication, 1–7–108, 103

mitigating measures on disabilities, 18–21

modified job duties as reasonable accommodation of religion, 136–137

modified work schedule

as disability accommodation, 90–92, 117

as religious accommodation, 129, 130–131, 134–136

monitoring prescription medication, 1–7–108, 103

multiple chemical sensitivities, employees with, 65

multiple disability accommodations, 104–105

N

new construction, access requirements for, 66–67

Ng, Edna, 138–139

non-disabled persons, provision of accommodations to, 27–30

non-traditional religious beliefs, 127

O

Occupational Safety and Health Act (OSHA) and ADA direct threat provisions, 8

P

parking access for disabled employees, 72–73

part-time work as reasonable accommodation of disability, 90–92

past misconduct, reasonable accommodation of, 106–107

pension and retirement plans, access of disabled employees to, 75–77

performance evaluations for disabled employees, 68–69

personal religious expression at work, 138–139

personal use items, 34

W

work schedule modification

    as disability accommodation, 90–92, 117

    as religious accommodation, 129, 130–131, 134–136

working, substantial limitation in, 16–18

workplace injuries, medical information about, 101

workplace policies

    disability accommodation, modification as, 94–95, 103

    on drug testing, 61–62

    religious accommodation, modification as, 129, 137–138

Practical, Time-Tested Guidance
For HR and Benefits Professionals —

ADA Compliance Guide

Helps employers understand, step-by-step, what they can and cannot do in their practices under the sweeping Americans with Disabilities Act.

Domestic Partner Benefits: An Employer's Guide

With an implementation strategy, model documents and much more, this resource is designed to guide you through the process of establishing and running a domestic partner program.

Employer's Guide to Military Leave Compliance

Explains employers' responsibilities under the Uniformed Services Employment and Reemployment Rights Act (USERRA), including the December 2005 final regulation

Employer's Guide to the Fair Labor Standards Act

Helps employers determine which employees are covered by the FLSA, compute overtime compensation, understand what constitutes hours worked and properly maintain employee records.

Employer's Guide to the Health Insurance Portability and Accountability Act

Explains HIPAA's portability provisions, including pre-existing condition exclusions, creditable coverage, special enrollment provisions, certificates of coverage, and more.

Fair Labor Standards Handbook for States, Local Governments and Schools

Offers public employers timely news, cost-effective guidance and expert analysis of federal wage and hour requirements under the FLSA.

Family and Medical Leave Handbook

Comprehensive guidance on the FMLA to help employers manage employee leave, reduce costs and minimize workplace disruption.

FLSA Employee Exemption Handbook

Enables private-sector employers to properly classify employees under the FLSA and other relevant federal laws.

Guide to Consumer-Directed Health Care

Shows employers how to save money and improve health through a combination of account-based and health and wellness programs, including the experience of early adopters.

HR Guide to Business Continuity Planning

Walks you through the planning process by providing strategies and expert guidance on how to implement your plan correctly and minimize the risks associated with an unexpected interruption.

HR Question and Answer Book

While most of the other question and answer books deal with generic hiring and firing issues, Thompson's *HR Question and Answer Book* covers the entire employment relationship with over 200 real questions. Not only does it answer your questions quickly and thoroughly, it provides you with the tools to move forward in the right direction.

Investigating Sexual Harassment: A Practical Guide to Resolving Complaints

Provides advice for employers on thoroughly investigating and resolving sexual harassment complaints under the evolving body of sexual harassment law.

Labor and Employment Law: The Employer's Compliance Guide

Uniquely organized around the employee life-cycle, the *Guide* provides instant access to key text and accurate answers on employment laws and regulations.

Public Employer's Guide to FLSA Employee Classification

Shows public employers how to properly classify employees, understand the executive, administrative, professional and other exemptions, and find remedies for a misclassification.

The Leave and Disability Coordination Handbook

Helps employers coordinate employee leave under the ADA, FMLA and state workers' compensation laws.

Thompson's Employee Handbook Builder

Create an expert employee handbook... completely online... in about an hour... and at a fraction of what an attorney or consultant charges.

Thompson's HR Employment Forms

Gathers over 300 HR forms, covering everything from hiring to retirement, in one easy to use resource- also includes a CD with electronic versions of every form in the book so that you can customize the forms to meet your specific needs.

Understanding and Preventing Workplace Retaliation

Describes the many forms retaliation can take and provides practical advice for safeguarding against incidents.

Workplace Accommodations Under the ADA

Helps employers to understand their obligations under the Americans with Disabilities Act and provides practical solutions to effectively handle accommodation requests from individuals with disabilities.

Workplace Privacy: Answers and Practical Solutions

Explains how to balance an employer's need to know what employees are doing with the employees' rights and expectations of personal privacy.

To start your RISK-FREE trial subscription:

- call toll-free: 1-800-677-3789
- order online at: www.thompson.com

THOMPSON